OTHER WORKS OF DR. ROBERT CROOKALL

Coal Measure Plants—Edward Arnold & Co. Ltd., 1929.

The Kidston Collection of Fossil Plants—H.M. Stationery Office, 1938.

"Fossil Plants of the Carboniferous Rocks of Great Britain", *Memoirs of the Geological Survey of Great Britain, Palæontology*, Vol. II, Section II, *ibid.*, Pt. I, 1955; Pt. II, 1959.

The Supreme Adventure—James Clarke & Co. Ltd., 1960.

Scientific papers in *The Geological Magazine,*
> *The Annals of Botany,*
> *Memoirs of the Geological Survey of Great Britain,*
> *The Naturalist,*
> *Memoirs and Proceedings of the Manchester Literary & Philosophic Society,*
> *Proceedings of the Geologists' Association,*
> *Proceedings of the Royal Society of Edinburgh,*
> *Proceedings of the Cotteswold Naturalist and Field Club,*
> *Proceedings of the Royal Physical Society,* etc.

WITH DR F. B. A. WELCH

British Regional Geology: Bristol and Gloucester District—H.M. Stationery Office, 1935.

THE STUDY AND
OF

SECAUCUS, NEW JERSEY

ROBERT CROOKALL

B.Sc. (Psychology), D.Sc., Ph.D.

Late Principal Geologist, H.M. Geological
Survey, London, formerly Demonstrator
in Botany, University of Aberdeen

PRACTICE
ASTRAL PROJECTION

THE CITADEL PRESS

A Citadel Press Book
Published by Carol Communications
Editorial Offices: 600 Madison Ave., New York, NY 10022
Sales Distribution: 120 Enterprise Ave., Secaucus, NJ 07094
In Canada: Musson Book Company
A division of General Publishing Co. Limited
Don Mills, Ontario
Manufactured in the United States of America
ISBN 0-8065-0547-8

8 9 10 11 12 13 14 15

PREFACE

RIGHTLY or wrongly—as the reader may decide—the writer considers that many, though not of course all, accounts which people give of having temporarily left their Physical Bodies in some sort of 'Spiritual Body' are basically true.

If true, these experiences are of great importance. In the first place, they provide material towards the answer to the Psalmist's question, 'What is man?' Secondly, they point unmistakably to man's survival of bodily death (since they are identical with those given by the 'dead'—see Appendix V). Thirdly, they suggest that our entrance into the 'next' world is no more (and no less) a religious matter than entrance into the physical world at birth.

In the various attempts that have been made to date to demonstrate the reality of out-of-the-body experiences reliance is chiefly placed on (1) cases in which the claim that a person is exteriorized in a 'double', or Psychical Body, seems to be corroborated by the fact that his apparition was seen by others, and (2) cases in which the experience is repeated experimentally. These evidences have not proved convincing to many.

On the other hand, we suggest that the cumulative evidence here adduced, though necessarily of an indirect nature, serves to establish the reality of out-of-the-body experiences quite as firmly as the theory of evolution is established (see Appendix IX).

Although a number of authors give methods for inducing astral projections, the present writer considers that, in general, these or any other psychic experiences, should not be forced in any way. If they come naturally and unsought it is a different matter. There is a time when an egg-shell can break and the chick emerge in comfort and safety.

Readers who have had out-of-the-body experiences, or who may encounter additional examples in print, are invited to send details to the writer. (A stamped addressed envelope would be appreciated.) The accounts should be exact, nothing being omitted and nothing inserted in an attempt to make them agree with those already published. Differences between narratives may be of great significance.

R. CROOKALL

12 Woodland Avenue,
    Dursley,
        Glos., England.

'He that answereth a matter before he heareth it, it is a shame and a folly unto him'—*Solomon*, Proverbs xviii, 13.

'A presumptuous scepticism that rejects facts without examination of their truth is, in some respects, more injurious than unquestioning credulity'—*Humboldt.*

'We cannot but speak the things we have seen and heard'—*St Peter and St John*, Acts iv, 20.

'How are the dead raised up, and with what body do they come? [In addition to the carnal, or Physical, Body] ... there is a Psychical and a Spiritual Body'—*St Paul*, I Cor. xv. 35, 44.

'Self-projection is the one definite act which it seems as though a man might perform equally well before and after bodily death'—*F. W. H. Myers.*

'When I consider Thy heavens, the work of Thy fingers, the moon and the stars ... WHAT IS MAN?—*David*, Ps. viii, 3.

'Nothing is too amazing to be true'—*Michael Faraday*. (But Faraday rejected supernormal phenomena: being committed to a sect with rigid Biblical views, he separated science from religion.)

'Sit down before fact as a little child. Be prepared to give up every preconceived notion, follow humbly wherever and to whatever abysses nature leads—or you shall learn nothing'—*Prof. T. H. Huxley*. (And he fulfilled his own prediction, since he failed to adopt his own advice. Huxley also wrote, 'Supposing the [psychic] phenomena to be genuine they do not interest me'.)

'Call it a sin to let slip a truth'—*Robt. Browning*. (But he did it himself. Browning failed to realize that D. D. Home was as honest as he himself and that the phenomena he produced were genuine.)

'Neither the testimony of all the Fellows of the Royal Society nor even the evidence of my own senses would lead me to believe in thought-transmission. ... It is clearly impossible'—*Prof. Helmholtz.*

'The very thought of thought-transference is "puerile" '—*Sir Ray Lankester*. (Yet Profs. C. D. Broad, H. H. Price, J. B. Rhine, Hornell Hart and many other eminent scholars are now convinced of its reality.)

CONTENTS

Page

PREFACE   v

ANALYSES OF CASE HISTORIES   I

A.—NATURAL OUT-OF-THE-BODY EXPERIENCES   3
    I. PEOPLE WHO NEARLY DIED, Cases 1–21   3
    II. PEOPLE WHO WERE VERY ILL, Cases 22–30   20
    III. PEOPLE WHO WERE EXHAUSTED, ETC., Cases 31–39   24
    IV. PEOPLE WHO WERE QUITE WELL, Cases 40–119   36

B.—ENFORCED OUT-OF-THE-BODY EXPERIENCES   118
    1. FIRST-HAND ACCOUNTS   118
        a. Caused by Anaesthetics, etc, Cases 120–145   118
        b. Caused by Suffocation, Cases 146–147   131
        c. Caused by Falling, Cases 148–152   132

    2. ACCOUNTS BY OTHERS   134
        a. Caused by Anaesthetics, etc., Case 153   134
        b. Caused by Hypnosis   135

CONCLUSIONS   140

APPENDICES   145
    I. History of the Subject   145
    II. Additional Details (Natural Experiences)   160
    III. Incomplete (or incompletely-remembered) Natural   177
        Experiences (Cases 154–160)
    IV. Certain 'Dreams' as 'Incomplete Natural Experiences'   183
    V. Statements of the 'Dead' regarding their Experiences   187
    VI. Statements of the 'Dead' regarding our Sleep-state   203
    VII. Arnold Bennett's Résumé of Theosophical Teachings   210
    VIII. 'Thought-forms'   219
    IX. Evidence, Direct and Indirect   226

ACKNOWLEDGEMENTS   229

INDEX TO CASES GIVEN IN THE TEXT   233

THE STUDY
AND PRACTICE
OF ASTRAL
PROJECTION

Analyses of Case Histories

SHAKESPEARE caused one of his characters to mention 'that undiscovered country from whose bourne no traveller returns'. Yet the world's literature contains innumerable incidental accounts of people who claimed temporarily to leave the body, to be conscious apart from it, and to 'return' and recount their experiences. The person who takes pride in his 'commonsense' outlook on life naturally regards such narratives as representing mere dreams. The present writer, who has studied them systematically over a period of many years, does not. He invites the reader to compare the accounts given in this book, to note the comments made [in square brackets] and to consider whether the concordances and coherences that occur can be explained except on the assumption that the narratives are, in fact, descriptive of genuine experiences.

A brief history of our subject is given in Appendix I. Many of these Case Histories were sent personally to the writer and are new to the literature. A questionnaire was submitted to correspondents and additional details were obtained (Appendix II). People often have incomplete (or incompletely-remembered) experiences of this nature (Appendix III), while many 'dreams' are obviously not fantasies but partially-remembered, out-of-the-body experiences (Appendix IV).

The writer has studied the supposed experiences of people who had left the body *permanently* (*i.e.*, died): he found that those who said that they died *naturally* described one series of experiences while those who said their death was *enforced* described another, a more restricted, series (Appendix V). Some of the 'dead' gave explanations of these differences. Their explanations are reasonable. Moreover, in some cases, they agree with the findings of psychical science. We therefore conclude that the accounts of the after-death experiences which we examined are very probably, indeed almost certainly, genuine. They are not, as is often supposed, mere products of the 'subconscious mind'.

The present book analyses the experiences of people who claim to leave the body *temporarily*. It is found that those who did so *naturally* typically describe one series of experiences, while those whose exteriorization was *enforced* typically describe another, a more restricted, series. It is further found that there is a remarkable correspondence between the accounts of those who claimed to leave the body permanently and those who claimed to leave it only temporarily. This correspondence in independent narratives seems explicable only if both sets of narratives are substantially true. No alternative explanation seems possible (*see* 'Conclusions', p. 140). We now proceed to the Case Histories.

A.—Natural Out-of-the-Body Experiences

(I) PEOPLE WHO NEARLY DIED

CASE No. 1—*Miss Elizabeth Blakeley*

MISS BLAKELEY'S narrative was published in *Prediction* for March, 1953. As a child she feared death. Her experience changed her whole outlook on life. She became certain that, 'The soul exists and is indestructible'.

Miss Blakeley became seriously ill. One evening she fell into a deep sleep, awaking to find the room in darkness. She continued, '*This awakening was not like the usual drowsy wakening from the sleeping state. The consciousness was strangely calm and clear. I was no longer in pain. ... Gradually the consciousness, which normally suffuses the whole body, became condensed in the head. I became all head, and only head. Then it seemed that 'I' had become condensed into one tiny speck of consciousness, situated somewhere near the centre of my head. ...* [Cf. Appendix V, Statement No. 13.] *Then I became aware that I was beginning to travel further upwards. There came a momentary blackout* [shedding the physical body, see Appendix V, Statement No. 9] *and then 'I' was free; I had left my body. I had projected in space somewhere above the bed upon which still lay my inert body. And I* knew—this is what the world calls the state of death. ... Contrary to general belief, there was no loss of consciousness. [There was no 'sleep' until 'the end of the age'—compare Statement No. 34.]

'*Again a timeless pause* [shedding the vehicle of vitality = the 'second death'—cf. Statement No. 23—and the cases of Miss Peters and Mrs Parker] *and then before my inner sight there flashed a complete series of pictures embodying the most important events of my life* [= the review of the past life, the 'Judgment'—cf. Statement No. 34]. *It seemed that I* became both actor and witness in these pictures, for I found that with clear reason, utterly devoid of all prejudice or hazy emotion, I became my own judge of my own actions, for good or bad, throughout my preceding life. *This judgment being over, there finally appeared to me only those people with whom there existed a true bond of love* [cf. 'Starr Daily's' experience]. And then I turned willingly and gladly to embark on this new life which was beginning for me. *Then came the Light. A brilliant, white Light, blinding in its unearthly radiance. ... It suffused my whole being, lifting me to the indescribable height of sublime ecstasy; complete at-one-ment*

3

with the Divine Essence, at the all-pervading consciousness of the Cosmic, of God [= 'mystical', 'cosmic' or 'spiritual' consciousness in the Spiritual Body].

'*Slowly began the return to my body and the world. Gradually I withdrew into my lifeless body. But the light remained, and, intuitively realizing, during this delicate operation, that it was of the utmost importance to retain as much as possible of its radiant life-giving vibrations, I concentrated my whole attention on it.*

'Once again my consciousness seemed to be located in that vital spot in my head. The life-force slowly infused the benumbed limbs. ... I had come back to life. ... *The wonder of this revelation continues to echo and re-echo down through the years of my life. Its memory lingers undimmed in my heart and mind, assimilated into the very depths of my being, beyond worldly scepticism, beyond intellectual doubt and argument, and beyond religious dogma.*'

CASE NO. 2—*Dr George Kelley*

This narrative was first published in *The Aquarian Age* by Mrs Kelley, who corroborated those of her husband's statements that were capable of corroboration. *Dr Kelley specifically disclaimed anyknowledge of psychical matters.* He was very ill. He said, 'The doctor saw me draw what he supposed to be my last breath; tests for life were made. He pronounced me dead. ... *There was a momentary darkness* [= while shedding the Physical Body—cf. Statements No. 3 and 9]. *Then I became aware of another presence in the room:* beside me stood my wife's sister who had passed away several years before [cf. Statement No. 18]. "Come with me," she said. I followed. I tried to inform my wife of my safety while absent, and to assure her that I would return. *I found communication impossible. I touched my wife, but she seemed unconscious of my presence* [cf. Statement No. 28]. Suddenly I realized that she thought I still occupied that inert body which was lying on the bed ... I became aware of a sudden swift movement. I knew then, beyond the shadow of a doubt, that my soul, free from the Physical Body, was about to enter another existence, entirely different from that of earth. *I was experiencing death and realized that it is not a thing to fear.* ... We entered a park [cf. Statement No. 32]. Men and women stood about singly and in groups. They were beautiful in their glistening soul-bodies. I found myself face to face with strange people. *I was one of them, yet quite apart from them.* [The intensity of his consciousness and the brightness of his Psychical Body were diminished by the vitality that passed from the Psychical Body, *via* the 'silver cord', to the Physical Body—cf. accounts of Gerhardi and Mrs Leonard, also Statement No. 1b]. *I cannot describe that bright, yet ethereal light—intense, yet* without the glare or the heat of the sun [cf. Rev. xxii, 5, and Wordsworth, 'The light that never was, on sea or land'].

'*As we entered the room where my body lay, darkness and oblivion claimed me once more* [= re-entering the body]. I awoke in bed and related my experience. ... *The knowledge I gained at that time assured me of a future life.*'

CASE No. 3—*Dr A. S. Wiltse*

The experience of Dr A. S. Wiltse, of Skiddy, Kansas, first published in *The St. Louis Medical and Surgical Journal* (1889), is also given in *Proc. S.P.R.* viii, p. 180. Like Kelley, Wiltse was thought to be dead. When, however, he recovered, he said that he had been fully conscious.

'*I looked,*' said Dr Wiltse, '*in astonishment for the first time upon myself, the Me, while the not-Me closed in upon all sides like a sepulchre of clay. With all the interest of a physician, I beheld the wonders of my bodily anatomy, intimately interwoven with which, even tissue for tissue, was I, the living soul of the dead body.*'

Wiltse heard and felt, '*the snapping of innumerable cords*' [cf. Statement No. 19], began to retreat from the feet towards the head of his Physical Body and finally emerged from the head [cf. Statement No. 13]. '*Then,*' he said, '*I floated up and down laterally, like a soap bubble attached to the bowl of a pipe, until at last I broke free from the body and fell lightly on the floor ...*' [cf. Bertrand, Case No. 4].

There were two men near the door of the room and one of them, without realizing it, passed his arm through the 'dead' doctor's Psychical Body. *Wiltse saw his own Physical Body* [cf. Statement No. 17] *and was surprised at its paleness. He tried to attract the attention of his wife, but failed* [cf. Statement No. 28]. *He realized, 'That* [Physical Body] *is not I; this is I, and I am as much alive as ever.*'

Passing out through the door and looking back, he saw 'a small cord like a spider's web' connecting his Physical and Psychical Bodies [cf. Statement No. 19].

During the period that he was 'dead', Wiltse saw much that went on in the room. Statements corroborating his were obtained from those present.

CASE No. 4—*The Revd L. J. Bertrand*

The experience of being almost dead also occurred to the Revd L. J. Bertrand who gave Dr Hodgson an oral, and Prof. Wm. James a written account: details were published in *Proc. S.R.*, viii, p. 194.

Bertrand was climbing in the Alps with a guide and a group of students; they were ascending the Titlis. Feeling tired, he allowed his companions to continue on two conditions, first that the guide took the students up by the left-hand track and returned by the right-hand track, and secondly that the strongest student should remain at the rear end of the rope. He then sat down. After a time, trying to light a cigar, he found that he could not discard the match; he was numb with cold, freezing to death. 'This is the sleep of the snow,' he said to himself. 'If I move, I'll roll down the abyss; if I don't, I'll be dead in thirty minutes.'

The first parts to freeze were the hands and feet. Then the head became unbearably cold and Bertrand found himself outside his body. *'Well,'* he said to himself, *'here I am, what they call a dead man—a "ball of air" in the air, a captive balloon still attached to the earth by a kind of elastic string* [= the 'silver cord' cf. Statement No. 19], *and, going up, always up.' Below him he could see his Physical Body.* He thought, *'*There is the corpse in which I lived. If only I had a hand and scissors to cut the thread which ties me still to it ... *I was never as alive as I am now'* [cf. Statement No. 26]. *Bertrand now became clairvoyant and saw that the guide had disobeyed his orders;* he had taken the students up by the right-hand path, and the strong student no longer brought up the rear of the party. Then Bertrand saw the guide secretly drinking Bertrand's own bottle of wine and eating the chicken reserved for his lunch. Rising still higher, he saw his wife (who was not due to arrive until next day) and four other persons in a carriage on their way to Lucerne, stopping at an hotel in Lungren. Then he felt as though someone were hauling down the 'balloon'. [This symbol for the exteriorized psychical body, that of a balloon, was used independently by several others who claimed to have left their bodies: they include Gerhardi, Helen Brooks, Frank Lind and Mrs R. Ivy 'Prothero'.] He awoke to physical consciousness to find the guide rubbing snow into his stiffened limbs.

'When I reached my body again,' he said, *'I had a last hope: the "balloon" seemed much too big for the mouth.* [He was reluctant to return to physical life: cf. Statement No. 8.] *Suddenly ... the corpse swallowed the "balloon", and Bertrand was Bertrand again.'* '*The guide told Bertrand that he had almost frozen to death, but he replied, "I was less dead than you are now* [cf. Statement No. 26]. The proof is that I saw you going up the Titlis by the right path when you promised to go by the left. Now show me my bottle of wine and we will see if it is full".' He also accused the guide of eating part of his chicken. Later, when they got back to Lucerne and found Mme Bertrand already there, he asked her, 'Were there five of you in the carriage, and did you stop at the Lungren Hotel?' 'Yes,' answered his wife, 'but who told you?'

CASE NO. 5—*Miss Gail Hamilton*

Miss Hamilton, the well-known American writer, told of her

experiences during apparent death. The account was first published in *Gail Hamilton's Life in Letters*, edited by H. Augusta Dodge (Boston, 1901) and later in Muldoon's *The Case for Astral Projection* (Aries Press, Chicago). She said, '*I felt myself sinking* [cf. Statement No. 9]. *There was no pain, no alarm, no fear* [cf. Statement No. 7]. *I had but one thought —that it would be a shock to the family to find me on the floor. ... So many friends were around me who had gone out of this world* [cf. Statements No. 3 and 18] *that it suddenly occurred to me whether I myself might not be already gone* ... [cf. Statement No. 31]. *It seemed, and it seems still, as if my spirit were partially detached from my body* ... *not absolutely free from it* [because of the 'silver cord'—Statements No. 19 and 20], *but floating about* ...'

CASE No. 6—*A Colonel*

Another experience due to serious illness (given in *Journ. S.P.R.*, xxxiv, 1948) concerns a colonel who had pneumonia. He heard the doctor say that he could do nothing for him and that he must fight it out for himself. He says, 'With what strength I had, I said, "You shall get better!" Now this was the crisis. *I left my body. I felt it getting heavier and heavier and sinking into the bed* [cf. Statement No. 9]. *I was sitting on top of a high wardrobe, looking down on myself in bed* [cf. Statement No. 17] *and the nurse sitting by me. I was disgusted at my unshaven appearance. I saw everything in the room. Fear was absent entirely*' [cf. Statement No. 7]. When told of his experience, the nurse said it was the effect of delirium. The colonel replied, 'No, I was dead for that time. I made myself go back.'

CASE No. 7—*Dr O. Rose*

Arthur J. Wills, Ph.D. (*Life Now and Forever*, Rider & Co., 1942) and E. H. Hunt (*Why We Survive*, Rider) cited the experience of Dr O. Rose, of Cheltenham, as follows. After being thrown from a horse and badly injured, he was 'picked up for dead' by two men who witnessed the accident. After five hours he regained consciousness. 'Although I was insensible,' he writes, '*I could see my body, lying there on the ground* [cf. Statement No. 17]. I could see the men pick me up, heard them say I was dead and saw them carry me into the house. I was able to see the doctors trying to bring me to, and all the time I was able to see myself lying there. *I seemed to be floating on a summer sea. I cannot describe the sensation of peace and happiness* [cf. Statement No. 26]. Yet someone seemed to tell me I had to go back.' He commented thus: 'Now, the points I wish to make are: First, I had never seen the men who picked me up, and have never seen them since, as they were strangers to the district, just passing through, yet I was able to describe them, their dress and also their horses. Secondly, although I was totally unconscious, I was able to tell the doctors everything that had taken place, and what my injuries were. *I am convinced that I was outside of my body, yet I was able to see and hear. It makes me certain that there is a life after death, which does not require a material body for us to be able to see and hear, and that we shall retain our personality.*'

Case No. 8—*Leonora Countess of Tankerville*

The Countess published her out-of-the-body experience in *Prediction* for June, 1952, under the title, 'Can we die twice?' She became unconscious and was expected to die. It was during the Boer War and she found herself out of her Physical Body and on a battlefield. She gave help to a newly-dead officer, encouraging and comforting him until 'strong and bright' discarnate helpers appeared and took him away. (This is an example of 'co-operation' between the 'living' and the 'dead'—see Statement No. 30, and compare the accounts of experiences by Jeffrey H. Brown and Wm. E. Edwards.)

'Only then,' said the Countess, 'did I realize that I too had crossed the "Great Divide" ' [cf. Statement No. 31]. She continued, 'At first the environment [= 'Paradise' conditions] proved so attractive that I thought of nothing else. *That marvellous atmosphere, the loveliness of green fields, the calm, the sense of freedom and the buoyancy of perfect health, all made for contentment.* ... Someone at my side confirmed the fact that I was indeed in the Spiritual World. "I must go back to my husband," I exclaimed. He replied, "You may return. You will live as long as the pneumogastric nerve [= the "silver cord": cf. Statement No. 20] holds out ...".'

Case No. 9—*Mrs Frances Leslie*

This experience was told by K. Frank Feldman in *Prediction* for December, 1952. Frances Leslie almost died. She was pronounced dead, but was revived by an injection. The account she gave is as follows.

'*I seemed to float in a long tunnel* [cf. Statement No. 9]. *It appeared very narrow at first, but gradually expanded into unlimited space* [= shedding the Physical Body—cf. Mrs Tarsikes and Miss Peters]. *There was some sort of a body* [cf. Statement No. 17]. *It seemed to defy all laws of gravity, simply floating onwards.* Then a voice called. It belonged to a man who had died years before. ... Then the colours blended and I was suffused with ecstasy. ... The brilliant shades gave one last glimmer and ... I felt as if my whole self were being split in two [= repercussion on rapid return—cf. Muldoon, Gerhardi, etc.]. An expression of sadness escaped from me [reluctance to return—Statement No. 8]. An iron hand had brought me back.' How near Mrs Leslie was to death during this experience is shown by the fact that she did die twelve hours later.

CASE NO. 10—*A patient with dysentery*

A case given in *Journ. S.P.R.* concerns a man who had dysentery. From instructions which he heard the medical officer give to the orderlies, he knew that they expected him to collapse, in which case they had to administer a saline injection. He gave the following account of his experience.

'Shortly after hearing these instructions, *I found myself lying parallel to the bed, about three or four feet above it and face downwards* [cf. Statement No. 16]. *Below me I saw my body and witnessed them giving the injection* [cf. Statement No. 17]. I listened to the conversation between two orderlies and a strange M.O., who was directing affairs. I found myself next back in bed. I told my story to the orderlies, who were sceptical. They said I couldn't possibly know of that matter as I was unconscious. I enquired about the strange M.O. ... There had been one. I never saw him again.

'*I have always been convinced that my soul had actually left my body, but returned as a result of the injection.*'

CASE NO. 11—*Mr John Oxenham*

John Oxenham, the well-known Methodist writer, who disclaimed 'any connexion with supernaturalism, spiritualism or psychical research', had a 'dream' four months before he died. In this he seemed to be exteriorized from his body and to have a foretaste of the after-life. Like all such experiences, it was so vivid as to be indelibly impressed on his memory. A narrative, entitled, 'Or out of the Body' was first published in the *Methodist Recorder*. Later, with the help of his daughter, the account was given in a book entitled, *Out of the Body* (Longmans, Green and Co. Ltd., 1941).

Oxenham was far from regarding his experience as a mere dream. It was his 'greatest wish' that his readers should accept it as a last message and as assuring them of the happy nature of the after-life. Such being the case, his insistence of his independence of spiritualism, etc. assumes importance, for the conditions he described are identical with those given in spiritualistic literature generally. They correspond to the 'Third Sphere', 'Paradise', or 'Summerland' State after death. Had this book been published anonymously, it might have been attributed to any spiritualistic writer.

Oxenham retired exhausted, knowing that his end was near. *He 'awoke' to find himself in a non-physical environment, with his sight and hearing greatly improved, and a feeling of 'perfect peace and abiding security'* [cf. Statement No. 26]. *His (deceased) wife was there* [cf. Statement No. 18]. *They were together amid scenes of exquisite beauty. When brought back by a loud noise, he was reluctant to return to the physical body.* He said, 'I had been elsewhere ... I had been vouchsafed a glimpse of a life sweeter than I had ever dreamed of. To be back in the bondage of the flesh was a sore trial' [cf. Statement No. 8].

Subsequent experiences were described in Oxenham's book. There were 'no shadows', since 'the strange rare light emanated from no one centre' [cf. James i, 17]. He said with regard to the newly-dead, 'After a certain time allowed for rest [cf. Statement No. 22], everyone had his or her chosen task, chiefly in connexion with those dear ones still struggling in the bonds of flesh, who could be helped, though not visibly, by suggestion and the influence of thought' [cf. Statement No. 28]. Communication between the 'dead' themselves was also by telepathy. One of the 'dead' told Oxenham that he himself was preparing for 'the next change'. [This 'third death' would involve the shedding of the Psychical Body, when True 'Heaven' conditions are entered in the Higher Mental, or Causal, Body. Oxenham was unaware of shedding the vehicle of vitality.]

Erica Oxenham, in the Epilogue to the book, said that, for the last few weeks of his life, her father had 'lived in the atmosphere of this book'. 'Now,' she said, 'he felt that his work was finished. ... Death for him had always meant New Life and a new Beginning. It was fitting that his last message should be such as this, and he and I both had the feeling that he was being given strength just to finish it.' It is further remarkable, in view of Oxenham's disclaimer of any connexion with 'spiritualism', etc., that three years later Erica Oxenham wrote an introduction to a typical spiritualistic account by Mrs L. N. Geldert (*Thy Son Liveth*, Frederick Muller Ltd.) which originally had been published anonymously in 1918.

It is significant that the orthodox and highly respected John Oxenham's descriptions of his experiences in *Out of the Body* agree in all essentials with those of spiritualists, Quakers, Anglicans, Buddhists, Hindus, agnostics, atheists and nondescript men and women who have claimed temporarily to leave their Physical Bodies.

CASE No. 12—*Bishop Eden's Case*

Canon Anson (*The Truth about Spiritualism*, Student Christian Movement Press Ltd., 1941) related an experience which was given him by Bishop Eden. The lady was pronounced dead. But, 'during that time she had *felt an extraordinary sense of freedom and elation* [Statement No. 26]. *She could look down and see her "dead" body lying on the bed, while she herself was bending over it* (cf. Statement No. 17]. *After a time she felt dragged back into a miserable prison-house* [cf. Statement No. 8 and note that Mme d'Espérance also called her body 'the prison']. *Then she heard the doctor saying, "She is coming round". This woman declared that she had passed beyond death, and would never dread it again.'*

CASE NO. 13—*Mrs Mary Tarsikes*

Mrs Tarsikes of Lanagan, U.S.A., sent the following account to the writer. '*I had read no books on these matters and had no other information when I had my first experiences. I do not belong to any spiritualist organization.* My first experience was when I was fifteen years old. I repeated it daily for several months. I felt like a bird leaving its cage. In 1911 my child was about to be born prematurely and I nearly died. My mother was at the bedside. *Suddenly I found myself raised above the head of the bed, looking down at my body* [cf. Statement No. 17] *and at my mother. She told me to return to life, and I did. In this experience I could see my Spiritual Body* (cf. Statement No. 31]. *I was clothed in soft white, slightly grey.* ... *There is no great pain at death—unless one struggles against death* [cf. Statement No. 7] ... *the thrill comes after death.* ...

'The surviving spirit thinks about his soul [here = the vehicle of vitality or 'body-veil']—he somehow sees that he needs his soul along with him. The soul [here = 'body-veil'] stays with the spirit [here = Psychical Body] at death. But when one projects while still in the Physical Body, the soul stays within the Physical Body. Only death takes the soul from the Physical Body. I believe there is a connexion [= the 'silver cord'—Statement No. 19] between the soul and the nerves of every living body. ... *Death, without a struggle to return, is like opening a closed door.* ... *Death was like passing through a thick dark wall of cloud with an opening about 1 in. in diameter. I passed through. I was asleep going through the wall* [cf. Statement No. 9]. Dying is also like sinking into a dark room and rising, as soon as the desire comes, into bright light [= 'Paradise' conditions cf. Statement No. 26]. *Returning to physical life was the hardest thing I ever did. But I will always remember with pleasure what I have seen'* [cf. Statement No. 8].

CASE NO. 14—*Mr 'S'*

Robert Owen (*Footfalls on the Boundary of Another World,* Trubner & Co., 1860) vouched for the genuineness of this narrative which he had received from a personal friend. It is here abridged. Miss 'A.M.H.' wrote as follows.

'A sick friend, "S", who was in a delicate state of health. He lived several hundred miles from us. We knew neither his home nor any of his family, our intercourse being by letter. One night ... I dreamed that

I had to go to the town where he lived. I seemed to arrive at a particular house, enter it, and go upstairs into a darkened chamber. *There, on the bed, I saw "S" as if about to die. I walked up to him, and, as if filled with hope, said, "You are not going to die. Be comforted. You will live." As I spoke I seemed to hear an exquisite strain of music sounding through the room.*

'On awakening, so vivid were the impressions remaining that I communicated them to my mother and then wrote to "S" enquiring after his health but giving him no clue as to the cause of my anxiety. In reply he informed me that he had been at the point of death and that my letter, which for several days he had been too ill to read, had been a great happiness to him.

'It was three years after this that my mother and I met "S" in London. The conversation turning on dreams, I said, "By the way, I had a singular dream about you when you were so ill," and I related it. As I proceeded, I observed a remarkable expression come over his face, and, when I ended, he said, "This is singular indeed: for *a night or two before your letter arrived, I had a dream the very counterpart of yours.* I seemed to myself on the very point of death. I was taking my leave of my brother. 'Is there,' he asked, 'anything I can do for you?' 'Yes, I replied in my dream, two things. Send for 'A.M.H.' I must see her before I depart.' 'Impossible,' said my brother, 'she would never come.' 'She would,' I insisted and added, '*I would also hear my favourite Sonata by Beethoven*'. ... *You walked up to the bed with a cheerful air, and, while the music which I longed for filled the air, spoke to me encouragingly, saying I should not die".'*

CASE NO. 15—*Miss I. V. Yeoman*

Miss Yeoman knew nothing whatever of spiritualism, etc. The account of her experience was published by Wm. Oliver Stevens in his book *The Mystery of Dreams* (George Allen & Unwin, Ltd., 1950). It is here abbreviated.

As a girl, Miss Yeoman feared the act of dying. Her fear was banished by the following 'dream'.

'I was lying in bed. The furniture of the room was familiar, but the room itself was strange. I felt desperately ill. *I knew that I was dying, but to my unbounded surprise, I felt no fear* [cf. Statement No. 7].

'At the foot of the bed stood my mother, a great friend, and a group of others whom I loved, and I knew that they were already in the Other World. (All but one of that group have since passed over.) They regarded me quietly, as if interested but not upset [i.e., they also were temporarily exteriorized from their Physical Bodies]. Then the door opened, and a little woman (whom I knew in my dream but was not afterwards able to identify) ran in, fell on her knees beside the bed and wept. She was followed by a doctor. ... *Those present thought I was quite unconscious, but mentally I was very much alert and (though too weak to turn my head and, indeed, I think my physical eyes were shut) could see perfectly all that was going on. My chief emotion was pity for those who sorrowed, so unnecessarily, as I thought* [cf. Arnold Bennett's account].

'*A curious sensation began at my feet* [cf. Elizabeth Blakeley, Bertrand, D. D. Home, etc.]. *It was almost like a tight glove being pulled from a finger.* [It is noteworthy that Miss Addison similarly said that leaving her Physical Body was like leaving a tight bathing-suit. Mrs Williams and Miss Johnson, who were conscious of the reverse process, namely, re-entering the Physical Body, independently described it as like fitting on a glove.] This pulling sensation travelled up my body until it reached my shoulder and throat. *Then came a second of blank unconsciousness* [= shedding the Physical Body—cf. Statement No. 9]. *I found myself standing beside the bed looking at the body on the bed* [cf. Statement No. 17]. ... *To my surprise I found that I still had hands and feet and a body, for I had always regarded the soul as something without shape, and void. I had read no spiritualistic books on after-death conditions. To find that, though dead, I still had form, was new to me. I looked with pity on those who were mourning me.* (See remarks under Case No. 133, Miss Hinton.)

'Then suddenly there appeared *an opening, like a tunnel, and at the far end a light* [cf. Statement No. 9]. I moved nearer to it and was drawn up the passage. I found myself standing at the top, on the summit of a hill covered with the greenest grass I have ever seen [= 'Paradise' conditions—cf. Statement No. 26]. The country was undulating and beautiful. Wooded scenery gave way to a glint of water here and there. *There was no sun visible, but the light had a wonderful and unusual quality* [cf. Rev. xxi, 23; xxii, 5].

'Beside me I found a tall veiled figure. I knew that he was a trusted friend. "Look back the way you have come," he said. I looked down the passage. My body still lay on the bed. My friends were still grieving for me. Then I was told to shift my attention, and immediately I found that I could see the entire world as clearly as I had observed the details of my own room [cf. Geddes's doctor-friend, etc.]. *The earth was shrouded in clouds of depression, fear and pain. My heart swelled with pity. I held out my arms to my friends in the world. "Look up! Look up! Can't you see that I am alive, well and happy? Far more alive than ever I was on earth. There is no death. Death is Life." Then I woke and the old terror had passed for ever*' [cf. Statement No. 26].

In the same book, Mr Stevens stated that no less than four of his friends had had a spontaneous exteriorization from the body. He said, 'It happened to one in a time of relaxation from weariness at the end of the day. Two others experienced it when they were desperately ill and were thought to have died at the time. Another, after a fall in which he sustained a severe blow on the head, said that *he felt himself out of his body which he could see lying on the floor.* One of these friends, when she lay at the point of death, made spontaneously a long journey out of the body to her home and brought back unexpected factual details which were later confirmed.'

CASE NO. 16—'*Janie*'

Elliott O'Donnell's account of the experience of an Anglican clergyman, an old friend of his family, with the dying 'Janie', was given in his *Ghosts with a Purpose* (Rider & Co., 1951). The narrative, here abbreviated, was headed, 'Was it projection?' The clergyman was staying with relations in Cornwall. Being out late one night, he lost his way among the disused mine-shafts on a lonely moor. He prayed for deliverance and groped his way cautiously until stopped by a low wall.

He was about to climb over this wall when a stone hit him softly in the back, causing him to look round. Confronting him was a girl with a lantern. She beckoned and he followed. The girl kept in front of him and did not speak. At length they came to a cottage and the girl pointed to the door. At that moment the moon shone out and the girl disappeared. The clergyman knocked to find himself in the presence of a weeping family. 'Heaven must have sent you, sir,' the man said. 'You have just come in time to say a few prayers to my dying Janie. We sent for our Minister, but he is ill.'

The clergyman, taken to the bedroom, recognized 'Janie' as his mysterious guide on the moor. She said, '*I dreamed I fetched you here. You are just like the gentleman I saw in my sleep. You were about to step into Pember's Shaft when I threw a stone to stop you.* ...' He remained with her until she passed peacefully away.

CASE NO. 17—*Dr Enid Smith*

Dr Smith's experience was described in *Psychic News*, July 3, 1954. Her enforced exteriorization (under an anaesthetic) is given as Case No. 124.

'This is what happened to me. Too ill for any hospital to accept, I had gone to California to die. It was a place where others were dying around me every day. One night I passed into the other world. *I seemed first to be cradled in a grey dawn. The next moment I seemed to be sinking into a dark river with folds of warm grey light above me. The water, kind and gentle, momentarily closed over my head. The swish of the waves seemed to whisper softly, comfortably, serenely in the silence.* [This is a typical description of temporary 'sub-normal' consciousness in the 'Hades' condition. Consciousness was enshrouded by the still-unshed 'body-veil' or vehicle of vitality. The 'greyness' and 'dark river' clearly represent the 'River Styx' of mythology which was supposed to encompass Hades. Descriptions by the 'dead' include all gradations of symbols from 'mist', through 'fog', 'a heavy murky atmosphere' to 'water' (see Statement No. 41). Dr Smith's account may be compared with those of Mme d'Espérance, Gerhardi, Sir A. Ogston, Miss Roos, Walter de la Mare, Frank Hives, Mrs I. M. Joy, etc., who temporarily quitting the body, were, for a time, aware that consciousness was enshrouded by the 'body-veil'].

I felt no pain [cf. Statement No. 7]. I rose quickly out of the water to a bank on the other side. *The scene had changed to one of light* [= 'Paradise' conditions—cf. Statement No. 26].

'A lovely figure ... was standing near in a radiantly white gown. He said, "Not yet. ... There is more work for you to do. You must return to earth." The next I knew I was back in my Physical Body. Shortly after that I was healed and at work again. *Death is like passing from twilight into the glories of the full midday sunshine.*'

CASE NO. 18—*Sir A. Ogston*

Sir Alexander Ogston (*Reminiscences of Three Campaigns*, Part II, *The South African War*, p. 222) had typhoid fever and was almost dying. He said 'In my delirium, mind and body seemed to be dual, and to some extent separate. I was conscious of the body as an inert, tumbled mass near the door; it belonged to me, but it was not I. My mental self used regularly to leave the body, always carrying something black and soft, I did not know what, in my left hand [= the 'silver cord'—cf. Statement No. 19 and note that a German author, Abdruschin, gave details from the 'dead' which are identical with those described by this British Officer] ... I wandered away from my body ... solitary but not unhappy, and seeing other dark shades gliding silently by until something produced a consciousness that the chilly mass (which I then recalled was my body) was being stirred. I was then rapidly drawn back to it. I joined it with disgust and it became I and was fed. When it was again left I seemed to wander off as before by the side of a dark, slowly-flowing, great flood [= 'Denser Between Worlds' = 'Hades' = 'earth-veil'—cf. Statement No. 41] ... and, though I knew that death was hovering about, having no thought of religion nor dread of the end [cf. Statement No. 7]. I roamed on beneath the murky skies, until something again disturbed my body where it lay, when I was drawn back to it afresh and entered it with ever growing repulsion [cf. Statement No. 8]. ... About the end of the term of high fever I was summoned back to the huddled mass with intense loathing. As I drew near I heard someone say: "He will live". The mass was less cold and clammy, and ever after that the wanderings appeared to be fewer and shorter, the body and I grew more together, and ceased to be two separate entities. ... *In my wanderings everything was transparent to my senses* [= clairvoyance]. I saw plainly, for instance, a poor R.A.M.C. surgeon, of whose existence I had not known, and who was in quite another part of the hospital, grow very ill and die. I saw them carry him softly out on shoeless feet, lest we should know that he had died, and the next night, I thought, take him away to the cemetery. Afterwards, when I told these happenings to the sisters, they informed me that all this had happened.'

CASE No. 19—*Geddes's doctor-friend*

Lord, then Sir Auckland, Geddes, medical man, and former Professor of Anatomy, in 1937, related a doctor-friend's experience to the Royal Medical Society of Edinburgh. His friend almost died but, when brought back to life, declared that he had been fully conscious. He dictated his experience and the account was read by Geddes to the Society. Extracts are as follows.

'I was very ill ... but suddenly realized that my consciousness was separating from another consciousness, which was also "me".' Distinguishing an "ego-consciousness" from a "body-consciousness", he said, "*The ego-consciousness, which was now me, seemed to be altogether outside my body, which I could see*" ' [cf. Statement No. 17]. He continued, 'Gradually I realized that I could see not only my body and the bed, but everything in the whole house and garden. There I saw not only things at home, but in London and in Scotland, in fact wherever my attention was directed [= clairvoyance].

'From now on the description is and must be entirely metaphorical. There are no words which really describe what I saw, or rather, appreciated. Although I had no [physical] body, I had what appeared to be perfect two-eyed vision, and what I saw can only be described in this way:

'I was conscious of a psychic stream flowing with life through time, and this gave me the *impression of being visible* [in the Psychical Body], and it seemed to me to have particularly *intense iridescence* [= which was luminous, a radiant body or a 'body of light'—cf. Matt. xiii, 43]. I understood from my mentor that all our brains are just end-organs projecting, as it were, from the three-dimensional [= physical] universe into the psychical stream, and flowing with it into the fourth and fifth dimensions. [Messages from ordinary 'dead' communicators commonly insist that this is the correct view of the function of the brain—that it limits while it defines thought but it does not create thought.] Around each brain, as I saw it, there seemed to be ... a condensation of the psychic stream [= the 'aura'] which formed in each case as though it were a cloud (only it was not a cloud). ... Then realized that I myself was a condensation, as it were, in the psychic stream, a sort of cloud that was not a cloud. The visual impression I had of myself was blue. *Gradually I began to recognize people and I saw the psychic condensation [aura] attached to many of them.* ... Quite a number had very little. ... "A" gave a visual impression of blueness; "B" gave blue and dark red; "C" pink; "D" grey-brown; "E" pearly, etc. ... Each of these condensations varied from all others in bulk, sharpness of outline and apparent solidarity.' (The 'psychic condensation' here described obviously represents the 'aura', part of the Psychical Body. The predominant 'colours' indicate the predominant desires, thoughts and feelings of the person observed. Compare Arnold Bennett, Appendix VII.)

'I saw "B" enter my bedroom. I saw her go to the telephone. I saw my doctor leave his patients and come very quickly and heard him say, and *saw him think,* "He is nearly gone" [= telepathy]. I heard him quite clearly speak to me on the bed, but I was not in touch with the body and could not answer him. *I was really cross when he took a syringe and rapidly injected my body with something which I afterwards learned was camphor.* [*The case of the supposed deceased 'Major P.' is very similar to this.* Both Geddes's doctor-friend and 'Major P.' expressed great reluctance to return to the Physical Body—cf. Statement No. 8. Although statements as to reluctance to return are understandable in the light of these accounts, they seem to be unbelievable otherwise: everyone clings to physical life.]

'*As my heart began to beat more strongly, I was drawn back, and I was intensely annoyed.* I was just beginning to understand where I was. ... *Once back, all the clarity of vision of everything and anything disappeared, and I was just possessed of a glimmer of consciousness* [cf. the *kenosis*] *which was suffused with pain. This experience has shown no tendency to fade ... as a dream would do ...*

'Thus ended the record,' concluded Lord Geddes; 'what are we to make of it? Of one thing only can we be quite sure—it was not fake. Without that certainty I should not have brought it to your notice. ...'

Case No. 20—*Mr Sylvan J. Muldoon*

Muldoon's first out-of-the-body experience occurred when he was aged twelve, long before he had heard that such things were possible.

Muldoon awoke from sleep. '*I knew,*' *he said,* '*that I existed some-where, but where, I could not understand* ... [cf. the 'partial awakening' which sometimes occurs after death—Statement No. 25]. *I was powerless. My entire rigid body (I thought it was my physical, but it was my astral), commenced vibrating at a great rate of speed, in an up-and-down direction, and I could feel a tremendous pressure being exerted in the back of my head. ... Then the sense of hearing began to function, and that of sight followed. When able to see, I was more than astonished: I was floating in the air, rigidly horizontal a few feet above the bed* [cf. Statement No. 16] ... *I was moving towards the ceiling, all the while horizontal and powerless. I believed naturally that this was my Physical Body* [cf. Statement No. 10]. ... *Involuntarily, at about six feet above the bed ... I was uprighted and placed standing upon the floor of the room* ... [cf. the accounts of Gerhardi, Bulford, Mr 'H' of Bournemouth etc.]. *Then I managed to turn around. There was another "me" lying quietly on the bed* [cf. Statement No. 17]. *My two identical bodies were joined by means of an elastic-like cable* [= the 'silver cord', cf. Statement No. 19] which extended across the space of probably six feet which separated us. ... My first thought was that I had died during sleep.'

Muldoon wished to go to his mother, who slept in another room, to tell her of his plight. He found himself passing through the door without opening it [cf. Statement No. 31]. 'Going from one room to another, I tried to arouse the sleeping occupants of the house. *I tried to shake them but my hands passed through them.* Then I noticed that the cable was pulling with a stronger and stronger tug. ... I was being pulled backwards towards my Physical Body. ... It was the reverse procedure of that which I had experienced while rising from the bed. Slowly the phantom lowered, vibrating again as it did so, then it dropped suddenly, coinciding with the physical counterpart once more. *At the moment of coincidence, every muscle in the physical body jerked, and a penetrating pain, as if I had been split open from head to foot, shot through me* [cf. accounts by Mrs Lester, Capt. Burton, Gerhardi, etc.]. I was physically alive again, as amazed as fearful. I had been conscious throughout the entire occurrence.'

After this, Muldoon had hundreds of out-of-the-body experiences during which he made all kinds of critical observations and experiments such as would be impossible in mere dream-states. Reading Dr Hereward Carrington's earlier books, he realized that he, a young and unknown man, without any instructions in these matters, probably had more real knowledge of this extremely significant phenomenon than anyone else in the world. Eventually, in collaboration with Carrington, he wrote *The Projection of the Astral Body*, a book of inestimable value.

In the Introduction to this book, Carrington maintained that so much evidence has now accumulated 'for the existence of some sort of an astral body [= the Psychical Body of St Paul—I Cor. xv, 44] that this evidence is now very strong.' (At a later date he went further and said that the existence of the 'astral body' is 'virtually proved'.) Prof. E. Bozzano (*Discarnate Influence in Human Life*, J. M. Watkins, 1938) pointed out that the conclusions which Muldoon and Carrington had published in 1929 had been arrived at by him, by a process of comparative analysis, and published in 1910.

Muldoon considered that he possessed a natural power to 'project' his 'double' from his Physical Body. This, however, states the case in reverse. Carrington, in the Introduction to their book, stated that the bulk of Muldoon's contribution to it was written when he was so ill that he could not get out of bed. He 'was never certain but that the next day might prove his last'. In other words, Muldoon, so far from possessing a natural power to quit his Physical Body, actually lacked the natural power, vitality or nervous energy, to keep his Psychical and Physical Bodies 'in gear'; he was, we may say, half-dead. Muldoon himself in another part of the book recognized the 'half-dead' condition (which he called 'the morbidity factor') as one of several features that predispose to exteriorization. It would appear that this condition, as well as prolonged fasting, tend to cause fainting and collapse, with the exteriorization of the Psychical Body from the Physical Body, because the Physical Body is 'vibrating' too slowly for their continued coincidence. But this is not the only possible cause of exteriorization. Mystics who are in robust health (as well as non-mystics who are 'half-dead') tend to have out-of-the-body experiences: the mystic's Psychical Body is temporarily 'vibrating' too quickly for it to remain 'in gear' with the Physical Body. Certain of the factors which affect temporary exteriorizations from the body modify, even nullify, the effects of others. The same statement is true of permanent exteriorizations—*see* Statements No. 1 and 24.

Muldoon described exercises that aid in the production of out-of-the-body experiences, inviting those who are sceptical about the genuineness of his experiences to investigate for themselves. He added a word of warning: 'If you are neurotic, easily influenced, lack "will", and are fearful ...; if you live in an atmosphere of discord, do not try to practise astral body projection. If you are of this type, never "think within yourself" and never "watch yourself in the process of falling asleep"; turn towards physical culture.' (This advice is in agreement with the statements of supposed discarnates: they say that a man who indulges in fearful thoughts or discordant emotions will, when freed from the insulating effect of his Physical Body, tend to create analogous conditions in the ideo-plastic environment [cf. Statement No. 10] and to attract others with similar defects. On the other hand, a courageous, well-meaning, generous, clear-thinking man, freed from his physical envelope, will automatically create happy conditions and attract high and helpful discarnate personalities; 'To him that hath shall be given'.)

CASE NO. 21—Mr Vincent Turvey

About the same time as Muldoon was experimenting with out-of-the-body experiences in America, Turvey was having involuntary ones in England. They were unknown to each other. Turvey also was 'half-dead' and had been very ill for many years. The first public announcement he made of his ability to 'travel' in what he called his 'mental body' was in an English newspaper in 1903. Six years later he gave details of his experiences and evidence in support of their genuineness in his book, *The Beginnings of Seership* (Stead's Publishing House).

According to Turvey, he 'travelled', in his 'mental body' at about two miles above the surface of the earth and at a velocity that rendered objects indistinct and blurred. He said, 'When I arrive at, say, Mrs Brown's house in Bedford, I am not only able to see into one room, but am able to walk about the house, see the contents of various rooms etc. In a few cases, "I" have been visible. "I" also hear parts of conversations …'

Turvey mentioned the 'silver cord'; he said, 'This cord appears whenever the "I" leaves the "Me." It seems to join one body to the other, passing from the solar plexus of the one to the back of the neck of the other. It is very like a spider's cord. *It is silver, tinged with heliotrope,* and it extends and contracts as does an elastic cord' [cf. Statement No. 19].

Turvey gave examples of veridical information which he obtained while out of his Physical Body.

Muldoon spoke of the total non-physical body ('phantom') as a unit; Turvey recognized three sub-divisions of his total non-physical body, (a) the 'energy-', 'vitality-' or 'etheric-' body (which evidently represents the vehicle of vitality and memory, *i.e.*, the 'body-veil'), (b) the 'astral body' (= the Psychical Body) and (c) the 'mental body' (= the Spiritual Body)—cf. Statement No. 1b.

(II) PEOPLE WHO WERE VERY ILL

CASE NO. 22—Mr G. J. Einarsson

EINARSSON cannot have been influenced by the accounts of others. He is an Icelander, ignorant of languages other than his own. No such accounts had been published in his language when, in 1910, he had his experience. The case was published by Muldoon and Carrington (*The Phenomena of Astral Projection*, Rider & Co. Ltd., 1951).

Einarsson felt weak and could not move. He said, 'I felt that some-one was coming. Then I saw a man come into the room. ... He seemed to read my thoughts, because he said, "You need not fear me. I invite you to come and see those places intended for you after death" ... [cf. Statement No. 3, regarding 'deliverers'].

'*All at once I found that I was standing upon the floor, looking at my own material body lying in the bed* [cf. Statement No. 17]. ... *The "I" who stood there on the floor, looking at the "I" on the bed, was so strangely light. I felt that it would be no effort to move.* ... "Now we start off," said the man, and no sooner had he said it than we were off. ... I saw how the fjord was shiny black, for the mountains were reflecting the sea. ... *We ascended slantingly into the air* [cf. Rebell, Sculthorp, Hout, etc.] ... *What I saw I shall not attempt to describe, because I lack words ...*' [cf. II Cor. xii, 4].

CASE NO. 23—*Miss Mollie Fancher*

Miss Fancher was bed-ridden for nearly thirty years, and lived almost entirely without food. Prolonged illness and fasting are among the factors that favour the production of these experiences.

Her case (*Mollie Fancher, the Brooklyn Enigma*, by Judge H. Dailey, Brooklyn, 1894) was supposed to include multiple personality. Mollie claimed that, when out of her body, in trance, she experienced two distinct conditions. She said, '*Sometimes the whole top of my head seems on fire with the influx of light; my range of* [clairvoyant] *vision is very great and astonishingly clear* [corresponding to 'super-consciousness' in the Psychical Body and to 'Paradise' conditions]. *Then again, it seems as if I were seeing through a smoked glass, and my vision, or consciousness, is dim and indistinct*' [corresponding to 'sub-normal' consciousness in the vehicle of vitality or 'body-veil' and to 'Hades' conditions].

Miss Fancher gave a number of examples of veridical information obtained while she was out of her body.

CASE NO. 24—*Mr Horace E. Wheatley*

'*I am not at present a spiritualist in the accepted sense of the term*,' wrote Mr Wheatley, though the experience he described was clearly of a nature that is usually regarded as typically spiritualistic. It was pub-lished in *Two Worlds*, Feb. 27, 1954 only because Mr Wheatley was concerned with the fact that so many people find it difficult to believe in an after-life. Like Oxenham, having had a 'vivid' experience of the after-death state, he felt it his duty to place it on record.

Writing from the Royal Sussex County Hospital, Brighton, where he was recovering from a coma, Mr Wheatley said, '*While I was still unconscious, I felt myself floating in an atmosphere of peace and serenity. ...*

While in this beatific sphere, a local government officer I knew quite well came forward to meet me. He greeted me ... "Welcome Wheatley," he said, and then continued, "I shall have to see you later". And he slowly faded from my view.

'*Now the interesting point about this "interview" is that at the time I did not know that this friend had "passed on".* I was told it afterwards by my wife.' [There are many cases recorded in which dying persons have claimed to see friends or relatives who have died, but of whose death they have not been told. They say, 'There is so-and-so. Why did you not tell me that he had died?' On the other hand, it is said that there is no case on record in which a dying person has said something of this nature by error, the person 'seen' being actually 'alive'.]

CASE No. 25—*Mrs Gussie Dowell*

Mrs Gussie Dowell, of De Lion, Texas, U.S.A., a nurse, informed me (*in litt.*) that she had had an out-of-the-body experience when she was *eleven years old*. Since then, although she has followed certain instructions for the production of astral projection, she has not succeeded in repeating the experience. She thinks that this is because she has learned 'how easy to go, yet how hard to get back'. She has observed many deaths in hospital, and, like the supposed discarnates who have communicated details of their 'passing', she said, '*Always it is a peaceful "slipping away" that seems to be absolutely painless*' (cf. Statement No. 7].

Mrs Dowell's experience was as follows. 'I had been stung at the base of the spine by some insect. I began to get sick. The doctor failed to find the trouble. I became desperately ill and he gave me a hypodermic injection. Before lapsing into a coma I told Mother I was going to die. I was unconscious until four o'clock the next day. When I came to, my father was bathing my face with cold water.

'*As long as I could feel anything, I suffered intensely. Then I became easy* [= had vacated the body] ... *I looked down and could see my body lying on the bed and my father working over me* [cf. Statement No. 17]. In later years I have read of the experiences of people who say that there is a "silver cord". I had no "silver cord". *I went to a place through a veil of mist* [= through 'Hades' conditions—cf. Statement No. 41] *high above the earth* [into 'Paradise' conditions—cf. Statement No. 26]. I spoke to the men who were standing about the entrance, but was told to come back and live the rest of my life. The walls around this "Heaven" are pearly and translucent. I started back and it was not long before I awoke in my Physical Body. *It seemed that I "blacked-out" at the same distance from my body when I approached it, and regained my consciousness, as when I left it.*' [This is an interesting statement: Mrs Dowell evidently not only observed the momentary coma that, according to those of the 'dead' who were conscious of the process, occurs during the shedding of the body—see Statement No. 9—but also had the same experience at the corresponding stage on returning. Mme d'Espérance was similarly conscious of both shedding and re-entering the body.] Mrs Dowell concluded, '*I am more understanding and sympathetic with people than anyone could be who had not had such a revelation. It made me a better person!*'

Case No. 26—*Mr J. Redgewell*

Mr J. Redgewell, of Parkhurst avenue, Barnehurst, informed me (in litt.) *that, at a time when he was ignorant of psychic matters, having read no books on astral projection, etc., he experienced an exteriorization.* Since then he has had several, though not deliberate ones.

Mr Redgewell was indeed a sceptic as regards the after-life. *When ill, lying in bed, he was 'scared' by feeling his Physical Body 'dropping' and his Psychical Body 'rising'* [cf. Statement No. 9]. *Although he realizes that he had not projected 'far', the experience convinced him of the truth of survival. He no longer feared death.*

While out of his Physical Body, Mr Redgewell tried, unsuccessfully, to attract the attention of his family by shouting at them [cf. Statement No. 28]. He found that he could jump over a wall which was much too high for him to clear in the Physical Body. He 'landed gently on the other side'. But this did not surprise him: he knew he could do 'seemingly impossible things'.

Case No. 27—*Mrs A. Land*

This case was published in *Prediction*, May, 1936: 'I was very ill. I fell into a deep slumber in which I seemed to be taken to the astral plane. An aunt who had died came and began to magnetize my arm (cf. Statement No. 3]. She took me with her and said, "This is the first stage when you come over here." It was very beautiful [= 'Paradise', cf. Statement No. 26]. I was there some time when I was told that I would have to return to my body. When I woke up, I found my mother distracted. She thought I had passed away. *I believe that my spirit ... was on the astral plane. It was a very similar world to this one but more beautiful* [cf. Statement No. 26]. *I know that death does not end all.*'

Case No. 28—*Mr Baeschly*

Richet (*Thirty Years of Psychical Research*, Collins & Co. Ltd., 1923, trans. by de Brath) gave the case of Mr Baeschly who, with his father, was awakened about midnight by great noises for which they could find no cause. Later they received a letter from America to say that Baeschly's brother had died, and that, shortly before his passing, he had awakened from a long coma saying, 'I have made a long journey: I have been to my brother at Brunatte.'

CASE NO. 29—*Capt. Burton*

This case was reported by J. Arthur Hill (*Man is a Spirit*, Cassell & Co. Ltd., 1918). Burton said, 'I had heart-failure. *I found myself standing at the foot of my bed, looking at myself and the doctor* [cf. Statement No. 17] *and feeling very well and bright* [cf. Statement No. 26], *though puzzled.* Then suddenly I found myself dragged violently over the bed-rail where I floated above myself; following which came a tremendous crash [= the 'repercussion', due to a rapid return of the highly 'vibrating' Psychical Body to the slowly 'vibrating' Physical Body the effect resembling that of a severe clutch on a motor car—cf. Muldoon, Mrs Lester, Gerhardi etc.]. Then I heard the doctor's voice: "He is coming round". He had considered me dead for some time.'

CASE NO. 30—*Mr Arnold Bennett*

Arnold Bennett (*The Glimpse*) gave a résumé of Theosophical teachings in the form of a personal narrative. We give extracts in Appendix VII.

(III) PEOPLE WHO WERE EXHAUSTED, ETC.

CASE NO. 31—*Mr Oliver Fox*

*F*OX *declared that he originally had no knowledge whatever of experiences such as he described.* He was delicate and had many illnesses. His experiences, which were described in *Astral Projection*, Rider & Co. Ltd., resembled those of Gerhardi by starting as dreams, and it was from a dream that he first 'woke' to full out-of-the-body consciousness: his awakening was accompanied by the use of his critical faculties, since he observed that his 'dream environment' differed from the physical world in certain respects—the paving-stones were not normally aligned. He thus found that if, during a dream, he could observe some incongruity, that is, *if he could begin to exercise his critical faculties*, he would become 'awake' to a non-physical environment. For example, in a subsequent dream, seeing a parrot fly through a wall, and realizing the physical impossibility of the feat, he 'awoke' to 'astral' conditions. *Like Muldoon and Turvey, Fox said that, when out of the Physical Body, he could 'do some intriguing little tricks at will, such as moving objects without* *visible contact* [telekinesis] *and moulding the plastic matter into new forms'* [cf. Statement No. 10]. *Like Muldoon, van Eeden and others, when outside, yet near, his Physical Body (within what Muldoon called 'the range of cord-activity')* he experienced 'dual' or 'alternate' consciousness, *being aware of both physical and non-physical environments.* He said, 'I could feel myself standing in the dream and see the scenery; but at the same time I could feel myself lying in bed, and see my bedroom' [cf. Statement No. 18].

Like Gerhardi and Muldoon, Fox decided to get further away from his Physical Body and see what happened. Then something seemed to 'click' in his brain, his Physical Body ceased to have a strong attraction for his Psychical body, and he was 'free' (cf. Muldoon and Ouspensky).

Walking along and seeing a man, he asked what time it was. But he was unseen and unheard [cf. Statement No. 28]. This made him feel lonely; he willed to awake in his Physical Body, and did so.

Fox made an experiment with chloroform. '*It seemed to me,*' he said, '*that I shot up to the stars, and that a shining silver thread* [= the 'silver cord'—cf. Statement No. 19] *connected my celestial self with my Physical Body.*' He only once saw (though often feeling) his Physical Body though he saw that of his wife. Muldoon commented, 'There are many reasons why this could be true'.

Fox cited one adventure in which he 'seemed to be earthbound' and then one (of a 'vast dream-London') which he considered was 'on some level of the astral plane' [here = 'Denser Between Worlds', 'earth-veil' or 'Hades']. He added, 'In the course of my various explorations of this place I have found that the astral counterpart (if such it be) of a city appears much larger than the earthly one; for *in addition to its present structures and features are to be found buildings, monuments, etc., which have no present existence on the earth. Some of these may have existed in the past; and others I suspect to be powerful thought-forms* [cf. Statement No. 10] ... *or perhaps the astral foreshadowings of earthly buildings yet to come.* ... If you can become connected up with the psychic trail of the forces governing Xtown Technical College, you may get a vision of the new buildings to be occupied by that institution in 1960—which is what a psychometrist actually does. ... *To the astral explorer, then, Xtown will seem at once both familiar and strange, a curious blend of the known and unknown ... and the general effect will be that the astral Xtown is much larger than the earthly one.* And as far as my experiences go, the investigator who makes his *n*th trip to the astral Xtown will still find the same features (non-existent on earth) that *puzzled him* on his first adventure.' (The fact that he was 'puzzled' indicates that his critical faculties were alert and that the experience was no mere dream. All the above is very similar to 'communications from supposed discarnates'—*e.g. Life Beyond the Grave.*)

Fox acquired the ability to leave his Physical Body through the head—through the 'door' in the pineal gland [cf. Statement No. 13]. Some of the 'places' he visited were on earth, others on the 'astral plane' [here = 'Denser Between Worlds' or 'Hades'] and he said, 'People who cannot forget or forgive poor Raymond's cigar will get very cross with me when I say that there are electric trams on the astral plane; but there *are* ...' He said, 'I have seen the body I travel in (etheric, astral, or perhaps mental) ... *Occasionally I have not been able to see any astral body when I looked for it—no legs, no arms, no body—an extraordinary sensation—just a consciousness, a man invisible even to himself, passing through busy streets.* ...' (We suggest that these were 'partial' or 'preliminary' awakenings—cf. Statement No. 25.)

Fox said, '*The experience is so extremely real that one who undergoes it may wonder if he is still walking in his sleep—if he cannot see his body upon the bed. His doubts will speedily be set at rest when he finds he can walk through the wall*' [cf. Statement No. 31]. Like Muldoon and Bulford, he gave directions as to how out-of-the-body experiences may be obtained. *Like them, Fox asserted that even a sceptic who persevered with the directions could satisfy himself that these are genuine experiences, demonstrating the existence of a soul able to function independently of the Physical Body.*

CASE No. 32—*Mr Wm. Gerhardi*, M.A., B.LITT.

Gerhardi had no previous knowledge of out-of-the-body experiences. In a prefatory note to his book, *Resurrection*, published in 1934 by Cassell & Co. Ltd., he insisted that, 'incredible as it may seem', what he described was 'a true experience'. He also published in *Prediction*, 1936 and 1939.

Gerhardi intended to write a book on the subject of immortality and went to bed in a state of nervous exhaustion. He dreamed that he had broken a tooth but that when he tried to pull it out, 'It came out easily, in a long sticky strand, like molten toffee'. *This awakening of the critical faculties during a dream (as with Oliver Fox) caused a real (yet not a physical) awakening:* that is, it caused an out-of-the-body experience. 'I *was* awake,' says Gerhardi, 'I knew, because I knew I was dreaming about that tooth. Therefore, dreaming though I still was, I had but to wake to ascertain that my tooth was sound. "Now wake," I said, "and find there is no need to worry about going to the dentist." And I woke. But I woke with a start. *I had stretched out my hand to press the switch of the lamp on the bookshelf over my bed, and instead found myself grasping the void, and myself suspended in mid-air, on a level with the bookcase. The room, except for the glow from the electric stove, was in darkness, but all around me was a milky pellucid light.* I was that moment fully awake, and so fully conscious that I could not doubt my senses. Astonished, I said to myself, "Fancy *that*! Now *would* you have believed it! Now this *is* something to tell. And this is *not* a dream." ... The suspension in mid-air lasted only a few minutes, during which I felt as if I were being suspended by a steel arm which held me rigid. [Others use this symbol of a 'steel arm'; it is clearly related to the cataleptic condition which is fairly common.] Then I was seized, pushed out horizontally, placed on my feet, and thrust forward with the gentle-firm hand of the monitor—"There you are, now proceed on your own" [cf. Muldoon, Bulford, 'Mr H.' and Hout]. *I stood there, the same living being, but rather less stable, as if defying gravity. If the whole world united in telling me that it was a dream, I would remain unconvinced. ...*

'I was in the body of my resurrection. "So that's what it's like? How utterly unforeseen." I staggered to the door. *I felt the handle but could not turn it* [cf. Statement No. 31]. *Then, turning, I became aware of a strange appendage. At the back of me was a coil of light* [the 'silver cord'— cf. Statement No. 19]. *It was like a luminous garden-hose resembling the strong broad ray of dusty light at the back of a dark cinema projecting on the screen in front. To my utter astonishment, that broad cable of light at the back of me illuminated the face on the pillow, as if attached to the brow of the sleeper* [cf. Gibier's engraver, Brunton, Mrs Joy and Mrs Larsen]. *The sleeper was myself* [cf. Statement No. 17]. ... *Who would have thought that I had a spare body at my disposal adapted to the new conditions?* But I was not dead; my Physical Body was sleeping peacefully, while I was apparently on my feet and as good as before. *Yet it wasn't my accustomed self. It was as if my mould were walking through a murky, heavy space which however, gave way easily before my emptiness.* [The 'murky heavy space' symbolized 'earth-veil' or 'Hades' conditions; compare 'the dark river' of Dr Enid Smith, the 'dark flood' of Sir Alex. Ogston, the 'River Styx' of mythology, etc. See also the accounts of Mrs Joy, Walter de la Mare, Miss Roos, etc. and Statement No. 41.]

' "Now, how will I get out?" I thought. ... At the same moment I was pushed forward. *The door passed through me, or I through the door* [cf. Statement No. 31]. I was in the corridor, dark, but illumined by a subdued light which seemed to emanate from my own body [cf. Statement No. 17], and the next instant I had entered my bathroom, affecting from habit to *switch on the light, but unable to press it down* [cf. Mrs Griggs, Mrs Larsen and Statement No. 31].

'*There was this uncanny tape of light between us, like the umbilical cord, by means of which the body on the bed was kept breathing* [this function, assigned to the 'cord', agrees with that given by discarnates; Statement No. 20], while *I seemed to be not walking but wading through an unsteady sea* [= 'earth-veil' or 'Hades' conditions—his Psychical Body was much enshrouded by the 'body-veil' or vehicle of vitality]. ... "*Now to be scientific,*" I said, "*this is one chance in a million. You must convince*

yourself so that nothing later will make you think it was merely a dream."
[These critical observations indicate that he was not merely dreaming—
cf. Statement No. 12.] All this I said to myself while going round and
collecting such evidence as: that window is open; that curtain is drawn;
this is the new towel-heater. It did not occur to me to cast a glance at
myself, but *I noticed a familiar outline of myself in the looking-glass'* ...
[cf. Miss Peters. Whether the 'double' is, or is not, seen in a mirror
might depend on its relative density. This feature in the accounts is
significant. We have already noted that Gerhardi's Psychical Body was
accompanied by much of the vehicle of vitality or 'body-veil', i.e. it
was relatively 'objective'. The same applied to Miss Peters (who, after
seeing her 'double' in a mirror, described the act of shedding the
(exteriorized) vehicle of vitality). On the other hand, Gibier's engraver,
who did not see his 'double' in a mirror, gave no indication that it was
impregnated with the vehicle of vitality. In Gerhardi and Miss Peters
the latter was relatively loosely associated with the Physical Body].

' "What evidence? What more evidence?" I kept asking myself, as I
passed from room to room. Here I noted which windows were shut,
then I tried, and failed, to open the linen cupboard [cf. Statement No.
31]. Then I noted the time. I could think of no other way of collecting
evidence to convince myself later, for my consciousness flared up full
and then grew so dim again that I was near to sinking back into my
dream [cf. Kelley, who realized that his condition approached, but did
not equal that of the dead and Mrs Leonard, who suggested that consciousness is reduced by the amount of vitality that passes along the
'cord']. And suddenly this strange power resumed its lead and began to
play pranks with me. *I was being pushed along like a half-filled balloon*
[cf. Bertrand, Lind, Helen Brooks and Mrs 'Prothero']. Out I flew
through the front door and hovered in the air, feeling an extraordinary
lightness of heart. Now I could fly anywhere, to New York, etc., visit
a friend, if I liked, and it wouldn't take me a moment. *But I feared that
something might happen to sever the link with my sleeping body. But when
my body obeyed and flew back and I felt it hovering over my old body on the
bed, drab disappointment came back to me* (cf. Statement No. 8]. *"Not
yet," I said. And again I flew off. When I flew thus swiftly, my consciousness
seemed to blot out and only returned when again I walked or moved at a
reasonable speed.* [Cf. Turvey's and Muldoon's accounts regarding
the effect on consciousness of speedy travel.] What was I going to do
now? Proof, I said. I wanted irrefutable proof which would convince
me and others when I came back into my body. ... Whom could I
visit? And that moment the thought occurred to me: let me visit my
friend Max Fisher at Hastings. ... My conscious-will flew out through
a window. But no sooner than the thought had occurred, doubt at
something too good to be true set in on its heels, and an instant later

back I came. But it *can* be done! I reassured myself, I am sure it can! *And again I flew off, this time again through the front door, so swiftly that my consciousness was blotted out.*

'*Consciousness returned suddenly. I was stepping lightly over an open patch of grass. ... The thought occurred to me: how do I know I am not dreaming this? and the answer: look for the lighted cord behind you. I looked round. It was there, but it was very thin.* [Cf. Muldoon, Bulford, etc.] That satisfied me that I was not dreaming, but so pale was my consciousness that it never occurred to me to ask myself where I was or why I had come. And my consciousness went out again like a lamp. When it returned it was so weak that I asked myself no questions, no more than you would in a dream. ... I was apparently hanging on to a thick brown beam on a white ceiling, effortlessly, like a bat, and in my enfeebled state of consciousness and the balloon-like lightness of my new body this seemed as unquestionable to the mind as it seemed natural to the body.

'*Then, with a jerk which shook me* [the 'repercussion'—cf. Muldoon, etc.], *... I opened my eyes. I was in my bedroom. ... Not a detail of my experience had been lost to my mind and there was quite another quality about it all, that of reality, which removed it from the mere memory of a dream* [cf. Statement No. 26]. *... We had a duplicate body all there and ready for use, the almost indistinguishable double of our natural body. ... It seemed that, for the first stage of survival at any rate, we already had a body, stored away, it is true, like a diver's suit, but nevertheless neatly folded in our own every-day bodies, always at hand in case of death or for special use. ...*

'*I got up, and went through the rooms, checking the mental notes I had made about which windows were closed or open, which curtains drawn; and the evidence in all cases proved correct.*'

Gerhardi cogitated as follows. 'I have always considered that, intellectually, the case for and against survival was pretty equally balanced. Now, after having surprised myself, with my senses and consciousness unimpaired, in a duplicate body, the scale went down heavily for survival. *... For if my body of flesh could project this other more tenuous and shadowy body, while I could still behold my flesh stretched out as if in death and of no more account to me than if it were my coat, then this subtler body, adapted to the subtler uses of another plane, was also but a suit or vehicle, to be in turn perhaps discarded for another ...*

'All experience,' continued Gerhardi, 'goes to prove a progressive discarding of so-called essentials. The essential to man has many embodiments; on each plane of life these embodiments are retained as hostages and slain: but the man behind the scenes does not appear till the end, and we do not know in what guise' [cf. the conception invariably given by supposed discarnates that death is a progressive unveiling]. Philosophizing further, he says, 'Gone, I reflected ... was the notion that death was eternal rest. ... Gone was the notion that the soul was like a little fleecy cloud. That twin body was real enough [cf. Statement No. 26]. *Perhaps it was rash to think that conditions beyond the grave were entirely different from ours. The surprise might be that they were the same. ...*' [Cf. Statements No. 10, 32, 33.]

On the second occasion that Gerhardi found himself out of his Physical Body, he was conscious of whirling blindly through his rooms and he 'felt too dim to realize what was happening'. He continued, 'Only when my own physical face looked back at me in dull but recognizable reflection was I sufficiently startled to say to myself: "But I am hanging on to the stained-glass fanlight over my dining-room door." ... How was it then that I managed to hold on by the finger-tips? The answer flashed across my mind: it was another astral projection. *And the proof was to see my body in bed* [cf. Statement No. 31]. *No sooner thought than complied with. But how queer! I saw myself in bed.* ... And suddenly I awoke. I was standing by the door in my bedroom facing the large mirror reflecting the bed with my sleeping body. I turned from the mirror and faced the bed: so it was. ... I walked round the flat, looked into the dining-room and noted the time. ... I went to my study, and sat in the chair at my writing-table. Here I sat, my own ghost, who could touch and feel his writing materials, but could not as much as lift a pencil. ... I suddenly saw Bonzo enter the room [cf. Statement No. 18]. "But how did you come in?" I exclaimed. "I heard the lift, but whoever opened the door to you?" "I don't use lifts," he said. ... Bonzo stood there, rather more smiling, more golden than ruddy, his face more transparent and frail than I had seen him before. "Well?" he said, "You're at it again, I see." "Yes," I replied. "Now you believe it, don't you?" "Well, yes, there's something in it," he smiled. ...'

Gerhardi next found himself in a field and again met Bonzo who said, ' "Whither, homing bird?" *"Why 'homing bird'?" "Because,"* he said, *"you are tied* [cf. Statement No. 19] *and we are free"* [cf. Statement No. 20]. ... *We had each projected ourselves from our natural bodies. ... Only, when turning a corner, I noticed the thin ray of light which extended from me, fading away into bright daylight. I also noticed that Bonzo had no such little tail of light.* ... Thus we came to Bonzo's house. ... We walked up the steps to Bonzo's bedroom, and there we stood. There I stood by his side and together we looked down at Bonzo's body on the bed. The man on the bed was not breathing. ... The Bonzo at my side, who looked at his double with an air of fastidious, almost quizzical dismay, was the living Bonzo. ...'

Gerhardi now had a review of his past earth-life [cf. Statement No. 5]. 'I,' he said, 'who had left my natural body on the bed, could now overtake the millions of untenanted bodies once mine, and tune-in with them. ... I took possession of one or the other of the milliard forms I had been at this or that instant of my past. I was re-living the authentic moment, not merely recalling it. ... I get up. I go out. Inconceivable happiness. I notice my extreme exhilaration and wonder whether I may not have really died unawares. I stopped, turned round. But the silver cord, faint and thin, was still there.'

Like so many who have had out-of-the-body experiences (and like those supposed discarnates who were brought back to life by injections etc.), *Gerhardi was reluctant to return to the physical body: he said, 'My heart quailed* [cf. Statement No. 8]. The return was with a jerk which shook me as if the machinery dropped into my bowels weighed a ton!

'After breakfast,' he said, 'I rang up Woburn Square. ... It was as I thought. A terrible thing had happened. The butler's voice broke into a sob. Bonzo had had his wrist smashed to be re-set. But he hadn't come round from the anaesthetic. ... At the grave everyone cried because they loved and missed Bonzo. But I did not weep, for I had stood with him and seen the almost quizzical look with which he beheld the prostrate companion of his earthly exploits ...'

CASE No. 33—*Mrs Eileen J. Garrett's nurse*

In her book *Telepathy* (Creative Age Press, Inc., N.Y., 1941), Mrs Garrett mentions that astral projection very often occurs in telepathic experiments. 'This projection,' she continued, 'should be more fully understood, for I am always coming into contact with people who have experienced it, and have been afraid to accept its significance. *I believe that projection takes place more often than any of us realize, and that it happens very easily when we are emotionally distressed, or when we are ill and the physical hold upon ourselves is less tenacious.*' (Muldoon, Bulford and others make similar statements. The present writer suggests that exteriorization may occur in illness because, although the 'double', or Psychical Body, may be 'vibrating' at or near its normal (relatively high) rate, the Physical Body is unusually sluggish and the two cannot remain 'in gear'. Exteriorizations that are due to drugs are similarly explained.)

Mrs Garrett cited the act of dying and extreme illness, in this con-nexion. She said, 'We have all heard of, and some of us have experi-enced, the apparition of someone at a time preceding his death, when the bodily-hold no longer controls the senses. Dancers, especially, are aware of this control, and I have heard Anna Pavlova say that she achieved her great spiritual beauty in the dance, and her phenomenal lightness, by the ability which she herself possessed of getting outside of herself, and demanding that her body portray perfectly the spiritual significance of the dance. ... Desire plays an important role in my own projection [cf. Muldoon, etc.], and I feel that this is true for everyone who is working creatively, and who wishes to relate an interpretation of a spiritual understanding to his work. ...'

She gave an example, from her own experience, of a projection caused by desire (and habit). It is as follows: (italics by present writer). 'While recuperating from an illness in the South of England, I was accompanied by a friend who desired to look after me through the nights. *One particular evening she seemed unusually tired, and as soon as dinner was over and we had reached our room, she expressed a strong desire to go to bed.* This we did, and she quickly fell into what seemed like a very heavy sleep. I was lying quietly in my own bed in the semi-darkness, when I became aware that my friend had risen and was moving with extreme care towards the dressing-table by the window. As she approached the table, she seemed to be bending low, searching for something.

'I addressed her quietly, telling her that she could put the light on, as I was still awake; but even as I spoke to her, I heard a moan coming from the direction of her bed. I sat up quickly, intending to put all the lights on. As I did so, I saw the figure by the dressing-table slide quietly toward the bed, while at the same time, I saw that my friend had not stirred, but was still sleeping. As the light flooded the room, she sat up very quickly, and seemed distressed. She looked in my direction, and breathed a sigh of relief to see me so close to her. Rubbing her eyes, she remarked that she had been dreaming that in the dream it was necessary for her to reach me, but something that she could not see [her Physical Body] held her back from being able to see or touch me. Still talking about her dream, she got out of bed and approached the dressing-table. *She poured out a dose of the cough-mixture that she had been in the habit of leaving by my bedside before she slept, and without further word to me, she went back to bed, and quickly fell asleep* ... [cf. the Grenside case].

'Next morning, on awakening, she retained no recollection of the incident of the night before, and neither could she recall the dream material that had obviously awakened her in the night.' Mrs Garrett said that the 'double', as seen in the dim light of the room, was by no means ethereal but apparently solid and real.

(The explanation of the above is as follows. Using Muldoon's terminology, the lady had a strong desire to perform that habitual act: as she was unusually tired, her 'double' was considerably detached from, or 'out of gear' with, its physical counterpart; the physical counterpart being 'incapacitated' so far as the desired movement was concerned, the 'double' [which was not incapacitated] went through the movements and was observed to do so by Mrs Garrett.)

CASE NO. 34—*Mr D. D. Home*

D. D. Home (*Incidents of my Life*, Pitman, 1864) described the following experience. '*I remember*,' he says, '*with vivid distinctness asking myself whether I was asleep or not, when, to my amazement, I heard the voice of one who, while on earth, was far too pure for such a world as ours.*' Home was told that he was about to have a foretaste of death [cf. Statement No. 3 regarding 'deliverers']. *He saw 'the whole of his nervous system, as it were, composed of thousands of electrical scintillations'*. [cf. the account of G. Costa and note that A. J. Davis reported a similar clairvoyant vision]. '*Gradually*,' Home continued, '*I saw that the extremities were less luminous* [cf. Bertrand, Miss Yeoman, Miss Blakeley, etc.] *and the finer membranes surrounding the brain became, as it were, glowing, and I felt that they were in a spirit body in every respect similar to the body which I saw lying motionless before me on the bed* [cf. Statement No. 17]. *The only link which held the two forms together seemed to be a silvery-like light which proceeded from the brain* [= the 'silver cord'—cf. Statement No. 19]. *The voice said, "Death is but a second birth, corresponding in every respect to the natural birth: should the uniting link be severed, you could never again enter the body"* ' [cf. Statement No. 20]. *During this experience, Home had a review of his past life* [cf. Statement No. 5]. *Later, he saw friends who had permanently left their Physical Bodies* [cf. Statement No. 18]. *He was most reluctant to return to his Physical Body* [cf. Statement No. 8].

CASE NO. 35—*Mr Edward Morrell*

A man may leave his Physical Body not only because he is more or less ill and physically exhausted but also because of either extreme mental or physical pain (or because of both, since physical pain usually causes mental pain). Mrs Eileen Garrett's out-of-the-body experiences, which began in girlhood, resulted from attempts to avoid mental pain caused by an unsympathetic aunt. The experience of 'Starr Daily' (*Release*, Arthur James, 1941), was due to physical, accompanied by mental, pain. It would appear that when pain gets beyond endurance there is a tendency for the sufferer to escape it by the simple expedient of quitting his Physical Body. (This agrees with the statements of supposed discarnates—cf. Statement No. 6—that about an hour before death a man may have left his Physical Body and stand, observing, beside it. This statement, in turn, agrees with No. 7 (that no physical pain is felt in the natural act of dying), No. 17 (that the Physical Body is often seen, from without, by the dying man, and No. 18 (that 'departed' friends are often seen before death actually takes place). Accounts of their experiences by men who have nearly been drowned, hanged, suffocated, electrocuted, etc., and yet recovered, support the above, since they include the statement that a point was soon reached when all pain ceased and, indeed, the sufferer became happy and free (cf. the cases of Georginus, No. 38, and Ellison, No. 36). It is probable that some people naturally escape from the body more quickly and more readily than others. The facility would be increased by age, ill-health, sedative drugs, etc.

Morrell's account was published in his book, *The Twenty-Fifth Man*. His statements were verified by the Governor of the State of Arizona. Morrell, in the State prison, was subjected to excruciating tortures. But as soon as the pain reached a certain intensity he ceased to feel it. *He felt as though his mind left his body in a 'mind-body' and, before long, was free of the prison. Morrell then saw, and later described, not only the Physical Body he had left* (cf. Statement No. 17) *but many things that he could not possibly have seen physically and that were actually happening at the time.* His Physical Body was in a windowless underground cell, but he was able to give accurate descriptions of people and events outside. He could not, however, leave his Physical Body at will—only involuntarily when pain became unbearable. Those statements of Morrell which were verified by others may be accepted, but other statements made by him appear to belong to a dream-consciousness.

CASE No. 36—*Mr N. F. Ellison*

The case of N. F. Ellison is given in *Journ. S.P.R.*, xxv, p. 126. He said, ' "H" and I were in the worst trenches we had ever been in. We were exhausted. *Several hours of this misery passed and then an amazing change came over me. I became acutely conscious that I was outside myself; that the real "me"—the Ego or Spirit—was entirely separate and outside my fleshly body. I was looking in a wholly detached and impersonal way, upon the discomforts of a khaki-clad body* [cf. Statement No. 17], *which, whilst I realized that it was my own, might easily have belonged to somebody else, for all the direct connexion I seemed to have with it* (cf. Statement No. 17]. I knew that my body must be feeling acutely cold and miserable, but I, my spirit part, felt nothing [cf. Statement No. 7].

'*At the same time, it seemed a very natural happening ... and it was only afterwards that I realized that I had been through one of the most wonderful experiences of my life. ... Nothing will shake my inward belief that my soul and body were entirely separated from each other.*'

CASE No. 37—*Anon.*

An anonymous contributor to *Fate* for Feb. 1953 gave the following narrative. '*That particular night I was especially tired. ... I sat staring blankly ahead, thinking of nothing. Then something made me look towards the door to the dining-room. As I turned my head, I felt as if a great weight were leaving me* [= shedding the Physical Body: the temporarily exteriorized Miss Kaeyer as well as several supposed discarnates gave this description. Conversely, Mrs 'X's body was 'heavy' when she re-entered it]. *There in the open doorway stood a perfect double of myself* [cf. Statement No. 17]. ... *My image stood smiling at me, and in an instant I was up in a corner of the room and could see both myself and the image in the doorway.* [This suggests a series of three bodies—see below.] In another instant I was back in my body and the image was gone. There ensued only a feeling of lightness: no fear. *At that time I knew nothing of spiritualism or of astral theories.* But years later I learned that, according to the Yogin teaching, each person has a corporeal body, an astral body, and a soul. Still I have never heard otherwise of a double projection.' [A number of others are given in these pages, e.g. Mrs Joy, Mrs Jeffrey, Miss Stables, Messrs Scunthorp, Turvey, Lind and Yram.]

Case No. 38—*Georginus*

This early case, one of exteriorization caused by pain, was given in Dr Kerner's *The Seeress of Prevorst* (printed in Germany in 1829, translated into English by Catherine Crowe and published by J. C. Moore in 1845). Georginus, persecuted for religion, was stretched on the rack at Prague. He 'became insensible to pain and appeared so lifeless that the executioners took him down and flung him on the earth for dead. After the lapse of some hours, however, Georgina returned to consciousness'.

Georginus said that, during the torture, he had had a 'dream'. He had been in a 'green and beautiful meadow' [= 'Paradise' conditions—cf. Statement No. 26] where there was a tree with 'a great deal of fine fruit and many birds.' Three men kept watch over it. Kerner said, 'He described these men and it is a remarkable fact that, six years afterwards three men, answering his description, were appointed to rule over the Church.' [According to the supposed discarnate Philip, communicating to his mother—*Philip in the Spheres*, Aquarian Press, 1952—the latter, during periods of deep sleep, used to 'visit' her son, though memories of such visits rarely 'came through' into 'normal consciousness': however, 'vague memories of green meadows' [= 'Paradise' conditions] were among the 'true ones'. 'Philip' said, 'vague as they are, they are not ordinary dreams ... this is the real beginning of true sleep-life-memory'].

The Seeress of Prevorst (Frau Hauffe) clearly had a loose vehicle of vitality or 'body-veil'—she was barely alive over a considerable period of time. She said '*It often appears to me that I am out of my body, and then I hover over it. This is not pleasant because I recognize my body.* ... The bonds of my nerve-spirit [= 'body-veil'] are becoming daily weaker.'

CASE No. 39—*Mr F. Huntley*

This case was given by J. Arthur Hill (*Man is a Spirit*, Cassell & Co. Ltd., 1918). Mr Huntley said, 'I had been under great mental stress. *I had not been indulging in psychism, had never attended a seance, nor had I been reading anything that might act as suggestion.*

'I woke from sleep to find myself out of the body. I was conscious in two places [= 'dual consciousness']—in a feeble degree in the body in bed, and in a great degree away from the body [cf. Statement No. 18]. I was surrounded by a white opaque light [cf. Geddes, Gerhardi, Oxenham, etc.—and Statement No. 26]. I felt absolutely happy and secure.

'*The whole of my personality lay "out there", even to the replica of the body* [cf. Statement No. 17]. I was not conscious of leaving the body, but woke up out of it. *It was not a dream, for the consciousness was an enhanced one, as superior to the ordinary waking state as that is to the dream state.* Indeed, I thought to myself, "This cannot be a dream", so I willed "out there!" As my spirit-self moved, so the body in bed moved. I was too happy to shorten the experience by moving further. It was very vivid. *I am sure that had a feeble thread* [= the 'silver cord'—cf. Statement No. 19] *between soul and body been severed, I should have remained intact* [cf. Statement No. 20]. *The grosser Physical Body is sloughed off for a finer one. ...*'

(IV) PEOPLE WHO WERE QUITE WELL

CASE No. 40—*The Revd Dr George Hepworth*

DR HEPWORTH had what he claimed to be a genuine out-of-the-body experience, describing it in his book, *Brown Studies*. He said, '*I seemed to step out of my body, and stand beside it, looking down upon it. I felt as light as air, and thought, "This must be what St Paul calls the Spiritual Body"*' [cf. Statement No. 17]. He was reluctant to return to 'the narrow quarters' of the Physical Body [cf. Statement No. 8]. 'I moved away from my Physical Body towards the door, and to my surprise, I found that the door was no obstruction whatsoever: I simply passed through it [cf. Statement No. 31]. *I knew that a cold wind was blowing ... but I was not chilled* [cf. Hives, Mme d'Espérance, etc.]. *Then I stepped back into the room to get another glimpse of the body. ... "It is not dead," I said to myself, "only I have stepped out of it. I shall have to return to it by and by," and at that thought I shuddered* [cf. Statement No. 8]. *... While I stood there, my dog Leo awoke. ... He approached my body in the usual way, with a wag of* *the tail, snuffed at my legs, and then appeared to be confused.* Something was not as he expected to find it. He then deliberately snuffed at my legs a second time. Not satisfied, he sat on his haunches gazing into the face. I thought that perhaps his confusion arose from the fact that the eyes were closed. On ordinary occasions, when he wished to wake me from a doze, he put his paws on my knees, and gave a quick, sharp bark, as though to say, "Come, master, rouse yourself!" But this time he exhibited signs of terror ... and uttered a mournful howl. *Then he apparently caught sight of me standing by the door. With a single leap, he reached my side, but turned instantly, took his place between me and the body, looked first at one and then at the other, and trembled in evident agony.* ...

'Just then the thought of my lost love came into my mind. An intense desire to see her seized me. ... It seemed to be an impelling force, and I flew with incredible speed through the darkness. The camp, the lake, the mountains were lost to view almost instantly, while other mountains and lakes came within range of my astonished vision. ... But I became so confused while journeying that I hardly noticed the landscape that lay far below me. ... I came to a certain point on the road. ... Something held me to the spot. ... "She is there," I said under my breath, "and is suffering. Will she be able to see me? Can I do anything to relieve her distress?" The next moment I was in the room. ... Margaret was sitting at the bedside of poor Edward, with her back toward me. ... I strode across the room ... and called out, "Margaret! Margaret!" For an instant I thought she heard me, for she raised her head as though in the act of listening. ... *I suffered tortures in the thought that I was invisible and could not make her recognize me* [cf. Statement No. 28]. I went to her side and placed my hand on hers, hoping that she would feel me near. Perhaps she did. At any rate, she looked up, then rose from her chair, went to the other side of the room, and stood there looking at an old photograph of me ... [This was the 'Call' —Statement No. 2—in reverse].

'Just before twelve, Edward roused. The last moments had arrived. ... He turned and his eyes rested on me. He stretched both arms in my direction and whispered, "Clarence! Clarence!" and then fell back in a stupor. I am sure he saw me. ... *That man's soul, half freed from his body, saw my soul standing at the foot of the bed, and, recognizing me, called me by name. I have no doubt of that.* [This was Statement No. 18 in reverse.]

'Then he whispered, "Paper and pencil." ... He wrote about two pages, signed the note, folded it, and said, "Margaret." "Yes, dear?" "An envelope." He placed the note in the envelope, sealed it, wrote someone's name on it, and handed it to his wife. "In good time," said the dying man, "you will find him. Deliver it to him." She shook her head ... but he said, "It is right, I wish it." With that he turned his head to one side, then all was still. ... Margaret thought she was alone with her dead. She was not, for I was there. ... I looked at the clock: it was three minutes past twelve. ...

'I was aroused by John saying: "I called, sir, and you didn't answer. Then I thought it best to wake you in any way I could. ..." "Yes, thank you, John. I never slept so in my life before. Is it late?" "Time for bed, sir." "What is the hour?" "Three and a half minutes past twelve, sir." Had I really made the journey from Florida to the Adirondacs in thirty seconds?

'After I retired I was unable to sleep. I felt that I should jot down my impressions, and the date and time when I saw Edward Waring die. ...

'It was on the 5th of March that this happened. On the 8th I received a letter from my cousin in Florida. "Ah," I said to myself, "Now I shall discover that it was only an unusually vivid dream." But I read these words: "Edward Waring has been a great sufferer since I last wrote you. ... He breathed his last on the night of 5th March, at three minutes past twelve." *It was clear that I had been by Edward's bedside and saw him die.'*

CASE NO. 41—*Dr P. Gibier's engraver*

Ralph Shirley (*The Mystery of the Human Double*, Rider & Co. Ltd.) gave the case of an engraver, first published by Gibier in his *Analyses de Choses*. He told the doctor, 'On returning home one evening, I experienced an extraordinary feeling of lassitude. ... I retired, lit my lamp and placed it on the table by the side of the sofa and rested my head on the cushions. *I became giddy* [= shedding the Physical Body—cf. Statement No. 9] *and found myself in the middle of the room. Looking round, ... I saw my body stretched on the sofa'* [cf. Statement No. 17]. *Approaching his Physical Body, he was surprised to find it still breathing. He tried to turn out the lamp but could not* (cf. Statement No. 31]. *His Psychical Body seemed to be clothed in white* [cf. Gerhardi, Lord Geddes's doctor-friend, etc.]. He stood in front of the mirror but did not see his own image.

'I remarked,' he said, 'the absence of light in my neighbour's apartments, but this caused me no difficulty. *I found I could perceive quite plainly by what appeared to be a ray of light emitted from my epigastrium which illuminated the objects in the room'* [cf. Gerhardi, Paul Brunton, Mrs Joy and Mrs Larsen]. It then occurred to him to go into his neighbour's apartment (into which so far he had only looked). '*I had hardly conceived the wish,'* he said, '*when I found myself there.'* ... [Many others say this—Hepworth, Muldoon, Gerhardi, Mrs Leonard, Geddes's doctor-friend, etc. Communications from the supposed dead include similar statements.] '*I passed through the wall easily'* [cf. Statement No. 31].

It was his first visit to these rooms and he knew that the owner was away in Paris. *He inspected the rooms with a view to recalling their contents and especially noted the titles of books on the shelves.*

He found that he had only to 'will' to find himself wherever he wished to be. He thus travelled, he believed, as far as Italy. On returning to the Physical Body he could not, however, remember all that happened. He took his neighbour's caretaker into his confidence and persuaded him to show him over the rooms that he had visited in his 'double'. 'I recognized,' he said, 'the pictures and the furniture which I had seen the night before, as well as the titles of the books which I had specially noted.'

CASE NO. 42—*A lady*

A lady described an experience in *The Spectator* of March 22, 1930. Her husband being ill in the next room, she intended to go to him if he grew worse. She slept. *She 'awoke' to find herself inside the doorway of her husband's room. The latter was filled with a bright light* (cf. Gerhardi etc.]. *She could see her Physical Body lying in bed* [cf. Statement No. 17]. She said, 'I was amazed. I particularly noticed a curious folding-back of the eiderdown. ... As I advanced, I seemed to fall asleep again [= re-enter the body]. *I knew that I had been out of the body with my full personality, living and intensely aware, with my husband's illness paramount in my thoughts. Some people might say I had only dreamed, but it was a real and very intense experience. ...'* A night or two afterwards she saw the eiderdown in exactly the same peculiar position in which it had been during the experience; she said, 'That took away my last lingering doubt. *I knew that I had stood there apart, yet a living person, that had looked upon my own mortality.'*

CASE NO. 43—*Mme d'Espérance*

Mme d'Espérance (*Shadow Land*, Redway, 1897) described an out-of-the-body experience as follows. '*I felt a faint sinking sensation.* The printed pages became indistinct. Everything became dark. The faintness passed away almost immediately [cf. Statement No. 9, with regard to shedding the Physical Body]. I glanced at my book; it now seemed far away and dim. I had moved away [in the 'double'] from the sofa, but somebody else [the Physical Body] was there holding the book. *I had a marvellous sense of health, strength and power. Every part of my body glowed with vigour, and a sense of untrammelled freedom. For the first time I knew what it was to live.*

'I moved towards the window. *My surroundings seemed dim. The walls appeared to approach me, then disappeared.* Nearby I saw a [discarnate] friend [cf. Statement No. 18]. He spoke, or perhaps he did not use language, though I understood: "Did I see where I was?" Yes, I could see though the sunshine had faded and we were in a narrow road. *Gloomy overhanging rocks were on each side, obstructed here and there by projections which seemed to block up the passage. It was dark and cheerless, surrounded by cold mist.* ... [= Symbolic representation of consciousness as limited by the unshed vehicle of vitality or 'body-veil' *i.e.*, in 'earth-veil' or 'Hades' conditions—Statement No. 39.]

'*I looked farther. Afar off, a brilliant gleam of light burst out, flooding the road with unconceivable glory.* ... *We turned aside.* ... *A sense of motion, increasing light, intense living radiance, and then—Who can describe the indescribable? Time had disappeared, space no longer existed. I knew that I was a part of this undying, infinite, indestructible whole; that without me it would not be complete.* [= Symbolical representation of consciousness in the Psychical Body with a minimum of limitation due to a small portion of the vehicle of vitality exteriorized, *i.e.*, in 'Paradise' conditions—cf. Statement No. 26.]

'*The light of this great life penetrated me, and I understood that thoughts were the only real, tangible substances* [cf. Sir Humphry Davy, etc.], *and why, between my* [discarnate] *friend and me, utterance was not needed.* The secrets of life and death were unveiled. The reasons of sin and suffering were evident ... [= the 'super consciousness' of the 'Greater Self'].

'I saw living, radiant beings ... while there were others for whom I felt an intense compassion and an irresistible desire to draw them nearer to me. They might come if they would. They could come to me, even as I could come nearer to those bright beings of love and truth. ...

'*The light had entered my soul and I was filled with joy ineffable.* It was mine, this new-born fire. It could not escape through all eternity. It was within their hands, too, but they had not laid hold of it. It was round about them, but they were not conscious of it. They were in the same position as I was when on the road. I prayed, "Help me to help others ...".

'*My interest in the mysterious dream-life drew me ... nearer to a misty cloud-like region in which one felt stifled* [= 'Hades' conditions—cf. Statement No. 41] *and cramped, as though the atmosphere had become close, thick and substantial. A feeling of almost fear and anxiety oppressed me, and I felt a desire to escape from the sense of heaviness which was gradually closing in. Yet the desire to learn was stronger and I combated the instinct which would lead to clearer air and freedom.* [Discarnate communicators from 'Paradise' conditions say that, in order to contact people in 'lower' conditions (including those in physical embodiment) and the 'earth-bound' (in the 'body-veil', delayed in 'Hades' conditions), they must attune themselves by 'lowering their vibrations'. This process tends to reduce their consciousness from the clear, bright and intense 'super-normal' type to the somewhat dreamy and confused 'sub-normal' type, while the environment tends no longer to be bright and clear but more or less 'misty', 'foggy' etc. (in extreme cases, 'dark'). Thus, those who come from 'Paradise' conditions to help either the 'earthbound' or mortals find the process neither easy nor pleasant: they say that they 'come at some cost'.]

'Something in the vaporous mistiness, in the forms and shapes, recalled the dream-life: I knew that in this region [= the 'earth-veil' or 'Hades' condition] the dream-life was lived. ... But I wondered why the objects were so different: these rocks, which before had seemed so solid [i.e., while she was in the corresponding bodily condition, namely, enshrouded by the 'body-veil'] were only vapours or clouds through which I now passed without resistance [i.e., when she was in the Psychical Body—cf. Statement No. 31].

'I saw that this life, which animates all things, is undying, immortal, that there is no death, no annihilation; that it is the same life which, circling for ever through form after form, dwelling in the rocks, the sand, the sea, in each blade of grass, each tree, each flower, in all forms of animal existence and culminates in man's intelligence. ... [Mme d'Espérance was here experiencing 'mystical', 'spiritual' or 'cosmic consciousness.]

'The longing to help these blind ones [the 'earthbound'] became intense. I became aware that, to come within their ken, I too must clothe myself with mist [= must assume material of 'body-veil' type]. It was a repugnant thought, yet I would do it [cf. the reluctance expressed by many narrators at having to re-assume the Physical Body—Statement No. 8]. The longing had taken me from a world of radiant light [= 'Paradise' conditions], of love and sympathy, and brought me to this dim, shadowy world to which the light could scarcely penetrate [= 'Hades' conditions].

'I must clothe myself with this mist. I would come back to these people of the mists, but first let me gather fresh strength from those radiant beings. I wanted freedom, yet I was like a captive being drawn back to the prison [of the Physical Body] from which I had escaped. As when I left [the Physical Body], the walls appeared to approach and recede through a mist [= entering 'Hades' conditions] and I stood looking at my own Physical Body lying still, book in hand, either sleeping or dead. That form was the prison from which I had escaped, and I must again become captive [cf. Mrs Tarsikes, who called the Physical Body a 'cage': Plato called it a 'tomb']. I had to show these poor struggling creatures that, beyond the shadows, there is a living reality, absolute and perfect, that the treasure I had grasped might be theirs also, that they might have freedom. Only clothed in these misty garments could I approach them and tell them these things (cf. I Peter iii, 19].

'The same sense of faintness and depression [= re-entering Physical Body: a similar description of the 'return' was given by others, e.g.

Mrs Dowell], and again I was conscious of lying on my couch. ... Had I not known better, I should have said that the earthly scenes were the realities and the world I had visited the dream-world. *But I know that spirit-communication is true, true as that God lives. They may say that my experience was a dream, but I know that it was a foretaste of life, real and indisputable. During the remainder of my journey through the shadows it will help me to bear with patience whatever may befall, and give me courage to fight to the end.'*

(Why should Mme d'Espérance (and a few others who left their bodies naturally) have consciousness first of 'Hades' and only later of 'Paradise' conditions, whereas most passed directly from 'normal' (= physical) to 'super-normal' (= 'Paradise' conditions?). The answer seems to be that these few exceptional people had a vehicle of vitality, or 'body-veil', which was in relatively loose association with the Physical Body: it therefore tended to leave the latter along with the Psychical Body, and, until shed, to restrict consciousness to the 'sub-normal' (= 'Hades') level. These few exceptional people (who exteriorized *naturally*) were thus temporarily in the same bodily condition (and therefore state of consciousness) as is typical for others whose exteriorization was *enforced*. The fact that Mme d'Espérance was a 'materialization' medium indicates that she had a loose 'body-veil'. (See also 'Conclusions'.)

CASE NO. 44—*Mrs Gladys Osborn Leonard*

Out-of-the-body-experiences were described by Mrs Leonard in *Brief Darkness* (Cassell, 1942).

Mrs Leonard awoke from sleep with 'double consciousness'. She said, 'I call it double consciousness because I was aware of the Spiritual, Astral or Etheric [here = Psychical] Body. She continued, '*For a few moments I lay in my Physical Body unable to move or speak* [cf. Muldoon, etc.]. *I found myself—my mind, my consciousness—gradually transferred to the Etheric Body. I moved easily and lightly in it.*' She saw her [deceased] husband [cf. Statement No. 18]. *His figure was self-luminous* [cf. Gerhardi, Brunton, etc.]. She also saw two friends who were still living on earth and who, like her, were temporarily exteriorized. Like Muldoon, etc., she found that '*strong emotion, such as fear or pity, brings one back to the Physical Body*'. This now happened to her. On other occasions, again like Muldoon, etc. [and many of the supposed dead— cf. Statement No. 9] she exteriorized from her Physical Body so gently that she was unaware of having left it. On such occasions she was rendered aware of being outside the body by critical observations: she noticed that her new environment differed from the physical—'*there is some subtle, yet definite, difference in the atmosphere* [elsewhere described by her as 'light' and 'beautiful'], a freedom of movement, a lightness of step, etc.' She also remarked the 'normal' and 'natural' appearance of everything [cf. Statement No. 26].

Once Mrs Leonard experienced a greater freedom and clarity of thought than she had ever felt before, and there was no 'pull' or influence from the Physical Body. She concluded that the 'silver cord' was either broken, or was about to be broken [cf. Statement Nos. 19 and 20], *and was 'overwhelmed with joy' at her release from the body. 'But,' she continued, 'with a shock, I gathered that I must go back. There was still something that I must do on earth'. Her (deceased) husband understood her reluctance to return* [cf. Statement No. 8].

Mrs Leonard knew that she seldom remembered the whole of her out-of-the-body experiences. Like Mrs Gilbert and others, she attributed this to 'dream-visions', *i.e.* to psychic impressions received in the 'sub-normal consciousness' caused by the 'body-veil': she said that she often had 'curious dream-visions' between the etheric [here = 'Paradise'] experiences and re-awakening in the Physical Body. She used the term 'dream-visions' to distinguish such impressions (many of which were prophetic) from 'pure imagination'.

Mrs Leonard also referred to these experiences in a book called *The Last Crossing* (Psychic Book Club, 1937). Like Muldoon, Fox and Simons, she observed that, 'As our etheric body approaches the physical counterpart, the astral (= 'silver') cord becomes shorter, thicker and less elastic ...' and, like discarnate communicators, she said that in natural death 'the cord wears gradually thinner and thinner' [cf. Statements 19 and 20]. She considered that 'the actual material elements' of the Etheric (here = Psychical) Body are watery substances energized by the electro-magnetic stresses. [Cf. certain psychics —Mrs Garrett, Dion Fortune, etc. and certain supposed discarnates, *e.g.* 'Philip'.] On this account, Mrs Leonard considered that the dying require much water (and little or no food). When she saw the 'double' of a person, she found it a sign that that person might make the transition 'within a limited time': in her experience the shortest interval was two days, but on two occasions it amounted to two years. (Exteriorization indicated that the 'double', or Psychical Body, was loosening from its physical counterpart and taking journeys 'on its own', 'as if it were trying its wings, or endeavouring to make itself familiar, with the new stage of existence. ...' [Supposed discarnates make identical statements —cf. Statement No. 26.] Mrs Leonard pointed out that the seeing of a person's 'double' did not necessarily indicate approaching death: on the one hand, the person might be 'proficient in exteriorizing'; on the other hand, the percipient might be clairvoyant.

The (discarnate) 'Private Dowding' and the (discarnate) 'F. W. H. Myers' described two 'cords' (in addition to numerous individual 'threads' such as are said to unite to compose the cords) connecting the 'double' to the Physical Body. Their statements are interesting in view of one made by Mrs Leonard in this book. She pointed out that many say that the cord unites the heads of the 'Astral' and Physical Bodies and added, 'Yes, I think this is so, but from certain experiences of my own, *I believe there is also a connexion of some kind with the solar plexus.* Later in the book she suggested that, while the 'double' usually leaves the Physical Body on temporary excursions by way of the head, under unusual circumstances it may leave by the solar plexus. She then said, 'I may be mistaken. An alternative explanation may be that ... the etheric body may "pull" on the solar plexus, though it actually leaves by the head.' Still later she described experiencing a severe shock in the solar plexus on returning to her Physical Body after exteriorization. (Supposed discarnates similarly say that the 'double' usually leaves the Physical Body *via* the head—Statement No. 13—but that with some people, who have some 'weak spot', it may leave by the chest, the feet, etc.)

Mrs Leonard was resting one afternoon in preparation for receiving two 'sitters', a lady and a gentleman. But her sleepiness vanished and gave place to 'a very calm feeling'. She said, 'Then I felt a tingling, as if a slight current of electricity were passing through my body, and the sensation of not resting on the bed. I held my mind quiet, saying to myself, "I will notice anything that happens, but will not anticipate or wonder."

'*I opened my eyes and saw my Physical Body resting on the bed* [cf. Statement No. 17]. *I, in my Astral Body, was resting above it. The head of my Physical Body was lying on a particular nightdress-case with an embroidered corner. I was surprised at seeing it there. I was not aware of its having been changed that morning for the one I had been using. I thought, too, how funny it was that my head was resting on it, because I don't usually do that. I was pleased with myself for noticing these things.*

'I felt my Astral Body getting further away from the Physical Body. Then I felt a little nervous—"Shall I be able to get back?" *That slight fear drew me back about a foot towards my Physical Body.* But interest overcame fear, and I determined, "Whatever happens, I will go through with it." At that moment my husband opened our flat door and spoke to someone in the hall outside. He spoke quietly so as not to disturb me. I thought, "I should like to see the caller" and found myself at once at my husband's elbow [cf. Hepworth, Muldoon, Gerhardi, etc. and discarnate communicators]. *The bedroom door was closed but I passed through it* [cf. Statement No. 31]. I saw that the caller was from the Gas Company. Just then a maid from an upstairs flat passed them, and I saw my husband, without speaking, take a coin from his pocket and hand it to her. I thought, "That's funny! Why did he give her a coin? I will remember that and ask him."

'*Then I found myself back in my bedroom. Clarity of thought was leaving me: I was less conscious, and thought it was possibly because I was returning to my Physical Body.*' ('René C.' also observed the effect of proximity to the Physical Body, though he expressed it in terms of the *density of the Psychical Body or 'double'*. Lt.-Col. Lester's (deceased) wife made the same observation regarding her husband's exteriorized 'double', but expressed it in still different terms, namely *the luminosity of the Psychical Body*. Costa also expressed the matter in the latter way; his own 'double', which was near his Physical Body, was dull; his mother's 'double', which was at a distance from her Physical Body, emitted a 'phosphorescent radiance'. See also the remarks made under the Brunton Case and note the *kenosis* in the sense of the limitation of consciousness as it operates through the various bodies, according to psychic communications. This is Statement No. 1b; limitation is at a minimum when the Higher Mental (= Causal) Body is used, giving 'mystical', 'cosmic' or 'spiritual' consciousness: restriction of consciousness is somewhat greater when the Psychical Body is employed, in which case telepathic, clairvoyant and pre-cognitive faculties are in evidence, giving 'super-normal' consciousness: it is great when the Physical Body is used, giving 'normal' consciousness. Our awareness is, however, at its lowest ebb when, stopping short of the Physical Body, it is limited by the vehicle of vitality or 'body-veil'. The latter, having no 'sense organs', is not a vehicle of consciousness: hence, there may be more or less brief periods (just before or just after deep sleep) of 'sub-normal', or 'dream' consciousness, a condition which also obtains in certain cases immediately after the permanent shedding of the Physical Body at death. It is especially liable to occur when a man dies in the prime of life and one is more or less 'awake': the Psychical Body is at first enshrouded by the 'body-veil'. Only when, at the 'second death', the latter is shed are 'super-normal' consciousness and 'Paradise' conditions entered.)

'I ceased thinking to facilitate return and, looking around, soon saw that I was in some room that I had never seen before. The lady and gentleman I expected that afternoon were there, talking to a gentleman unknown to me. My name was mentioned. They were inviting the stranger to share their "sitting" that afternoon. I thought, "I must be dreaming: these people would not do this." Then I found myself half-way down a staircase. At first I thought it led to our lower floor. Then I heard singing and music that seemed to be coming from my bed-room. There is no piano in my bedroom and that told me that this could not be my bedroom. Looking up, I saw the (deceased) son of the "sitters" whom I was expecting. (I had seen him clairvoyantly at one of our earlier sittings.) I said, "Hullo, Philip, who is that playing and singing?" He replied, "It's Gertrude." "Who is Gertrude?" I asked. He answered, "When she was on earth she used to come every week and play and sing to us. Now she sings for me."

'I went into the room. It was not my bedroom. There was a piano and, seated at it, a young lady. I felt that she and Philip were somehow different from the people I had seen earlier (who, I knew, were on the earth-plane). I felt that Philip and the young lady were people who had "died". I said, "Is that Gertrude?" He said, "Yes." Then I seemed again to lose my power of thinking correctly. *When I resumed consciousness I was back in my bedroom, lying in my Astral Body just over the Physical Body.* My astral felt quivery and I thought, "There is going to be difficulty in returning." Then I said, "Keep calm and you will slip back." I seemed then to slip lower and lower and suddenly found I was resting on the bed again: I was back in the physical. I went downstairs. It was 3 p.m. My husband had prepared tea.

'When I told him I had heard him speaking to someone at the door, he said, "Oh yes, but you may have been half asleep." I said, "Yes, but it was the Gas-man to whom you were speaking: I saw his uniform." Next I told him about seeing the servant and his giving her a coin. Then he admitted that I must have seen him. He said that while he spoke to him, he had given the girl a sixpence for some trifling service she had done two or three days before, when he did not happen to have change. He had forgotten about it and, seeing the maid passing, remembered it. Then I told him of the strange gentleman I had seen with my "sitters" and said I heard him invited to come with them that afternoon. My husband said, "Well, that is bound to be wrong. They would never let anyone else come to their "sitting." I gave him a description of the man and told him about "Philip" and "Gertrude".

'Then the door-bell announced the arrival of my "sitters". My husband, who let them in, came and said, "You were right—they have brought that gentleman you described." I went into the room. The stranger was the man that I had seen when in my astral body. The lady explained that he was her brother. ... I gave the "sitting" and the brother left. Thereupon I recounted my experience. The lady said, "Philip had a cousin, Gertrude, who came over weekly to play and sing to us. She passed over six years ago." '

CASE NO. 45—*Miss Dorothy Grenside*

Dorothy Grenside (*The Meaning of Dreams*, G. Bell, 1923) told of an airman who was unconscious for some days after an accident. On recovering, he insisted that, *immediately after the crash he was standing beside his unconscious body and wrecked machine* [cf. Statement No. 17]. 'Thus,' concluded Miss Grenside, 'two phrases in common use—"He is beside himself", and "He is wandering"—may have originally held a literal meaning.' That author also mentioned a friend who awoke to see both her husband apparently standing by the window, and his Physical Body asleep beside her. She shook the latter and instantly the 'double' left the window and, rushing towards the sleeping body, disappeared. The husband awoke but knew nothing of the matter.

Case No. 46—Miss 'P.L.'

Miss 'P.L.' told H. E. Hunt (*Why We Survive*, Rider & Co. Ltd.) that once, when she 'awoke' from sleep, *she saw a 'cord' which was looped over the roof. Following it, she found that it led to the bed on which lay her sleeping body* [cf. Statement No. 19], seeing which, she awoke in it to physical surroundings.

Case No. 47—Mrs 'M.A.E.'

Mrs 'M.A.E.' wrote to tell the writer that she had out-of-the-body experiences before she had heard of such phenomena. The available details correspond with those of others. She said, 'At a certain time of night, it was as much as I could do to stop my Real Self from drifting away. *It was as if another body slowly rose up from my natural body coming out at the top of the head* [cf. Statement No. 13]. *I could see the natural body* [cf. Statement No. 17]. Then the Real Self, or Soul-Body, floated through the walls and up into the air' [cf. Statement No. 31]. Her route corresponds with that of Muldoon, Mr 'H', etc.—'After going up it was necessary to float across.'

Case No. 48—Miss Dorothy Peters

Miss Peters published accounts in *Two Worlds*, Aug. 1952. She said, '*My first experience occurred before I had heard of astral projection*.' She had floated up to the ceiling. In the second, like Mrs 'M.A.E.', *she evidently left her body by way of the head* [cf. Statement No. 13]. *Exteriorized, she also took the same route as that described by Muldoon, etc.* Miss Peters said, 'I was roused to awareness by ... a tremendous pulling of the head. I was out of, and above, my Physical Body, turning round at right angles to it [cf. Statement No. 17]. It felt so strange that I said, "Oh!" and returned smoothly to the body ... I was annoyed at having thus ended the experiment.' In her third experience Miss Peters found herself out of bed at about 6 a.m. *She felt 'curiously light and springy'.* She saw her reflection in a mirror [cf. remarks under Gerhardi]. Miss Peters made critical observations: opening a drawer she found everything disarranged, whereas it had been left in good order. The incongruities between the physical and non-physical environments made her realize that 'things were not normal' and that she was outside her body [cf.

Fox, etc.]. The fourth experience began with 'a sensation of ascending' [cf. Statement No. 9 regarding the shedding of the Physical Body], and Miss Peters found herself on a roof-top. The height caused no fear. Descending, she stood 'at the entrance to *a dark tunnel*' [= shedding most of the *vehicle of vitality* (that had been exteriorized along with the Psychical Body, as with Miss Blakeley and Mrs Parker). Mrs Leslie, Mrs Tarsikes, etc., used the symbol of a tunnel for shedding their *Physical Bodies*—cf. Statements Ib and 9.] It was, no doubt, the presence of the vehicle of vitality that had rendered Miss Peters' 'double' visible in the mirror [cf. Gerhardi]. On the other hand Gibier's engraver could not see his 'double' in a mirror. Miss Peters entered the 'tunnel' and 'sped through it' to find herself over a sea. There she did experience fear. It brought her to land. [When the writer read this, he thought that he had found a discrepancy between this and other accounts, but Miss Peters later (without specific reference to the matter) provided an explanation, namely, that on this occasion 'hasty return was prevented by invisible operators']. She saw children who, however, could neither see nor hear her [cf. Statement No. 28]. On this occasion her 'costume' combined leather snow-boots with a summer dress! Like Fox, etc., she found that such incongruities awoke her from the dream-state to full consciousness. She considers that in these experiences she was assisted, as part of her education, by discarnate 'guides' [cf. 'deliverers'—Statement 3].

CASE No. 49—*Mr J. H. Dennis*

The experience of Mr Dennis was given to me in a letter. He had read no literature on this subject and had attended no spiritualistic meetings. He had no interest in survival. Before having this experience, Mr Dennis often awoke to find himself unable to move (= catalepsy). He noted that this occurred when he lay on his back (cf. Mrs Gilbert, 'René C.', etc.). Actual exteriorization occurred after a period of sleep. (This is commonly the case.) Mr Dennis said, 'I awoke and saw my wife's mother, who had died a year before, standing beside the bed [cf. Statement 18]. *I felt a great purring in my ears like vibrations at high impulse* [cf. Muldoon, Fox, etc.]. *I felt myself rise, lying level as I was on my back, to about eighteen inches above the bed* [cf. Statement No. 16]. *Then my feet swung round and I landed standing on the floor beside my mother-in-law. There was a white haze; everything was bright. I returned by the way I went out. My head was the last part to re-enter my body* [this is Statement No. 13 in reverse]. *A click occurred and I thought, "Is that me?" The vibration was terrific.* Then I became conscious.'

CASE No. 50—*Mr S. R. Wilmot*

This case was given in *Proc. S.P.R.* (vii, p. 41) and in Myers's *Human*

Personality (I, p. 682). Wilmot sailed from Liverpool to New York, encountering a great storm. His account is as follows.

'Upon the night following the eighth day of the storm, the tempest moderated. ... Towards morning I dreamed that I saw my wife, whom I had left in the United States, come to the door of my state-room, clad in her night-dress. At the door she seemed to discover that I was not the only occupant of the room, hesitated a little, then advanced to my side, stooped down and kissed me, and after gently caressing me, quietly withdrew.

'Upon waking, I was surprised to see my fellow-passenger, whose berth was above mine—but not directly over it, owing to the fact that our room was at the stern of the vessel—leaning upon his elbow, and looking fixedly at me. "You're a pretty fellow," he said at length, "to have a lady come and visit you in this way." I pressed him for an explanation, which at first he declined to give. *At length he related what he had seen while wide awake, lying in his berth. It exactly corresponded with my dream. ... I questioned him about it, and on three separate occasions he repeated to me the same account of what he had witnessed.*

'*The day after landing, I went to Watertown, Conn., where my children and wife had been for some time. Almost the first question my wife put when we were alone together was,* "Did you receive a visit from me a week ago Tuesday?" "A visit from you?" *said I,* "we were more than a thousand miles at sea." "I know it," *she replied,* "but it seemed to me that I visited you." "That wouldn't be possible," *said I.* "Tell me what makes you think so."

'My wife then told me that, on account of the severity of the weather ... she had been extremely anxious about me. On the night previous, the same night when, as mentioned above, the storm had just begun to abate, she had lain awake for a long time thinking of me. *About four a.m. it seemed to her that she went out to seek me. Crossing a wide and stormy sea, she came at length to a low, black steamship, whose side she went up, then, descending into the cabin, passed through it to the stern until she came to my state-room.* "Tell me," *said she,* "do they ever have state-rooms like the one I saw, where the upper berth extends farther than the under-one? A man was in the upper berth, looking right at me. For a moment I was afraid to go in, but I soon went up to the side of your berth, bent down and kissed you, and embraced you, and then went away".'

'The description given by my wife of the steamship was correct in all particulars, though she had never seen it.'

Replying to a question, Mrs Wilmot said, 'I had a very vivid sense, all that day, of having visited my husband: the impression was so strong that I felt unusually happy and refreshed—to my surprise.' The shipping information was checked with the files of the *New York Herald*. Dr Hodgson got into touch with Mr and Mrs Wilmot and with Wilmot's sister (who was on the ship with Mr Wilmot). Miss Wilmot remembered the other passenger asking her if she had been to see her brother: on her answering in the negative, he had told her what he had seen.

This case is of interest in several respects. *Mrs Wilmot had a sense of travelling* (cf. Walter de la Mare, though that feature alone is not significant). In addition, she saw objects (unknown to her) that were intermediate between her Physical Body and that of her husband. Comparison may be made with the account given by Mrs Eileen Garrett, who is not only able to exteriorize at will and to see intermediate objects, but to distinguish such experiences from somewhat similar ones that are due to telepathy and/or clairvoyance and not to the exteriorization of a 'double'. Mrs Wilmot both saw and was seen and that not only by her husband, but by a stranger. She realized the presence of that stranger, in the state-room, and knew that the bunks had a peculiar arrangement. At first sight the experience might be referred to telepathy and/or clairvoyance (though the mutual aspects render this most improbable). *However, the correct knowledge of successive intervening objects (that were not in the perception either of the husband or the stranger) shows it to be almost certainly an actual visit in a 'double' which has objective reality.* Comparison may also be made with Dr Van Eeden's account.

CASE No. 51—*Dr Paul Brunton*

An exteriorization described by Brunton in *A Search in Secret Egypt* (Rider & Co. Ltd.) was also given in *Prediction*, Sept., 1950: it occurred when he spent a night in the Great Pyramid.

Brunton said, '*I gazed down upon the deserted body of flesh which was lying prone on the stone block* [cf. Statement No. 17]. *I noted a trail of faint silvery light* [the 'silver cord'—Statement No. 19] *projecting down from me, the new me, to the cataleptic creature who lay upon the block. Then I discovered that this mysterious psychical umbilical cord was contributing towards the illumination of the corner of the King's chamber where I hovered, showing up the wall-stones in a soft, moonbeam-like light.*' [Compare the accounts of Gerhardi, Gibier's engraver, Mrs Joy, Mrs Larsen, etc. and note that many of the 'dead' state that the 'double', and the 'silver cord' by which it is attached to the physical, is luminous. There is, indeed, some experimental evidence of its radio-activity. Col. de Rochas, the French experimenter, said that if screens were coated with calcium sulphide, they glowed when approached by a 'double' exteriorized (in this case by hypnosis) from its physical counterpart. Similarly, Dr Omoda found that when Eusapia Paladino was in a normal state she had no influence on the electroscope, but when her 'double' was exteriorized from the physical (in trance) she could affect it. Moreover, if her exteriorized hand touched photographic plates that were wrapped in opaque paper, finger-like impressions appeared on the plates. Such phenomena indicate radio-activity in the trance-state (see, *e.g.*, Ceasare Lombroso's *After Death—What?*, T. Fisher Unwin, 1909). Those who claim to have out-of-the-body experiences say the same as the supposed dead. Mrs Larsen, for example, found that her exteriorized 'double' was luminous, while Gerhardi, like Brunton, noted the luminosity of the 'silver cord'. Conversely, Lt.-Col. Lester, exteriorized from the Physical Body, was described by his 'dead' wife as 'vanishing' suddenly when he returned to physical embodiment. This is precisely what the supposed dead say—that *the rapid 'vibration' and high luminosity of the 'double' (with which is correlated 'super-normal' consciousness) is necessarily more or less 'quenched' when the 'double' is near, and still more when it is 'in gear' with, the Physical Body.* See also observations under the Leonard case and note that psychics (who owe their abilities to their being less immersed in the Physical Body than non-psychics) are more or less visible to discarnates, especially during intense thought or emotion: it is, indeed, noteworthy that psychics are often described by independent communicators simply as 'lights'. Here is a whole complex of statements, given independently, that exhibit a remarkable coherence and concordance.]

'I knew at last why the Egyptians of old had given, in their hieroglyphics, a pictured symbol of the bird to man's soul-form. ... Had I not risen into the air and remained floating above my discarded body, even as a bird rises into the sky and remains circling round a point?

'Yes, I had risen into space, disentangling my soul from its mortal skein. ... *I experienced a sense of being etherealized, of intense lightness, in this duplicate body which I now inhabited. A single realization now overwhelmed me. "This is death. Now I know that I am a soul, that I can exist apart from the body".*'

(Brunton commented on the bird as a symbol of the soul to the ancient Egyptians, on account of its ability to 'fly' and the freedom that accompanies that ability. He might have added that, for the same reason, the Greek symbol for the soul generally bore the wings of a butterfly, while the Burmese was a butterfly.)

CASE NO. 52—*Miss Margaret Newby*

Following the description, by Muldoon and Carrington, in *Prediction* (Feb. 1951), of exteriorizations, Miss Newby described her experience (in March). *She clearly knew little of these matters beforehand.*

Miss Newby was worried and fell asleep 'worn out by purposeless thinking'. Her narrative continued: 'I awoke ... but it was in another world. I may have been conscious of being slightly out of alignment with my body. My memory of recent events was distinct, but my Physical Body was sound asleep.

'Often in the past I had been conscious of dreaming; I had amused myself by practising levitation, knowing that my dream-body could come to no harm. *But now I experienced the continuity of consciousness between waking and dream-life and was aware of two bodies, one lying inert, while the Real Me occupied a body of a different texture* [cf. Statement No. 17].

'Cautiously I got up—or rather, *no sooner had I thought of getting up than I stood in the centre of the room* [cf. Hepworth, Muldoon, Gerhardi, Mrs Leonard, etc.]. I was anxious to make the most of the opportunity [cf. Gerhardi, Mrs and Miss Griggs, Mrs Leonard, etc.]. In a flash my mind was made up. I would go into the street and ask the advice of the first man I met. ...

'Negotiating those familiar stairs was no simple matter. I had not sufficient command of my light-as-air body to fly from top to bottom; nor, since *my dream-body was not subject to the law of gravity*, could I walk down in the usual way. Finally, I walked down very slowly, pausing on each stair, otherwise my feet would slide from under me, leaving me suspended in mid-air until I floated gently down again. Outside, I saw a woman and children filing through the gates of a spacious park. A man ... stood silently at my left side.

'I considered returning home to find out whether my body still breathed, but remembered in time that I might be drawn in and so lose part of the rare experience. ... If this were death who could tell what possibilities lay beyond this park? But I had an urge to return to physical life and clean up the mess I had made of things. My companion said, "You know you are going downhill." Then I realized that he was the man for whom I was looking and that he knew all about my difficulties. I could return and continue my life ... and I was once more in bed.

'I lost no time in finding out what others say on astral projection. I was not aware of any "clicking-in" sensation on returning to my body, nor had I noticed the "silver cord". ... *But, although aware of my body in bed, I had not looked closely at it; nor, during my journey, had I once looked behind me. Had I done so, I too might have seen the cord.*' [Fox did not always see his 'cord' and probably for the same reason.]

Case No. 53—*Miss Marjorie T. Johnson*

Miss Johnson informed me (*in litt.*) that she had had several experiences of this nature. She said, 'In 1935, I cut my finger and fainted. I found myself sitting in a lovely meadow full of sunshine, and felt very light and happy [= 'Paradise' conditions—cf. Statement No. 26]. *I was quite free from pain* [cf. Statement No. 7]. *I heard the sound of children's voices. Then I seemed to be drawn back down a dark tunnel.* [Cf. Statement No. 9 and note that the symbol of a 'tunnel', used by dozens who were conscious of *leaving* their Physical Bodies is used by Miss Johnson to describe *re-entering* the body. That symbol is also used by supposed discarnates in their accounts of the act of dying. More significant still is the fact that discarnates who 'enter' the body of a medium (vacated in trance), in order to communicate with mortals, use the same symbol. This employment, by independent persons, of a single term in describing identical processes, as seen from different angles, indicates something real and objective.] *I found myself in the room at home again. The room seemed very small and dark, and at first my parents looked unfamiliar.'* [Mrs Piper, returning to her Physical Body from trance, similarly described people's Physical Bodies and material objects as 'dark' (in comparison with Psychical Bodies and the 'Paradise' conditions she had just left). She referred to those (discarnates) she was just leaving as 'white people', while those to whom she was returning appeared 'black' to her. This refers to the relative *luminosity* of the bodies. Similarly, with regard to weight: the Psychical Body is described as 'light' and 'balloon-like' in contrast with the Physical Body which is 'heavy'—cf. the accounts of Bertrand, Gerhardi, Lind, Helen Brooks, Mrs 'Prothero', Miss Kaeyer and anon. Case No. 37. The effects which the denser Physical and the subtler Psychical Bodies are said to have on *consciousness* are also significant: the Physical Body limits consciousness considerably, acting like 'blinkers' etc.; the Psychical Body, more responsive, permits telepathy, clairvoyance and pre-cognition.] *'I hated to come back'* [cf. Statement No. 8].

'My first experience was on Sept. 21, 1935. I had the sensation of slipping down into my own body, which lay on the bed. *When I reached the "legs" part of me, it was like fitting myself into a tight rubber skin* [Mrs H. D. Williams gave a similar description of *re-entering* the body, while Mrs Parker spoke of entering a 'bag': on the other hand, Miss Yeoman described *quitting* her body as 'like a tight glove being pulled from a finger']. Then I seemed to "come together" and was fully conscious, but my brain still felt rather scattered and my teeth were clenched. *Suddenly cold air* [ectoplasmic phenomena] *began to waft over me as strongly as if an electric fan had been turned on, and the room seemed full of mist.* [The environment was obscured by part of the 'body-veil']. *Every atom of my body tingled with a feeling of exhilaration* [cf. Mme d'Espérance, etc.]. *I was for a time, super-conscious: my mind was clearer than it had ever been* [cf. Statement No. 26]. For the rest of that day I knew only peace and joy, and seemed to be literally "treading on air". The experience was repeated several times, and always when I was lying on my back [cf. Muldoon, Mr Dennis, etc.].

'On July 25, 1939, as I lay in bed, I felt the same rushing sensation inside me, but that time *I was moving upwards, not downwards. Then everything was blotted out for a while* [cf. Statement No. 9]. *Then I found myself flying through space. I seemed to have a companion.* A voice said, "Where to?" and I answered, "Paris." I was not afraid, but before I reached my destination I lost consciousness again. *These travels were always characterized by the cold "air" and the rushing "Spirit-of-the-Wind"* sensation [ectoplasmic phenomena from the 'body-veil'], *followed by a heightening of the faculties and indescribable peace and exaltation'* [= 'supernormal' consciousness in 'Paradise' conditions].

CASE NO. 54—*Mr Cromwell F. Varley*, F.R.S.

Cromwell Varley, well-known engineer and inventor and a member of the Committee appointed in 1869 by the London Dialectical Society to investigate Spiritualism (*Report on Spiritualism of the Committee of London Dialectical Society*, J. Burns, 1873, 3rd ed.) gave evidence which included accounts both of natural and enforced exteriorizations.

Describing a natural experience, Varley said, 'I had a nightmare and could not move a muscle [= catalepsy]. While in this state, I saw the spirit of my sister-in-law whom I knew was confined to her bedroom. She said, "If you do not move you will die." But I could not move, and she said, "*I will frighten you and then you will be able to move ...*" [she realized that fear would cause him to return to his body]. She suddenly exclaimed, "Oh, Cromwell, I am dying." That frightened me exceedingly, throwing me out of my torpid state, and I awoke in the ordinary way.

'My shouting had aroused Mrs Varley; we examined the door and it was still locked and bolted, and I told my wife what had happened, having noted the hour (3.45 a.m.) and I cautioned her not to mention the matter to anybody, but to hear her sister's version if she alluded to the subject. In the morning, the latter told us that she had passed a dreadful night, that she had been in our room, greatly troubled, since I was nearly dying. This was between half-past three and four a.m. and she had aroused me by exclaiming, "Oh, Cromwell, I am dying".'

The other natural experience occurred when Varley had to catch a steamer early next morning. He had often successfully 'willed' himself to awake at a necessary time and this he did now. However, although he himself was awakened, his body remained asleep and cataleptic; he saw it lying inert on the bed [cf. Statement No. 17]. He could not arouse it. Then he saw a timber-yard in which two men were moving planks and conceived a method of awakening his body from its torpor. The method significantly enough, as in the experience just cited, involved the use of fear. Varley said, 'It occurred to me to make my body dream that there was a bomb-shell thrown in front of me. ... When the men threw down a plank I made it dream that a bomb had burst and cut open my face. This woke me. ... I leapt out of bed, opened the window, and there was the yard, the timber and the two men, just as I had seen them. I had no previous knowledge of the locality. It was dark the previous evening when I entered the town, and I did not know that there was a yard there. I could not see the timber until I opened the window. I had seen these things while my body lay asleep.'

CASE No. 55—*Miss Helen Brooks*

Helen Brooks (*Prediction*, 1949, 1950) had several exteriorizations. On the first occasion, she awoke to find the legs of her 'double' protruding through the eiderdown and at first mistook them for her physical legs. She said, 'I was mystified that there was no rent in the eiderdown. It dawned on me that I was exteriorizing. My astral legs were waving backwards and forwards. *Then I glided up to the ceiling. When I got perturbed, I immediately lost consciousness and found myself back in bed.*'

Miss Brooks also said, 'I was struck, on my first visit, to the astral [here = 'Paradise' condition] by having to pass through one plane beforehand, where everyone and everything seemed to be in semi-darkness and completely unaware of anything. [Much of the 'body-veil' had been exteriorized from the Physical Body along with the Psychical Body, so that both the consciousness and the environment were more or less enshrouded. Miss Brooks was, therefore, temporarily in 'earth-veil' or 'Hades' conditions and her consciousness was of the 'sub-normal', or dream-type—cf. the accounts of Mme d'Espérance, Gerhardi, Ogston, de la Mare, Hives, Mrs Joy and Miss Johnson.] People in this condition just walked right through me and seemed not to know they were even there. Evidently they were not trained enough to remember the sleep-state [cf. the Biblical account which, no doubt, applies to many of the 'dead' who are in the 'Hades' condition—'The dead know not anything'—Eccles. ix, 5]. When [after shedding the enshrouding portion of the 'body-veil'] I got to the astral proper [here = 'Paradise' conditions] I was shown round by a Guide ...'.

On the second occasion, Miss Brooks found herself exteriorized and watching some sleeping children. She said, '*I noticed a misty vapour emanating from the tops of their heads* [cf. Statement No. 13]. It teemed with life and I saw what they were doing astrally, for, reflected in the vapour, were the activities of their astral bodies [cf. Frank Lind's account]. I thought, "That must be how we are able to remember our 'dreams'." *Through the connecting link, or cord, to their heads, these children were able to record their astral experiences as dreams, and remember them, according to their capacity, next day.*'

When exteriorized, Miss Brooks made many journeys, like Muldoon, Fox and others, travelling at 'terrific' speed and 'sailing' through houses etc. Like Muldoon, Mrs Garrett, Dr Leaf, etc., she considered that 'astral travelling is done by everybody, though few are aware of it'.

CASE NO. 56—*Mrs Caroline D. Larsen*

Mrs Larsen (*My Travels in the Spirit World*) whose accounts of the out-of-the-body experiences were published in 1927 by The Tuttle Co., Rutland, U.S.A., said, 'I have no doubt that what I have experienced is real, very real. *Nothing in all my life has made such a lasting and vivid impression upon my mind. ...*' Her first projection was as follows. 'I had been enjoying Beethoven ... when suddenly I had a feeling of oppression and apprehension as though I were about to faint. ... *Soon numbness crept over me* ... [= shedding the Physical Body—cf. Statement No. 9]. *Next I, I myself, was standing on the floor beside my bed looking down at my own Physical Body* [cf. Statement No. 17]. ... *Everything appeared to be natural* [cf. Statement No. 26]. There was the table with books, trinkets, etc. ... The music from downstairs continued. ... Then I walked towards the door, passed through it and into the hall. ... Through force of habit I went through the motions of turning on the electric light, which, of course, I did not actually turn on [cf. Gerhardi and Mrs Griggs and cf. Statement No. 31]. *But there was no need for illumination, for from my body and face emanated a strong whitish light that lighted up the room brilliantly*' [cf. Gibier's engraver, Brunton, Gerhardi, Mrs Joy, etc.]. Mrs Larsen walked downstairs, but a 'spirit' ordered her back into her Physical Body. When she awoke to the physical world she learned that what she had 'heard' agreed to the smallest detail with what had actually transpired. *Her account includes a reference to the 'silver cord': she said, 'a current of mysterious influence united astral and Physical Body*' [cf. Statement No. 19].

CASE NO. 57—*Miss Sigrid Kaeyer*

Sigrid Kaeyer's account was given in *I was in the Spirit*, Rider & Co. Ltd. A Bachelor of Music and a member of the Church of England, *Miss Kaeyer said that she had read no books on mysticism or spiritualism.* She commented: 'I am glad that such is the case, for in my mind, anyway, my experience is all the more trustworthy, since it has not been coloured by anything I have read. Whether or not, therefore,' she continued, 'what I have seen and heard corresponds to the visions and revelations of others, I do not know. Nor do I know whether what I get agrees with doctrinal beliefs. It makes no great difference so far as I am concerned; there must be more of truth than what is set forth in theological treatises.' Her 'absolute honesty, sincerity and deep spiritual nature' is vouchsafed for by her pastor. She described her experiences as follows.

'*As my bodily senses become dulled, I begin to live in another body, which seems to take flight. I have a sense of lightness and of ascension* [cf. Statement No. 9]. With that comes the consciousness of contact with cosmic power. The world of sense is blotted out ... *I seem to move through space, where I see the spiritual universe, indescribable, beautiful. ... Indeed, what I see is the only Reality; Everything we see in the physical world is but the shadow of the real* [cf. I Cor. xiii, 12]. ... *Time and space are no more. My Soul Body, or Spiritual Body, becomes transcendent. It has broken through the thin barrier of the physical and I am in my true home* [cf. Heb. xiii, 14]. *St Paul was right when he said, "There is a natural* [= Psychical] *body, and there is a spiritual body"* [I Cor. xv, 44]. *The Spiritual Body is mine now, and it is for use. It is also the body in which our loved ones dwell. I have seen them again and again. ...*

'*There is still a connection* [= the 'silver cord'—cf. Statement No. 19] *between my two bodies, and I sometimes feel something holding them together. If they were not still united thus, I am sure my Spiritual Body, and therefore my Soul, would not return from these ascensions it makes. This is what death means.* [Compare this, written by one who has no knowledge of spiritualistic literature, with statements by the supposed dead with regard to the 'loosening' of the 'silver cord'—Statement No. 20]. *There was a time when I almost rebelled when I had to come back to earthly life* [cf. Statement No. 8].

Later, describing another experience, Miss Kaeyer said, 'I seem to be actually passing through death. ... A moment's blackness [cf. Statement No. 9], *then the feeling of letting go something dense and heavy. It is my Physical Body* [note that 'Mrs X', re-entering her body, described it as 'very heavy']. *I look down and see it kneeling in the Church* [cf. Statement No. 17]. *I am in a new body—my real body; I feel light, as if I could fly anywhere. The blackness of unconsciousness was just long enough for my soul to escape from the physical. ... There is one I recognize, my cousin who was afflicted in mind and in body. How lovely she is! Her mind, shut up so long, is now free to think. She is among her own people* [cf. Statement No. 18]. *... So, this is death! Oh, death, what a fraud you are! You are the opener of the gate which sets us free. ... There is something greater in life than what is seen and experienced in earthly living. There is a larger life which is our possession now, a new existence which belongs to man in this present world. ...' *Miss Kaeyer continued, 'I feel a strange atmosphere around me. Where are we? ... People, people, a new world of people. They are* *alive; they are real beings! Absolutely no difference from the human world; at least, none that I can see* [Statement No. 11]. ... *Again I ask not to be taken back to earth. Truly I belong here*' [cf. Statement No. 8].

CASE NO. 58—*Miss Monteith's doctor-friend*

A friend of Miss Mary Monteith (*A Book of True Dreams*, Heath Cranton, 1929) was sometimes aware, as he awoke, that he had been traversing different 'planes' of consciousness. Similar experiences occurred under nitrous oxide. He carefully observed each 'plane' and tried to impress his observations on his memory for future reference. Like Dr Van Eeden and others, when outside the Physical Body, he noticed 'a new aspect of things' and 'had to observe everything from a different angle'. On one occasion, when his return to the Physical Body was retarded, like Fox, Muldoon, etc., *he had 'dual consciousness': he was not only 'able to see, to hear and to reason, apparently out of the body' but was also aware of 'the familiar surroundings' of his room* [cf. Statement No. 18: the 'dead' state that 'dual' or 'alternate' consciousness may occur so long as the 'cord' is still unbroken].

CASE NO. 59—*Mr F. Hives*

Frank Hives (*Glimpses into Infinity*, John Lane the Bodley Head Ltd., 1931) was having out-of-the-body experiences in 1908, more than twenty years before Muldoon published his account. He referred to long journeys made through space. These excursions were made at night, except once (when he was ill). He said, 'While travelling I see everything absolutely clearly, and what occurs seems always to be perfectly normal. The people I see are recognizable and the places sometimes quite familiar. ... *When I see people whom I know, they do not appear to see me, or to be aware that I am near* [cf. Statement No. 28]. *But I can see my own body ... and I can hear—or at any rate understand—what people say to each other* [cf. Statement No. 17].

'*When I am away on these journeys, anyone seeing my body would think I was dead. ... The sensation is one of gliding away, very slowly at first but gradually gaining speed until I am travelling very fast. At first I speed through darkness, nothing being visible; then there is a feeling of falling, feet first, into space* [cf. Statement No. 9]. *Gradually light begins to show and I am in a thick grey mist, with a mighty wind sweeping past me* [= 'Denser Between Worlds', 'earth-veil' or 'Hades' conditions]. Then I begin to see through the mist, many shapeless forms that appear in front, drift past and vanish again in the white fog. These I see, as they become clearer, have human heads but their bodies tail away into indefiniteness [= 'astral shells' or isolated 'body-veils', *i.e.*, partial corpses]. Suddenly I begin to rise [the enshrouding 'body-veil' has been shed = the 'second death' or 'unveiling' cf. Statement No. 41]. The sensation of rising gives me indescribable pleasure.

'*The mists* [= the 'earth-veil', 'Hades' or 'Greylands'] *disappear and there is a bright light all around me* [= 'Paradise']—*though nothing is visible by it* [= partial awakening—cf. Statement No. 25]. *Then something seems to snap* [cf. Muldoon, Dennis, Fox, Miss Price, etc.], *there is a singing in my ears, and at once I am in some place on earth* [in Psychical Body]. *I then feel perfectly normal, except that when walking, or gliding, I do not need to avoid obstacles; I pass through them* [cf. Statement No. 31] ... Having seen the things I came to see (things that may be in the past, in the present, or yet to come), my Doorkeeper [cf. Statement No. 3 regarding 'deliverers'] bids me return; and the journey back to my body is the reverse of what it was when coming. *I always experience a sense of reluctance to leave the place where I have been* [cf. Statement No. 8]. ... But always I retain a very clear recollection of everything I have seen. ...'

In 1908 Hives was in Nigeria as political officer: he had been away from his headquarters for some weeks and had had no letters. He said, 'So far as I knew, my brother was in New Zealand where he had been settled. I had no idea that he intended visiting England. He had not been in my thoughts, for we had little in common. ...

'I gave my servants instructions to call me at five. Then I turned in. Gradually I lost consciousness of my surroundings and, without warning, I felt myself gliding away. I knew that another journey had begun.

'*After passing as usual through the great mist and the rushing wind* [= 'Hades' conditions], *I emerged into light* [= 'Paradise' conditions]. Then, suddenly, I stood in a field, which I recognized. It was in the meadow adjoining the churchyard at Breamore, in Hampshire, the parish where my brother-in-law was the Rector. *The ground was covered with snow, and I glanced at my tropical kit—bush shirt, khaki shorts and putties—and wondered why I did not feel cold.* [The latter were 'thought-forms'—cf. Statement No. 10, and compare Hepworth who made a similar critical observation.]

'I glided through the thick hedge without feeling that it was there, and then through a two-railed fence. I could see these obstructions quite well, and they looked quite solid; but it was just as if nothing had been there when I advanced [cf. Statement No. 31]. Then I found myself in the churchyard. ... "Walk on," said my Guardian. *I proceeded along a narrow path leading to the main entrance of the church, noticing as I went that my feet left no marks in the snow.* Between this entrance and a small door opening into the chancel, stands a yew tree. Beneath this tree stood seven or eight people, every one of whom I knew well. *I moved a little nearer so that I was close to my sister who was one of the group. I spoke to her but she took no notice; nor did any of the others show that they were conscious of my presence* [cf. Statement No. 28]. ... "Look down," said my Guardian. I did so, and saw the top of a coffin on which was a metal plate; on it was my brother's name and date of his birth. I knew that he was dead. ...

'Then I felt I was sinking, my Guardian being close beside me. After this came the return journey through the mist, the rushing wind and drifting wraiths [= 'astral shells', seen in 'Hades' conditions, exactly as described by Mme d'Espérance] followed by darkness [= while re-entering the Physical Body—cf. Statement No. 9]. Slowly I came to my senses. ... I told my brother officers about my experience, that I was sure my brother was dead, and was buried in Breamore churchyard the day before. I wrote a description and made a plan of what I had seen. The officers signed both. A month later all the details were confirmed in a letter from my sister in England. My brother had returned to England from New Zealand quite unexpectedly, and had gone to stay for a few days at Breamore with my (and his) sister. He had contracted a chill, which had developed into pneumonia. From this he had died, a fortnight later, and had been buried in Breamore churchyard on the same day that my ego had been present at the funeral.

'As soon as she received my letter, which of course crossed hers in the post, my sister confirmed every other point and circumstance I had mentioned in my letter.

'Several months later I returned to England and went to stay at Breamore. There I visited the churchyard with my sister and two of the others who had been in the group. *I showed them the place where I had passed through the hedge and fence.* Following this I walked over the ground my ego had covered, under the guidance of my Doorkeeper, and as we came round the church I saw the grave, over which the grass had by then grown. It was not at that time marked by a headstone, but I went straight to it and indicated that it was my brother's. And I was quite correct; it was!'

Case No. 60—Dr Horace Leaf, PH.D., F.R.G.S.

With Dr Leaf (*What Mediumship Is*, Spiritualist Press Ltd., 1938), the exteriorization of the astral body from the physical body does not take place at will. He says, ' *It has always occurred unexpectedly or during sleep, out of which I have awakened to find myself either floating over my physical organism or standing beside it, my body meanwhile lying asleep. Nevertheless, I have always been aware of being out of my physical body.* On one occasion I tried to make it speak whilst I was extruded. The effort was quite successful, and I heard my own voice speaking in clear but distant tones. This effort brought me back to normal. ...'

Dr Leaf pointed out that 'the most common form of transportation is that of floating by a mere effort of the will', and that, 'the individual may be quite unaware of the direction in which he wished to travel, yet will find himself in the right place.' He continued, 'This, you will observe, is one of the characteristics of telepathy and clairvoyance. The telepathic thought finds the person to whom it is "projected" wherever he may be, and similarly, the clairvoyant locates the person who is the subject of the vision' [cf. the accounts of Hepworth, Hives, etc.]. In Dr Leaf's experience, 'Surprisingly few ever experience complete separation of the two bodies; and when that has occurred, it has usually been unexpected. Mostly it has been accompanied by catalepsy, either before or after, but generally before. Partial extrusion does not deprive the individual of his normal awareness and he functions through his brain the whole time, although the tendency in some instances is towards unconscious trance [*i.e.* partial exteriorization may involve 'dual consciousness'—cf. Statement No. 18]. *The indications of partial extrusion are a feeling as if falling downward, forward, backwards or sideways, or of being elevated above the Physical Body* [cf. Statement No. 9]. *Another frequent feeling is that of swaying to and fro whilst in the Physical Body* [cf. the accounts of Muldoon, Mrs Gwen Cripps, etc.]. *When the separation of the two bodies is complete, and the individual fully aware of it, he may notice a cord-like connexion between them, stretching from head to head. This is the "psychic cord" or "psychic umbilical cord"* [cf. Statement No. 19]. *It supplies vitality from the astral to the physical body* [cf. Statement No. 20]. Dr Leaf pointed out that "astral projection" is the best explanation of some apparitions of the "living" and especially of apparitions manifesting at the moment of death. He said, "*Careful investigation goes to show that a large number of apparitions occur immediately before, or immediately after, death. The Astral Body* [here = vehicle of vitality or 'body-veil'] *not only exists during life-time, but continues to exist after death; not, it is maintained, indefinitely, but as long as the physical organism exists. According to some, it disintegrates step by step with the coarser body. It is therefore, conceivable, that it may retain vitality for a short time after physical death and, during that period, make an appearance".'

CASE NO. 61—*Mr Fred Rebell*

As a relief from these studies, the present writer, on one occasion, turned to a book of adventure. This is what he found.

A Latvian, Fred Rebell (Escape to the Sea, Youth Book Club Ltd., 1951) was a sceptic of twenty-five years standing. He became a firm believer as a result of certain 'dreams' that clearly included out-of-the-body experiences. These occurred while he was sailing across the world, alone, in a small boat. Rebell obviously had no knowledge of psychic matters, though he does not specifically say so.

On one occasion, Rebell said, 'I dreamed one night that I was float-ing in the air above the dark ocean. I knew myself to be roughly a hundred miles to the N.N.E. of my boat's present position. There on the ocean, on the dark water below me, I saw a curious hull which I took to be a derelict. As I looked at it, the light increased and I made it out to be a ship with a stumpy mast and the Captain's bridge aft resembling a hen-coop. ...'

This was no mere dream, since Rebell continued, 'The next morning, as I took my first peep outside my berth, I saw, about a mile ahead, the very duplicate of the ship I had dreamed about. She looked like a steamer, but there was no smoke coming from her stack. I wondered if she was in fact a derelict. But no: she was moving. It was not till I drew closer that I was able to make her out to be a diesel-engined freighter with a deck-cargo of timber. ... Never till that moment had I passed a ship of any kind on the high seas. ... At the time I dreamed of this steamer she was far below the horizon, and it was not till next day that our paths crossed.'

He commented, 'If dreams like this mean that the soul wanders from the body, it is a curious fact that the soul nevertheless remains clearly conscious of just where the body is at the time.' In this connexion, it may be said that Rebell's description of a subsequent 'dream' indicates why this is possible. In this latter experience he was aware of the presence of the 'silver cord' uniting his physical with his non-physical body. Others who are conscious when exteriorized from the physical bodies realized that it was this feature which carried sensory stimuli from the Physical Body to the 'soul' (which uses the Psychical Body) and ideas, observations, etc. from the 'soul' to the Physical Body, so that there is awareness of two bodies and of two corresponding environments.

With regard to his second experience, Rebell said, 'I seemed to be above the deck: and *with a clearness quite unusual in a dream*, I saw the moonlight playing upon the hood of my boat. ... But there was some-thing mysterious about the scene: for though I could see the bellied sail, I could feel no breeze; though I could see the rippling ocean, I could not hear the wavelets lapping. [Cf. Hives's critical observa-tions.] ... Then I found myself rising *obliquely*: and, from an elevation of about one hundred feet, I caught sight of the boat once more. ... Higher and higher I seemed to rise, through clouds and mists, till at last the horizon disappeared. Then at last there was nothing above me but the moon shining out of a clear sky: and beneath me an ocean, not of water, but of clouds. ... Yet I rose still higher ... *I felt as if I were carried in the hands of some very powerful friendly being: but I could not see him* [compare Muldoon, Fox, etc.]. *Neither could I very well see my body or whatever visible shape my soul might then be wearing. For my body seemed to be garbed in a sort of a night-shirt from which came a faint light;*

[the Psychical Body was luminous—cf. Gerhardi, Brunton, etc.] *and rom which there spread downwards, in the direction I had come from, a thin, slightly wavy and speckled, luminous ribbon* [the 'silver cord'—cf. Statement No. 19].

'Tremendous as the distance seemed, I must have traversed it with the speed of thought. It did not take me half the time to travel it that I have taken to relate it now. ... I cannot say how long I tarried in this state of happiness: all I know is *I wanted to remain there for ever* [cf. Statement No. 8]. But consciousness was stealing upon me that I could not do so as yet. Some bond [the 'silver-cord'] seemed to hold me to an earthly existence: I felt that I had still something to do in the world. At that, presently I found myself sinking, sinking, and again sinking ... and I awoke to find myself in my bunk aboard the *Elaine*.'

CASE NO. 62—*Lt.-Col. Reginald M. Lester*

Lester, prominent journalist and Founder of the Churches' Fellowship for Psychical Study, described out-of-the-body experiences in his *In Search of the Hereafter* (Harrap & Co. Ltd., 1952). *Originally a sceptic, Lester eventually concluded that sleep differs from death chiefly in that 'the astral cord' remains attached.* During early experiences he had difficulty in distinguishing between 'real astral travel' and 'mere dreams'. Later he distinguished them by two criteria: in astral travel events occur in proper sequence and the details are so vivid that they remain almost permanently in the memory; dream-memories, on the other hand, are 'always confused' and tend to fade on waking.

Most of Lester's out-of-the-body experiences took place 'on our own' (earth) plane but in some *he visited his (deceased) wife in the 'etheric world'* [here = 'Paradise' conditions]. *He 'co-operated' with her in 'rescue work'* [cf. the Countess of Tankerville, Edwards, Brown, etc. and Statement No. 30]. Part of his wife's duties were said to consist in helping people who, having been suddenly killed in accidents, 'did not realize where they were' [cf. Statement No. 42. While many people (of average type) who die naturally in old age fail, at first, to realize that they have shed the Physical Body, this applies to most people (of average type) whose death is enforced. The latter require special help and this is often most effectively given by others who are newly-dead]. His wife told him that when she took him beyond the 'astral' plane [here = 'Hades' conditions] to her own world ['etheric' here = 'Paradise' conditions] it involved much preliminary work by way of 'thinning' the density of his Psychical Body [in communicators' terms, 'raising his vibrations']. In their (more numerous) earth-journeys, they re-visited familiar scenes. Lester mentioned the interesting point noted below (as well as examples of veridical information obtained in the course of his out-of-the-body experiences).

Lester was puzzled by one matter: as he awoke, he would remember that he had been with his wife, happy in a beautiful country [= 'Paradise' conditions], 'when,' he said, *'suddenly she would collapse in my arms as though stricken with sickness.'* He asked his wife, if he were really with her in his sleep-hours, how could she possibly be taken ill there? She told him that the 'picture' of illness was 'flashed across' his sub-conscious mind 'at the impact of waking'. This may be true, but it is not an explanation. In view of numerous psychic communications, an actual reason is suggested. It should be noted that the remembrance of the illness which caused his wife's transition came to him after a period in the Psychical Body and just before he entered his Physical Body, that is, during a brief period of consciousness in the 'body-veil'. In other words, *Lt.-Col. Lester's experience was an example of the 'taking-on', by psychics, of the illness-symptoms (etc.) of their communicators.* This well-known phenomenon seems to be due to a communicator in 'Paradise' conditions contacting the vehicle of vitality and memory, the 'body-veil', (the organ of detailed memory) of the psychic, which contact vivifies certain memory-traces of the deceased, causing certain experiences to be 'remembered' by both communicator and psychic. The phenomenon is related to the vivification, by a medium, of the memory-traces in 'astral shells', the effect being to simulate truncated communications. The latter is, of course, the basis of the 'Mindlet' or 'Psychic Factor' Theory. Here the medium unconsciously 'reads' the memory-traces of an astral corpse: in the 'taking-on' of symptoms (as in Lester's case), he 'reads' the memory-traces of the non-physical body actually in use by a discarnate person. Lester's account is, therefore, highly evidential.

A second interesting feature mentioned is that his (deceased) wife reported that, during his earlier 'astral' visits, when the time arrived that he must return to his Physical Body, he 'vanished' suddenly. Later she noted that, *just as he was about to 'vanish' in this manner, the 'colours' of his 'etheric body' began to dim and fade away.* The husband replied, 'That's an interesting point that I've not heard stated before'. Although he did not see the implication of his wife's observation, it seems clear in relation to what is said in numerous psychic communications: the increasing influence of the Physical on the Psychical Body reduced the 'vibrations' (and consequently the brilliance of the latter) until *it was quenched as it re-entered the Physical Body.* Lester's Psychical Body, visible to his wife so long as it was exteriorized from his Physical Body, became dim as he approached it, and disappeared as they coincided. The same phenomenon was noted by Mrs Leonard and Mr Sculthorp, but they expressed it in terms of the clarity of consciousness.

Costa made the interesting observation that his mother's Psychical Body (which was at some distance from her Physical Body) was luminous, but his own (which was near to its physical counterpart) did not glow.

Matters which are either misunderstood or only partially understood by an author, his communicator, or both, and yet which are concordant with the general philosophy of communications may have additional significance on that account: they are 'pointers' to the truth.

CASE No. 63—Miss 'W.S.'

Frank Lind (*My Occult Case Book*, Rider & Co. Ltd.) gave the experience of a woman which was earlier published in *Prediction*, Sept. 1950. Her mother had died after a long illness. She repeatedly 'dreamed' of her mother as ill, and finally dreamed that she got away from her mother (in an effort to escape infection) and soared to the ceiling. (Here exteriorization was caused by fear. In Muldoon's terminology, her Physical Body was 'incapacitated' but her Psychical Body was not.) *She patted the ceiling several times 'in order to fix upon her mind that she had been able to do it'* (i.e., *she sought experimental evidence that she was exteriorized from the Physical Body*). So strong was the impression that, although she knew it was absurd to try, she endeavoured to touch the ceiling the next day [cf. Gerhardi and Miss Sime]. She asked Lind what the dream meant and why it should occur after her mother had died and she had ceased grieving for her. Mr Lind considered, first, that she was exteriorized from the Physical Body in her 'double' (a conclusion with which we would agree); secondly, that she had continued to dream while thus out of her Physical Body in her 'double'. *We suggest, however, that the image of her mother as in her last illness, was not a dream but was due to the (deceased) mother impressing her presence on her daughter and incidentally contacting the latter's 'body-veil': this process caused a partial review of the last illness in both their minds.* Similarly, the (deceased) Mary Lyttleton (*Proc.* S.P.R., 52, p. 170) was sad only when, in order to communicate, she contacted earth-conditions and therefore revived a sad earth-memory.

CASE No. 64—Mr F. C. Sculthorp

Mr F. C. Sculthorp informs me (*in litt.*) that, when exteriorized, he 'visited' places both on earth and in 'astral' spheres, pleasant and otherwise. *Like Muldoon, Fox, Miss Peters, Hives and others, he noted 'incongruities' during his out-of-the-body experiences.* For example, he says, 'Walking on the edge of a pond with thick mud, my boots were quite clean—to my surprise.' [The explanation of this, and similar incongruities, seems to be that the pond and mud were physical but the 'boots' in which Mr Sculthorp 'walked' were mental images or 'thought-forms']. *A description that agrees with those of Muldoon, Wiltse, Mrs Boorman, Miss Addison, etc. concerns the vibrations that may be felt in the Physical Body while the non-physical body is in process of separating from it.* Mr Sculthorp said, 'At first the astral body left the Physical Body vibrating as if being drawn over a corrugated surface.' (Muldoon said, '... my entire rigid body—I thought it was my physical, but it was my astral—commenced vibrating at a great rate of speed in an up and down direction. ...' Dr Wiltse was 'rocked to and fro', Miss C. Addison experienced' vibrations' that 'increased in intensity', and 'a rocking movement'.) A third point of similarity is that Mr Sculthorp described his 'astral' body as leaving the earth 'at a *tangent*' [Einarsson, Hout, Rebell, Mrs Parker, 'Betty' and all others who mentioned the direction of its movement said it was 'oblique', 'spiral', etc., never vertical].

Like Turvey, Lind, Mrs Jeffrey, Zoila Stables, Mrs Joy, Yram, etc. Mr Sculthorp found that his total non-physical body was divisible. On two occasions it was 'made into two distinct bodies' and he found himself looking at himself. This experience gave him 'the impression that the etheric body could be made into several complete bodies, according to advancement, each body capable of awareness and activity on its own plane and always connected to a central body'.

When out of his Physical Body Mr Sculthorp met discarnates [cf. Statement No. 18]. They were interested in his appearance, a fact which he could not understand for some time. He said, 'One night I had projected to a hospital where my wife, who had passed over, was helping. I saw a young lady and told her whom I wished to see, but she was more interested in something above my head. *I at once realized that she could see the "silver cord" that went from my head to my Physical Body on earth.* ...' [cf. Statement No. 19].

As with Muldoon, Mrs Leonard, Helen Brooks, Varley, etc., strong emotion caused Mr Sculthorpe to re-interiorize. The operative emotion with Muldoon was fear: that with Fox was love. Sculthorp's return was due to annoyance. Seeing something that made him 'very annoyed', he was 'drawn back into the Physical Body at once.' His explanation is that, 'There seems to be a law that does not allow the feeling of annoyance in the etheric body'. But it seems more likely that the cause of return lies in the nature of the emotions while one is exteriorized but still connected with a Physical Body—that emotions are near-physical, or 'semi-physical', in nature. It should be noted that emotions of desire, dislike, admiration, etc., seem to be important factors in the production of supernormal photographs. Mrs Cripps (*in litt.*) sent the writer an interesting suggestion: it was that since fear tends to involve the idea of flight, to experience that emotion while exteriorized, tends to cause concealment by interiorization.

Like Muldoon and others, Mr Sculthorp found that 'discomfort or noise near the Physical Body generally caused a return'. Like many others also, he experienced 'astral catalepsy': he said (after a noise had caused re-interiorization), 'As is usual when returning from a projection, I was unable to move at first. ...'

Mr Sculthorp described 'dual consciousness' [Statement No. 18]. Like Muldoon, Fox, etc., he was aware (*via* the 'silver cord') of both a physical and a non-physical environment. He said, 'Discomfort in the Physical Body is registered in the same part of the Etheric [here = Psychical] Body through the connecting 'silver cord'. This I experienced when talking to a soldier, an acquaintance while on earth, in the 'astral'. I felt an increasing numbness in my right arm and knew that my Physical Body in bed was overlaying an arm. I tried to dismiss the feeling, but the discomfort became so great that I told the soldier that I must go. Concentrating, I returned to my body, sat up in bed and rubbed my right arm.' [Compare the experiences described by Dr van Eeden.]

Mr Sculthorp 'experimented in several ways during projection' but not with the 'etheric' body—his 'feelings of well-being and solidity' deterred him. He said, 'In my first projection I thought I was experiencing clairvoyance (which I often get before going to sleep), but an experiment which I tried convinced me that I was indeed out of my body.' He also made an interesting point when he said that, *when exteriorized, consciousness is, in general, more vivid than ordinarily, but that in his case, 'consciousness is not even and regular (as on earth), but seems to wax and wane according to the life-force reaching it through the astral cord'.* Mrs Leonard made the same observation [cf. also the accounts of Col. Lester and 'René C'. The amount of 'life-force' that is transmitted by the 'silver cord' is said to vary according to several factors.]

CASE No. 65—*Mr Frank Lind*

Frank Lind (*My Occult Case Book*, Rider, 1953) gave extracts from first-hand descriptions of astral projection that were published over many years in *Prediction*. Illustrating the role of symbolism in projection, he cited a woman's 'dream' as follows. 'Again and again I have dreamed I was flying. The dream usually starts with my being trapped in a small room by enemies. They have left a window slightly open at the top, and I float up and slip through this tiny space. Soon I am very high in the air and rising higher every minute. ...' Lind commented, '*The "room" in which the dreamer was "trapped" was a corporeal prison. She was not the first to escape from those symbolical enemies—warders, comprising the lower emotions* [fear, anger, sensuality] *which would prevent the* *"double" from leaving its narrow cell* [others use such terms as 'prison' and 'cage']—*through that slightly open "window" (in reality, the head)'* [cf. Statement No. 13]. *Again Lind pointed out that the symbols for the shedding of the Physical Body include 'dreams' of falling out of a cart, of floating through a doorway and of floating through an open window. Again, 'a constant preliminary to loss of consciousness is the symbolic passing through a pitch-dark tunnel'* [cf. Statement No. 9]. *Mr Lind also said, 'Fright invariably exerts a sharp pull upon the cord'.*

One of Lind's correspondents wrote, 'I was in a narrow, dimly-lit passage ... [= 'tunnel' = the Physical Body], down both sides of which was a row of black doors. A child's dress came flying through the air towards me. It got wrapped around my head, but I threw it off and drifted out through the doors into an empty room where I sank on the floor'. Then there was a return to physical embodiment. Lind commented, 'When this lady reached the room and fell down, she had, as Mr Fox allegorically expresses it, forced her "incorporeal self through the doorway of the pineal gland". The impression that something like a child's dress got wrapped around her head, was produced by the final effort of her exteriorized consciousness to detach itself completely from the physical brain [cf. Statement No. 13—(?) or from the vehicle of vitality]. Astral projection may be caused by the brain remaining active while the Physical Body is exhausted. Sometimes one thinks one hears a sharp snap as the "double" interlocks with the latter' [cf. Muldoon, Fox, Dennis, Hives, Miss Price, etc.].

Some men, while 'out', can, while others cannot, be seen in a mirror: some can, and some cannot, pass through walls, etc. A somewhat similar phenomenon is mentioned by Mr Lind. *When 'out', Yram once received a slap in the face. Apparently it did not affect his Physical Body. However, a correspondent of Lind's, when 'out' received a similar blow that did affect his Physical Body and the mark could be seen for days.* [Compare the experience of Wills while normally exteriorized and that of Adèle Maginot while under hypnosis. The 'repercussion' in 'materializations' and in witchcraft are clearly of a similar nature. The differences here noted are presumably due to the different densities in the total non-physical body (or to 'layers' of the latter) as projected, either by different people, or by one and the same person at different times. They are among the indications that the non-physical body is objective and that it is not simple but consists of components of various densities.]

Another point made by Lind is that, '*As the astral body is the servant of suggestion, objects take shape or dissolve in obedience to every play of fancy. It is this ready response to suggestion while out in the "double" which, for the beginner, is the cause of fright.* The dread of attack by entities of a peculiar astral type brings them, by the law of attraction, into temporary existence by one's own creation' [cf. Statement No. 10]. Mr Lind has himself had a number of exteriorizations and, while he has many times experienced 'thistle-down lightness' he says, 'One does not enjoy it until one has overcome the breathless astonishment first felt at being lifted off one's feet and "carried away", as by some forceful emotion, which it is one's instinctive urge to resist: that, of course, brings one's "double" rushing back into its material sheath.'

One night Lind 'travelled, with breathless swiftness, through houses, shops, lamp-posts, etc.' to a friend's house a mile away but was invisible to anyone there. However, on another occasion he says, 'I paid an un-invited visit to another friend's house and was afterwards informed that my presence there had been sensed'. [Either his 'double' was relatively dense on this occasion, or the percipients were sensitive to psychic impressions.] *The return from out-of-the-body experiences was made 'regretfully'* [cf. Statement No. 8].

We have referred above to claims that the total non-physical body or 'double' consists of a series of progressively subtler components (or alternatively, that man is equipped with a series of successively subtler 'bodies'). This plurality of bodies is mentioned independently by Turvey, Bennett, Yram, Mrs Jeffrey, Mrs I. M. Joy, Mr Sculthorp, Zoila Stables, etc., and we find it given (without mention of these similar cases or of its significance in connexion with the bodily consti-tution of the observer) by Mr Lind. He stated, 'I was definitely awake; yet became aware that I was watching the process of a dream in forma-tion. Indeed, as soon as I caught myself slipping back into the dream-state, immediately I put on the brake; consequently, I found myself a second time, not merely recalling, but actually watching, in a strictly detached way, the unfoldment of a dream. And I could check, in a measure, its action backwards and forwards. Or more correctly, it moved in a series of connected pictures as if revolving on the surface of an immense oval-shaped bubble. This "bubble" was, no doubt, my partly-projected "double" [cf. the accounts of Gerhardi, Helen Brooks and Mrs "Prothero"]. Strangely enough consciousness seemed to have shifted from one centre to another more remote; that is to say, out of the Physical Body to one more in contact with the dream phenomena, but still not within the film-like oval reflecting them [= part of the vehicle of vitality or "body-veil"]. The auric oval swayed with the beats of my heart. ... It responded to the pulsations of my heart in the manner of an air-balloon on the jerks of a hand holding it by a thread. And I soon became aware that the closer I fixed my attention upon the bubble, the nearer the centre of my consciousness moved towards it— and out of the physical; so I concluded that, with sufficient concentra-tion, I might become fully conscious inside, and not outside, the dream-world of which I was viewing certain faint and shifting reflections.'

CASE NO. 66—*Mrs E. F. Sheridan*

Mrs E. F. Sheridan informed me (*in litt.*) that she has had exterioriza-tions that were usually assisted by discarnates [cf. Statement No. 3 regarding 'deliverers']. In one, she saw her (deceased) brother (cf. Statement No. 18]. In another *she saw her Physical Body (looking down on it from somewhere about the ceiling)* [cf. Statement No. 17]. *Fear then caused re-interiorization. She was reluctant to return to physical life* [cf. Statement No. 8]. With regard to one occasion she said, 'I hated leav-ing the "heavenly" condition to take up earth-life again.' Like others who claim to have had such experiences, she was 'conscious of physical things actually present in the room, things that could not have been visible unless one was out of the body, because of the complete absence of ordinary light.'

CASE NO. 67—*Mrs Peggy Roberts*

Mrs Roberts informed the author that she had read no books whatever on this subject. The experience came as a complete surprise. She said, 'Since my first experience I have read of other cases, but I have never met anyone who could understand what I meant when I told them about it.

'My first experience was seven years ago. I was dozing in an arm-chair when I found myself floating about the room. I was also con-scious of the fact that I was unable to move my Physical Body or open my eyes [= catalepsy]. I became frightened and began to think I had either had a stroke or passed away. I also wondered how I would open the front door when my children came home from school. With that [wish] I gradually felt myself returning and able to use my body.

'After this sort of thing had happened a few times I saw a book called *The Projection of the Astral Body* by Muldoon and Carrington. The descriptions given were almost identical to my own experiences.

'*Projection begins when I am dozing: a kind of whirring begins in my head, and I know I am "off". It is as if I am floating over strange countrysides and cities.* So far I have never met any other beings on my travels. I am no longer afraid and look forward to it happening, though that is not often. Projection is quite different from ordinary dreaming. *It has taught me belief in life after death. Before, I always thought this the only life.* If people could experience astral travel, they would lead better lives and lose all fear of dying, knowing that we do not die.'

CASE NO. 68—*Mrs D. E. Boorman*

Mrs D. E. Boorman 'had read no books on the subject'. She wrote (*in litt.*) 'I was resting in bed. *There was first a stillness* [= shedding the Physical Body—cf. Statement No. 9]. *Then there was a swaying of what I thought was my Physical Body* [cf. Muldoon, Sculthorp, Wiltse, Miss Addison, etc.] *and I rose horizontally above it. "Enough," I cried, and stopped a foot from the ceiling. Looking down, I saw my Physical Body lying on the bed* [cf. Statement No. 17]. *I also noticed a silver light* [the 'silver cord'— cf. Statement No. 19] *between me and my body. A bluish light seemed to permeate everything; everything seemed alive, glowing and pulsating. I was filled with wonder.*

'*Wishing myself back, I felt what was like a violent push in the chest. It then felt like slipping into a coat, and I found myself back in my body.* [Miss Johnson described *re-entering* the body as like entering '*a tight rubber skin*'; Mrs Williams said it was like slipping the hand into a glove; Mrs Parker said it was like entering a bag. Conversely, Miss Yeoman described *leaving* her body as like pulling off a glove and Miss Addison said it was like being drawn out of '*a tight rubber bathing-suit*'. It is, the writer considers, correspondences such as these that indicate that these people were, in fact, outside their Physical Bodies in an objective 'astral' body. Such converse descriptions cannot be explained as images. On the other hand, the fact that a percipient claims to see the projected person is not, *by itself*, evidence that he was there in a non-physical body. The percipient might be psychic and see a 'thought-form', etc.]

'*After getting over the shock, I was delighted and awed. I have had plenty of astral travelling since then. These experiences did a great thing for me: I did not believe in survival before, but now I know, I am convinced and am no longer afraid to die.*'

Asked if she thought she might be dreaming, Mrs Boorman replied 'No—because it was more real than the matter of this world in which we dwell' [cf. Statement No. 26]. In answer to my questions about the 'silver cord', she said, 'Is it a cord? To me it's just a stream of light. I take no notice of it, coming from behind. I should say it is joined to the head.' Asked about the sensations on leaving the Physical Body, etc., Mrs Boorman said, 'The sensations of leaving the body are of floating and rising [cf. Statement No. 9]. Once one is partly out, the room, the atmosphere and articles of furniture glow. One feels soothed. Coming back is often more abrupt. Your body seems to jerk a little' [= the 'repercussion'—cf. Muldoon, Gerhardi, Mrs Lester, etc.].

CASE NO. 69—*Mrs Howard W. Jeffrey Sr.*

Mrs H. W. Jeffrey Sr., of Rockdale, New York, who furnished me with the following particulars of her experiences, knew practically nothing of psychical matters. She said that she had 'heard of "H. H. Home"' (meaning, of course, the famous D. D. Home).

'I sit in a chair and the other-me floats out of me. *Floating out of the body, and re-entering it, is rather like swimming.* It does not hurt [cf. Statement No. 7]. I suppose I am aided in leaving my body, but, if so, it is not by anyone on earth. I cannot go out at will, though I know when it is about to take place.

'I seem to leave from the middle [cf. Mrs Garrett], though I am told that in India this is considered a dangerous thing to do [this is not true, of course], and one is supposed to go out by the top of the head [most people do]. A woman told me that if I left from my middle my heart would stop—but I answered, "How can I get up to my head, when my middle is much closer?" I guess perhaps that when it comes to these matters we do the easiest way for us [cf. Zoila Stables's account]. That woman told me that she used to climb through her head [cf. Statement No. 13] and go to China, etc.

'*I watch what goes out of me like white intestines and floats under the door and goes away, and I get from "me" and leave too.* (I don't see those white intestines again. I don't like seeing them. If they come back in— and I suppose they do—well, I never know when).' [These 'white intestines' clearly correspond to (1) the 'violet gaseous counterpart of the Physical Body', or 'pale, greyish heliotrope form' described by Arnold Bennett; (2) to the substance often seen leaving the bodies of dying men and (3) to that seen emerging from 'physical' mediums in trance to form the basis of 'materializations'. It has been called ecto-plasm. Ectoplasm (from the vehicle of vitality) is variously described by supposed discarnates, and by more or less clairvoyant observers of the process of dying, as (1) a 'vapour' ('a pearly vapour', 'a thin violet vapour', 'a fine luminous vapour', etc.) a 'mist' ('a deep violet mist', 'a light haze or mist', 'a mist-like wraith', etc.) a 'cloud' ('a thick white cloud', 'a cloud-like form', etc.) and a 'substance' ('a curling, shadowy grey substance', etc.). These are also descriptions of ectoplasm as seen (and photographed) at seances. Supposed discarnate communicators say that it is a product of the vehicle of vitality. It is remarkable that these accounts agree so closely, yet Mrs Jeffrey had no knowledge of psychic matters (as indeed her narrative shows). She therefore saw part of the vehicle of vitality, or 'body-veil', leave the Physical Body and presumably she saw this (as well as the temporarily discarded Physical Body) from the Psychical Body.] Mrs Jeffrey said, 'I get away from me [the Physical Body] as well as exteriorizing the "white intestines".' [*That is, she recognized three 'bodies'. So did Mrs Joy—'There must have been three of me'. Others in whose accounts a plurality of bodies is claimed include Miss Stables, and Messrs Yram, Sculthorp, Turvey, and Lind and the anonymous Case No. 37.*]

'*In earth-life you listen to people speaking with their mouths—in floating you know what their brains are thinking. You hear what people are saying to each other, and what their brains are thinking at the same time. It is amusing,* for they do not say what they think.' [Compare the statement of the anonymous communicator of *Life Beyond the Grave*, E. W. Allen, 1876, regarding, it should be noted, those sub-average 'dead' who are 'earthbound', delayed in 'Hades' conditions. He said, 'We can hear all that a mortal gives utterance to through the body, and a good deal that he does not utter through the body, for we hear his thoughts as words.']

'*The floating-me,*' continued Mrs Jeffrey, '*is white. It is very happy and knows more than the earth-me could ever know. It talks with those who have "passed over"* [cf. Statement No. 18]. I have seen nothing but earth-scenes and people.'

CASE No. 70—*Mr Wm. E. Edwards*

Mr Wm. E. Edwards (in litt.) informed me that, prior to an exteriorization, he had no knowledge of, or interest in, psychic phenomena and had never heard of the subject of astral projection. He was against such things, since he belonged to a religious sect that took that attitude. He described his 'first outstanding experience' as follows. 'I awoke in a dream and realized that I was not (as I should have been) in bed. Everything, including the scenery, was one-hundred per cent. reality [cf. Statement No. 26]. I think I must have been somewhere on earth. As I pondered the situation, I suddenly felt, as it were, a pull of a powerful force which literally hurtled me back through space towards my body. I hovered above my body for a second or so. *Then I felt the pull of the cord as though it were made of stout elastic. It was pulling from the centre of my forehead* [cf. Statement No. 19]. *Then catalepsy. Then noises in my head. Then the two bodies coincided and I opened my eyes, though I was already awake.*'

'This,' said Mr Edwards, 'was the only occasion on which I have felt the pull of (as it were) a cord. Since then, I have had thousands of experiences of allied phenomena. I have been able at times to leave my body at will, fully conscious, and so to return.

'*There are two kinds of projection, one to places on earth, the other to the astral world.* The latter has occupied the great majority of my experiences, and I have met and spoken with the "dead" [cf. Statement No. 18] and seen the other worlds, both the great heights and the terrible depths. *I have been used in giving healing in the sleep-state and also in rescue-operations* [= 'co-operation—cf. Statement No. 30 and compare the accounts of the Countess of Tankerville, and Messrs Lester and Brown]. Also, in my sleep-state, I have been shown all that was to be ahead of me, so that I knew things that were to take place.'

CASE No. 71—*The Revd Dr J. R. Staver*

The Revd J. R. Staver, PH.D., of Saginaw, Michigan, informed me (*in litt.*) that while his first exteriorization was of an involuntary nature, he subsequently left his body deliberately.

He said, 'I felt a very urgent impulse to go and lie down on my bed, though I did not feel tired. Almost at once my consciousness was projected into the dining-room of an acquaintance some six miles distant. From the adjoining living-room I could hear this man and his wife, discussing the status of a young man who worked for them, whom they were deciding to discharge. At no time did I actually see those who were talking, but every detail of the dining-room in which I was could be distinctly seen. Later I verified the appearance and arrangements of this room. ...

'Within a year I resolved to attempt the voluntary experience of astral projection. I selected as my goal the residence of a lady in Connecticut with whom I was then in correspondence. I made arrangements with her as to time, etc., and, since she also was a psychic, I asked her to endeavour to see my astral form on the occasion of its presence in her home. *The result of this experiment was that while I was able vividly to see both the appearance of her home, interior lay-out, the several items of furniture, etc., etc., she was unable to see me, though she declared that she distinctly felt my presence.*

'In the latter experiment, immediately after I returned, I wrote a complete description of all I had seen, all of which was verified, with the exception of the direction towards which the house faced. ...'

CASE No. 72—*Miss Zoila C. M. Stables*, B.A.

Miss Stables, of Brisbane, wrote (*in litt.*) 'My first projection was in my early teens. *I had not then heard, nor read, nor had the slightest inkling of projection, or any other psychic subject.* We lived then on a small selection in the empty western grazing areas, and were 200 miles from the nearest town.' She continued. 'One night I had what I then considered a dream, but what I now believe to be a genuine projection. I simply woke to find myself flying through the air at a considerable height above the ground. ... There was a strange glamour about the experience—a kind of unreasonable and unprecedented rapture, that engraved it on my memory. It was not until thirty years later that I saw Muldoon's book, *The Projection of the Astral Body*, I remembered that early flight and set out to experiment according to the instructions given—with some result.'

Miss Stables continued, 'Usually I have awakened out of a dream to find myself projected; but an infinitely more interesting, and difficult, achievement is to project oneself from the waking condition. My method is to imagine the astral body vibrating faster and faster—to imagine it so hard that I can actually feel it.' Mentioning the methods recommended by Muldoon and others, she stated, 'They are all methods of keeping the attention "at home", as it were; of keeping the mind alert and focused on its own mental sensations—if that is not a contradiction in terms. It is just as if the astral body were a train seeking an opportunity to slip away without its passenger—which does seem to be the case, for I find that if I let my attention wander for only a moment, all is lost, and I am asleep.

'*When, however, I do manage to project by my own efforts, the final sensation before floating free is invariably a jolt in the feet, as if that were the last point to separate. Sometimes it is quite severe, a kind of grinding jerk (not painful), sometimes only a light tap, but always there.* [The 'dead' occasionally describe exteriorization by way of the feet.]

'*Another very frequent sensation (after getting free this time) is that of going down a long tunnel* [= shedding the vehicle of vitality—cf. Miss Blakeley, Miss Peters and Mrs Parker]. ... *It is usually going down a creek with high banks, or sometimes down inside a long pergola: but it is too frequent a happening not to have some correspondence with reality.*

'Another rule that I have discovered for myself is that if the Physical Body lies on its back, the phantom may go to any height and be in any position but if the Physical Body lies on its side (either side), the phantom floats face downward and only about a foot above the ground. Of course, this may be true only for me.

'Once, while floating in a horizontal position, I looked down and saw a luminous outline (following the contours of my body), about six inches below me.' [This suggests three bodies—the Psychical, the vehicle of vitality (and memory) and the Physical Body.]

CASE NO. 73—*Mr Jeffrey H. Brown*

Mr Jeffrey H. Brown had astral projection experiences since six or seven years of age, but did not recognize them for what they were until the age of thirty. He had neither read any books on the subject nor discussed it with other people until then. He published an account of an exteriorization in the *Psychic News* for May, 1952 which included fore-knowledge. He mentioned several features that strongly suggest an actual out-of-the-body experience and not mere clairvoyance or telepathy: they include the cataleptic condition and the 'silver cord' [cf. Statement No. 19]. He obtained veridical information about a house that he had never seen while he was in the flesh.

In an article headed 'Some Psychic Experiences' and published in *Light* in September 1946, Mr Brown gave further details. He said, 'I have always been an astral projectionist ... but it was not until I began the serious development of the psychic faculties that I found it possible to control this erstwhile liability, and even now there are occasions on which I fail to control the situation. Sometimes the experiences seem to be directly under my control, whilst at others they appear to be directed by another intelligence, and sometimes it would appear that the projection is purely spontaneous and without a definite end in view.'

Mr Brown gives an example of 'directed' projection—'with the object of assisting spirit helpers' [= 'co-operation'—cf. Statement No. 30]. The abbreviated account is as follows: 'I became aware that I was out of the Physical Body and far from my bedroom at home. From the difficulty experienced in walking, I knew that I was still on the earth-plane. I seemed to be alone and could see nothing in the darkness. Then I heard a voice, though I could not see who spoke: it said, "You are in the North of England and have been brought to assist us. An accident is going to occur on the railroad".' Mr Brown 'saw' the accident happen, but no one seemed to be seriously injured. The voice next told him to return, and he says, 'Then, as so often happens on such occasions, I felt myself drawn upwards and backwards [compare Muldoon, etc.], losing all control over my actions, but not of consciousness. ... Slowly I sank down until I seemed to be lying on my bed. I suddenly regained the ability to control my body, sat up in bed, ascertained the time, and told my wife, who had also awakened, of my experience.' Mr Brown then cited a newspaper paragraph describing the accident he 'saw' during the night hundreds of miles from his Physical Body.

With regard to another experience, Mr Brown said, 'I became conscious to find myself apparently floating over my Physical Body at a height of five to six feet [compare Statements No. 16 and 17]. The fact that I could see told me that it must have been the early hours of the morning. I willed myself to move forward in the air, in a horizontal position, feet first [compare Muldoon, Mr 'H', etc.] until I was quite clear of the house; then I seemed to change direction, turning over on my face, and moved forward as if swimming. *Very quickly I seemed to find myself moving through what appeared to be a light blue mist which I apparently mistook for water* ['Denser Between Worlds' or 'Hades' conditions—cf. Statement No. 41]. I recall trying to swim through it, although I was surprised to find that I remained dry. After travelling for some time I reached a shore the sands of which were golden in colour. *Climbing out of the "mist", I looked round and saw groups of people standing about as if waiting for somebody. An atmospheric vibration extended in every direction and the blueness created a feeling of rest and calm.*' [Compare *Blue Island*, said to be communicated by the supposed discarnate W. T. Stead. The latter, newly-dead, described an 'island' with a general condition of 'blueness' while Sir Arthur Conan Doyle, commenting on the communication, said, 'The colour blue is, of course, that of healing, and an island may be only an isolated sphere—an ante-chamber to others.']

'I looked behind,' continued Brown, 'but I could see nothing except the swirling mist, which now seemed a much lighter blue when com-pared with the island, as I now called it. Suddenly I heard a voice but, as so often happens, could not see who spoke [compare Muldoon, etc.]. "You have visited the Plane of Healing [compare experiences of Miss Peters and Mrs Cripps]. You must now return." I was literally swept off my feet and propelled backwards through the air, ultimately find-ing myself back in my bedroom and passing through the now custom-ary sequence of becoming cataleptic, being lowered towards the body, re-linking with the latter and remaining unable to move for about a minute, finally awakening to normal consciousness with a start' [the 'repercussion']. *Mr Brown, like Muldoon, Bulford, Mrs Cripps, etc. miti-gated the effect of the repercussion.* He said: 'I have now learned the futility of struggling against the cataleptic condition, for to do so only makes matters worse and the discomfort greater. So now I wait, more or less calmly, for the condition to break naturally.'

Like Mrs Cripps and others, Mr Brown found that 'as life on one plane is succeeded by life on another, all our senses become more acute and we are, consequently, more sensitive both to beauty and ugliness'.

CASE NO. 74—*Dr R. B. Hout*

Dr R. B. Hout, a medical man, published an account of his out-of-the-body experiences in *Prediction*, 1936 and in the *National Spiritualist*, 1937. He said, 'I had placed myself in a comfortable position for a few moments of relaxation. ... George, my trusted etheric friend [cf. Statement No. 18] appeared. ... He asked whether I would go with him. I acquiesced and felt myself drawn out of my body [cf. Statement No. 3 regarding 'deliverers']. ... I just stepped away from the reclining physical form, turned to view it [cf. Statement No. 17] and then floated upward, out and away from the material room. ... *Then I found myself in a new but very natural environment. It was a grove or park* [= 'Paradise' conditions—cf. Statement No. 26]. *And there was George, seated opposite me.* ... *Here were my departed friends and here also, was my-self, able to function actively there for a limited time and in a feeble manner'* [cf. Kelley, Gerhardi, Mrs Leonard, etc.]. After a time, 'I was pulled *obliquely* downwards [cf. Rebell, Sculthorp, etc.], out of the etheric realm ... back through the walls [cf. Statement No. 31], into my study. Then, as the pull of the body became stronger, *I suddenly stiffened in my astral form, assumed a position parallel to and immediately above the physical counterpart, and dropped into it* [cf. Gerhardi, Muldoon, Bulford, Mr 'H', etc.]. The re-association of the two vehicles occasioned a slight jolt [= the 'repercussion']. ... These out-of-the-body experiences are real and objective. In them I meet people living in a real world, doing natural things. *Until I had my first visit I could not possibly have understood the objectivity of the next world.*'

CASE NO. 75—*Mrs Eileen J. Garrett*

Mrs E. J. Garrett (*Awareness*, Creative Age Press Inc., N.Y., 1943), President of the Parapsychology Foundation Inc., N.Y., is a famous sensitive. She takes an objective and thoroughly scientific attitude towards psychic phenomena. *Mrs Garrett had out-of-the-body experiences long before she had heard of their existence.* Since childhood she had observed the 'double', 'aura', 'surround', 'astral body', etc., sur-rounding living creatures and found it difficult to believe that others were unaware of that feature. Mrs Garrett had an experience identical with one described by Mme Hauffe. She said, 'I was one day surprised and disturbed to perceive a shadowy replica of myself at some distance in front of me. After observing it for a moment, I rose and attempted to approach it; as I did so, it lost outline and drew back towards me. It was my own "surround".'

In an earlier book (*My Life as a Search for the Meaning of Mediumship*, Rider & Co.), Mrs Garrett told how she had learned when very young, consciously to project a 'fluid' part of herself into a tree, a flower, or even a rock. Later she did this with persons. As a child she used the ability to dissociate in order to avoid mental pain: when her aunt spoke unkindly she quietly dissociated and, though seeing the aunt's lips moving, she heard no word. In adult life she not only had many voluntary out-of-the-body experiences but studied these experi-ences in a scientific manner and underwent systematic investigations. *When Mrs Garrett projected a 'double' involuntarily it was sometimes unable to pass through physical objects, but when she projected a 'double' deliberately it could always do so, i.e.* as with Yram, etc. This indicates that the 'double' which is exteriorized by one and the same person may be of different density (according to circumstances) and the conclusion is supported by two other observations: (1) while some (*e.g.*, Gerhardi, Miss Peters) saw their own 'doubles' in mirrors, others (*e.g.*, Gibier's engraver) did not; and (2) in some few cases (*e.g.*, Maginot and Lind) 'repercussion' can have physical effects, though in most instances the 'double' cannot affect physical matter (Statement No. 31).

Mrs Garrett said, '*Everybody has a double of finer substance than the Physical Body; it is referred to either as the astral or as the etheric body by some scientists. This is not to be confused with the surround* [= the vehicle of vitality, 'Denser Between Body' or 'body-veil'] *which remains in position enveloping the human body, while the double* [= the Psychical

Body] *can be projected. I never forget the smallest detail of any such experience which has come to me through conscious projection, though in ordinary daily living I can be quite forgetful. ...'*

Proceeding to describe an example of projection, Mrs Garrett said, 'In my projected state in that place in Newfoundland, where the experiment was set up, I found myself not only at the place of the experiment, but *before I entered the house, I was able to see the garden and the sea, as well as the house I was supposed to enter;* I sensed the damp of the atmosphere and saw the flowers growing by the pathway [cf. Van Eeden, Mrs Wilmot and Hives]. Then I passed through the walls [cf. Statement No. 31] into the room in which the experiment was to take place. There was no one there and I looked up the staircase searching for the experimenter. ... He walked down the stairs at that moment, and entered the room which I knew had been selected for the experiment. What took place then included not only telepathy, but the entire range of super-normal sensing, including clairvoyance, clair-audience and precognition. The doctor in this experiment himself had powers of super-normal sensing, and was obviously aware of my presence and that the experiment had begun. In what I am about to relate, the proof of our mutual awareness will soon become evident.

'Speaking aloud and addressing me, he said, "This will be a successful experiment," and I, sitting in a New York room, was able to receive this speech, seemingly, through my physical hearing. The investigator in Newfoundland addressed my "double" which I had projected into his study, and said, "Now look at the objects on the table." I followed his direction from that moment on ... I could see the objects on the table, not by means of ordinary sight, but through clairvoyant vision; I then gave a description of what I saw to the note-taker with me in New York. I heard the doctor say, "Make my apologies to the experimenters at your end. I have had an accident and cannot work as well as I had hoped." I transmitted what I was hearing in Newfoundland to the note-taker in New York, in the exact words which had been spoken to me, and I also described the bandage on the doctor's head. This had scarcely been done, when I heard the experimenter in New York comment, in an aside, "This can't possibly be true, because I had a letter a few days ago and the doctor was quite well then."

'The experiment continued and I remained in my projected state; I followed the activity of the investigator in Newfoundland. The next thing he did was to walk slowly to his book-case in his room; before he reached it I knew that he was thinking of a certain book and I knew its position on the shelf; this was telepathy. He took it down and held it up in his hands with the definite idea that I, being present, could read its title and then he opened it and without speaking, read to himself a paragraph out of this volume. The book was about Einstein and his theories of relativity. The paragraph he had selected, he read through silently, and as he did so, I was able to receive, from his mind, the telepathic impressions of what he read. The sense of his reading, I reported in my own words to the stenographer in New York. In the meantime, the experimenter, speaking aloud, told me in my projected state, that during this experiment, he too had projected himself into the bedroom in New York of the psychiatrist who was his co-experimenter. He proceeded to describe the two photographs that he had actually seen there on his previous (physical) visit to New York, but he now explained in Newfoundland, that these photographs had been put away, and that the bedroom of his friend had been redecorated since his actual physical visit.

'This was the end of that experiment, and the recorder commented when it was over, that the entire proceedings had taken fifteen minutes. Had this experiment rested on telepathy alone, I could never have reached nor seen the experimenter, the locality or the room and set-up for the experiment. All that pure telepathy could have produced would have been the thoughts in the experimenter's mind, and the impressions of the words he spoke aloud to me. ... The record of the experiment in New York·was posted that night to the doctor in Newfoundland. Next morning a telegram was received from him; in it, he described an accident which had occurred just before we began our experiment, and a day later a letter was received from him, listing the steps of the experiment as he had planned it. The telegram proved that I had not only heard his message correctly, when he spoke to my "double" there, but I had actually perceived his bandaged head. Remember, he opened the experiment by predicting that it would be successful; this prophecy was more than justified by our unusual results. I had succeeded in catching and relaying this prediction telepathically, so that in this case precognition and telepathy occurred simultaneously. From his letter, we learned that he had used a table and placed upon it a series of objects which I had seen correctly by means of clairvoyance; every step of my description of his behaviour turned out also to be correct. The book he removed from the shelf, the title and the subject matter he read to himself, were as I described them when received through my own conscious projection, and my application of clairvoyance and telepathy.'

Mrs Garrett did not describe seeing the 'silver cord'. It is evident however, that like many others who did not report perceiving the 'cord' she felt its presence, since she said that, in her case, the 'double' was projected from the centre of the chest [cf. Miss Stables] *and added the following significant phrase: 'From the moment I begin to project, I am aware, at this point, of a pull, accompanied by a fluttering ...'*

Apart from any other considerations Mrs Garrett's experiences are of the first importance since they show that the 'double' [= 'astral body' = 'Psych-ical Body', etc.] *is objective* [*and not, as some orthodox investigators believe, no more than a mental image of the Physical Body*], *since she made effective use of her exteriorized 'double' as a mirror, an operation which would be impossible with a mere image.* She said, 'I could see myself clearly at any time. Whenever I wished to assure myself that my personal appearance was in order, I need never glance at a looking-glass; I could use my lipstick or powder my nose in the reflection of my own "surround".' Mrs Garrett's statement has the support of statements made independently by several others. For example, Dr Hout saw a patient brought into an operating theatre: the Physical Body, being 'swathed in sterile sheets', was not visible, but the doctor could see, from the exteriorized 'double' that it was an elderly lady. Either this or Mrs Garrett's use of her own 'double' as a mirror would be impossible with a mere image: it indicates something of an objective (though of non-physical) nature. In the same way many others who claimed to see their exteriorized 'doubles' observed details of which they had no information *via* the physical senses and which was later known to be true. The objectivity of the 'double' is similarly strongly suggested by the fact that, although few of us have any clear mental image of what we ourselves look like (and are often quite surprised at a side-glimpse we may get in passing some shop window) and few of us are trained artists with good visualizing powers, yet 'doubles' (and these are most commonly seen a short time before or a short time after death) exhibit all details necessary for their identification with the Physical Body to which they correspond.

CASE NO. 76—*Mr B. B. Wirt*

In Dr J. M. Peebles's *Immortality* (5th ed., Boston, 1883) B. B. Wirt, of Ohio, is described as deliberately leaving his Physical Body. Wirt said, 'I desire, and become conscious that I am about to leave my body. I feel that my body is not 'me' but my dwelling-place. ... *After a few moments I feel the approach of spirit intelligences* [cf. Statement No. 3 regarding 'deliverers']. ... *Seemingly, I float out of and away from my fleshy form. ... I now look back and see my body lying in bed* [cf. Statement No. 17]. *And, further, I see the silver cord or chain connecting my spiritual body, or myself, with the earthly body* [cf. Statement No. 19]. ... *After becoming accustomed to these excursions, I so far experimented as to find that I could pass through doors, etc.*' [cf. Statement No. 31]. He declared, 'If I know anything absolutely, I know that I have left my body and that hundreds of times and, while on these journeys, have investigated the grades and conditions of spirits in the spirit-world.'

CASE NO. 77—*Mrs Alice Gilbert*, B.A.

Mrs Gilbert (*Philip in the Spheres*, Aquarian Press, 1952) described a number of out-of-the-body journeys. She lay flat on her back (a position found by 'René C.', Mr Dennis, etc. to facilitate exteriorization), with palms upwards. She emptied her mind of everyday thoughts, relaxed, drew deep rhythmic breaths and (much as is suggested by Muldoon) visualized her Psychical Body emerging from her head [cf. Statement No. 13] and floating above her Physical Body. 'Suddenly,' she said, 'this was not an imagined vision. I, the essential Me, was no longer on the divan but outside it. *On the bed was stretched my discarded form* (cf. Statement No. 17] *with a cloudy-looking cord extending between it and my etheric self'* [cf. Statement No. 19]. *Floating horizontally, she passed through the roof* (cf. Statement No. 31] *and out into the night. Then she met the object of her journey, namely, Philip, her son who had died some time before but with whom she was often in telepathic communication* [cf. Statement No. 18]. They saw the 'astral counterpart' of the earth [= 'The Denser Between Worlds', 'earth-veil' or 'Hades']. On another occasion Mrs Gilbert left the 'astral counterpart' region for 'higher' ones [= 'Paradise' conditions—cf. Statement No. 26]: she said, 'The earth was behind us, vanishing into a grey yet glowing mist. Around us seemed to be pure ether, intersected by myriads of rays. The light was intense ...' [cf. Gerhardi, Oxenham, etc.].

CASE NO. 78—*Miss L. M. Bazett*

Miss Bazett (*Beyond the Five Senses*, Basil Blackwell, 1946) undertook 'travelling clairvoyance' only under expert direction [cf. Statement No. 3 regarding 'deliverers']. She said, 'When entirely quiescent, one seems to move out of the Physical Body.' Like Mrs Leslie, Mrs Tarsikes, Miss Peters, Miss Stables, Miss Yeoman, etc. *she experienced leaving the body as 'like going through a tunnel'* [cf. Statement No. 9]. On one occasion she found herself looking down, from a great height, on a beautiful city and knew it was in the Mediterranean area. Then she was on ground-level in Paris. She did not move by walking but 'floated'. On another occasion she visited a Tibetan monastery, and brought back veridical information, since the details she described were corroborated by someone who was familiar with Tibet. Miss Bazett, like Muldoon, etc., stood in her 'etheric' [here = Psychical] Body at the foot of her bed and *saw her Physical Body on the bed* [cf. Statement No. 17]. On another occasion she felt that her Psychical Body was lying horizontally about three feet above the physical [cf. Statement No. 16].

CASE NO. 79—*Dr Frederick Van Eeden*

Van Eeden's experiments with his 'dreams' are mentioned by Carrington (*Higher Psychical Development*, Kegan Paul, 1929) and by Mary E. Monteith (*A Book of True Dreams*, Heath Cranton, 1929). He maintained that the soul, in the 'dream body' [= the Psychical Body] dissociates from the Physical Body and that in dreams it is more or less completely re-integrated in a non-physical environment. When out of the Physical Body (which, he was aware, was asleep), Van Eeden found that the 'dream body' still enabled him to see and hear, but *objects were somehow seen from a different angle than normally* (an observation that is paralleled by Miss Monteith's doctor-friend, etc.). He passed from place to place by 'floating' or 'flying' and observed that *the perspective of branches etc. changed in a normal manner as he passed the trees that bore them*. [This strongly suggests a definite journey and not mere telepathy and/or clairvoyance—cf. the accounts of Wilmot, Hives and Mrs Garrett.] On one occasion when 'out', he (like many of the newly-dead) experienced 'dual consciousness' [cf. Statement No. 18]: *he was aware that his Physical Body was lying on its back and his dream body was lying on its chest* (see also below). Like Muldoon, Gerhardi, Simons and others, Van Eeden took a critical attitude towards out-of-the-body phenomena, initiating specific experiments to elucidate them. *He deliberately awakened slowly in order to make careful observations* [cf. Eden , Yram and Miss Addison]. *he had 'the feeling of slipping from one body into another' and 'a distinct recollection of two bodies'.* This conscious transition from one body to another occurred more than once. He was aware, for instance, that his Physical Body was asleep in bed, the arms being folded, while at the same time, he, in his 'dream body' was looking out of the window [cf. Statement No. 17: note also that others, *e.g.* Sculthorp, described his Physical and Psychical Bodies as being in different positions]. Van Eeden was, indeed, seen looking out of the window by a passing dog [cf. Hepworth]. Then he glided towards his Physical Body, lay down beside it, entered it, and woke up to the physical world.

CASE NO. 80—*'René C.'*

P. E. Cornillier (*The Prediction of the Future*, Author-Partner Press Ltd., 1947) gave the out-of-the-body experience of a young French scientist, 'René C'.

'I lay awake in bed, on my back [cf. Mrs Gilbert, Mr Dennis, etc.], all muscles relaxed. I experienced giddiness, the forerunner of conscious detachment. I remained passive. *The giddiness increased, there was a momentary clouding of consciousness* [= shedding the Physical Body—

cf. Statement No. 9]. This rapidly cleared. I was standing in my room, detached. My thoughts were extremely lucid. I fully realized my state and carefully analysed my sensations. This was no dream or vision. ... *I was in a fluidic body of human appearance* [cf. Statement No. 26]. I could move about, either by walking or sliding along the floor. *I saw my Physical Body, lifeless as a corpse, on my bed* [cf. Statement No. 17]. I realized that, though detached, I was on a very material plane, close to the physical, and *I reflected that I could retain greater materiality in my room and near my Physical Body than away from them.* [Mrs Leonard and Mr Sculthorp made the same observation as to the influence of the Physical Body, though they expressed it in terms of *clarity of consciousness.* Col. Lester's (deceased) wife described the effect on her (exteriorized) husband's 'double': she gave it in terms of the *luminosity of the exteriorized 'double'* (not of its *density*). These three features, the density of the 'double', its brilliance and the intensity or clarity of consciousness are, of course, directly inter-related. Their appropriate occurrence in independent accounts is not explicable on the basis of telepathy, clairvoyance, body-images or 'split personalities'. It seems, indeed, explicable only if the accounts are directly related to fact.]

'*The idea then struck me that I might make some experiments. A paper, open, lay on the table. I resolved to attempt to read a few lines. ... I did it with ease.*' Then he experimented with the creation of mental images, creating first an image of a work-table and later images of objects on it. He realized that some mediums might mistake such images for objective environment [cf. Statement No. 10].

CASE No. 81—*Miss Nancy Price*

Nancy Price (*Acquainted with Night: A Book of Dreams*, George Ronald) mentioning the difference between the physical senses and those that she used in her 'dreams', made the following observation. 'It seems as though I have another body which has a different method of sensing sound than from vibrations on the ear-drum.' Like Van Eeden, she called this body the 'dream-body'. Miss Price found that, 'In dreams one is not exactly anywhere in particular, because one experiences constant transport of mind and body.' *In one of her 'dreams' she saw her (deceased) mother* [cf. Statement No. 18]. *The latter told her daughter that she was surrounded by 'a web'* [= a relatively large proportion of the vehicle of vitality or 'body-veil'], *that rendered her a 'half-way' person. It was difficult for her to 'get through' this 'web'* [into 'Paradise' conditions], *though each attempt made it easier.* Just as she seemed to be succeeding in breaking through it, she awoke in the Physical Body.

One of Miss Price's experiences was as follows. 'Suddenly I was afraid, so afraid that I seemed to be fighting that part of myself which wished to go on. And then the most peculiar thing happened, something which, when I try to describe it, sounds ridiculous. There was a sort of cracking sensation in my body, as if something were struggling to free itself [cf. the 'click' which, in the cases of Muldoon, Fox, Hives, Lind, Ouspensky, Dennis etc. accompanied the release of the 'double' from (or its return to) the Physical Body]. Then there was a sound like the tearing of silk. *I felt a strange lightness and I saw my own body* ...[cf. Statement No. 17]. *It looked to me particularly distasteful and I had a remarkable feeling of exhilaration in that I could leave it there. I was seized by an overmastering pity for this shell of myself, which I resented and fought* [cf. Statement No. 8]. I held it closer and closer, and then gradually I felt my two selves merging into one ... I woke.'

CASE NO. 82—*Mme David-Neel's statements regarding the Tibetans*

Mme Alexandra David-Neel (*With Mystics and Magicians in Tibet,* first English Ed., 1931; Penguin Books Ltd., 1936) pointed out that the Tibetans, like the Chinese and Egyptians, believed that we possess a 'double', an 'astral' or Psychical Body. She stated the Tibetans' views as follows. 'During life, in the normal state, the "double" is closely united with the material body. Nevertheless, certain circumstances may cause their separation. The "double" can then leave the material body and show itself in different places: or, being itself invisible, it can accomplish various peregrinations. With some people the separation of the "double" from the body happens involuntarily, but trained people can effect it at will. *The separation of the "double" from the Physical Body, however, is not complete, for a strand* [= the 'silver cord'— cf. Statement No. 19] *subsists, connecting them. This link persists for some time after death* [cf. Statement No. 21]. The destruction of the corpse generally, but not necessarily, eventually brings about the destruction of the "double". In certain cases it may survive its companion [cf. Leaf].

'In Tibet, one meets people who have been in a state of lethargy, and described various places in which, they say, they have travelled. Some have only visited countries inhabited by men, while others can tell of journeys in the paradises, the purgatories, or in *the Bardo, an intermediary region* ... [= 'Hades'—cf. Statement No. 39].

'These travellers are called "delogs", which means: "those who have returned from the Beyond". *Though the "delogs" vary in their descriptions of places and events* [according, in part, to the conditions contacted, as just noted], *they usually agree in depicting the feelings of the pseudo-dead as definitely pleasant*' [cf. Statement No. 26].

A woman told Mme David-Neel that she had been out of her

Physical Body in a body which was remarkably light, agile and rapid in its movements [cf. Statement No. 17]. *She had only to wish herself in a certain place to be there at once. But she found it impossible to cut 'an almost impalpable cord that attached her ethereal being to her Physical Body'* [cf. Statement No. 19]. *She saw the latter sleeping upon the couch* [cf. Statement No. 17]. The cord lengthened indefinitely; nevertheless, it sometimes hampered her movements; she would 'get caught up in it', she said. A man gave a similar account.

CASE NO. 83—*Mr Richard Wilhelm's statements regarding the Chinese*

Doctrines similar to those of ancient Tibet were held both in ancient China and ancient Egypt. Esoteric Taoist teachings which date back to the 8th century were written on wooden tablets in the 17th century and printed in Chinese in 1920. They are found in *The Secret of the Golden Flower. A Chinese Book of Life* [meaning Superphysical Life], translated and explained by Richard Wilhelm, with a European Commentary by C. G. Jung (Routledge and Kegan Paul Ltd., 1931). This was translated into English by C. F. Baynes. *'The Golden Flower' is described as representing the 'Immortal' or 'Spiritual'* [here = the Psychical] *Body and the powers of people who function therein.* The expression 'Golden Flower' includes the word 'Light', referring, of course, to 'Spiritual' Illumination, or wisdom. Average followers of these doctrines used talismans, written charms, prayers, sacrifices and mediumistic seances to obtain results of a psychical nature (they evidently concentrated on the development of 'physical' mediumship, with the exteriorization and control of much of the 'body-veil' and the ectoplasm therein—the 'Bardo' Body of the Tibetans). Advanced disciples employed meditation to develop, organize and eventually exteriorize the 'Spiritual' [here = Psychical] Body, the 'Golden Flower', in which they had 'super-conscious' (clairvoyant and other) experiences.

According to this book, the first stage of meditation consists in 'gathering' the [super-physical] Light. Then, 'Within the Physical Body we must strive for *the form* [= Psychical Body] *which existed before* [the physical] *heaven and earth were laid down.'* The breathing must be rhythmical. The attention being fixed on a point between the eyes [= on the 'Spiritual' eye], Spiritual Light streamed into the soul. The use of effort defeated its own end. The 'new body' then formed by the spirit crystallizing in 'the place of power' [= the solar plexus]. *Then the Psychical Body exteriorized from the Physical Body. It left by way of the head* [cf. Statement No. 13]. The Hui Ming Ching includes illustrations of the stages here outlined. The final drawings depict the exteriorized 'Spiritual' [here = Psychical] Body. When the disciple succeeded in the above, he might (1) become clairaudient or clairvoyant, (2) 'Everything before him may become very bright, and equally bright' [cf. Geddes, Gerhardi, Huntley, Oxenham, Mrs Boorman, etc., and cf. Rev. xx, 5] and (3) 'The Physical Body may shine' [⇒ 'transfiguration'].

CASE No. 84—'Yram'

Practical Astral Projection, by 'Yram', published by Rider & Co. Ltd., is a translation from the French Le Médicin de L'Âme. In it are described out-of-the-body experiences that occurred over a period of fourteen years. Whereas with Muldoon, Turvey, etc., the chief predisposing cause to such experiences was a Physical Body with relatively low 'vibrations', in Yram's case it was a Psychical Body with relatively high 'vibrations'. This reflected his moral nature. In either case the Physical and Psychical Bodies are 'out of gear', causing exteriorization.

'Yram' said that most of us can have these experiences and so prove survival but the timid person must first acquire courage and calmness: excesses of all kinds, including over-eating, must be avoided: the psychological state must be one of earnestness, peacefulness, gentleness and patience: the 'man of the world' constantly tries to live with the maximum of comfort and the minimum of consideration for others, an attitude that must be reversed [cf. Lind]. Prayer and meditation are essential. The psychic aspect of the self-training is represented by intense concentration of thought and the ability to relax thereafter.

Most people, 'Yram' found, are convinced of the reality of an out-of-the-body experience when they are a few feet from the Physical Body. He said, 'You leave your Physical Body with greater ease than taking off a suit of clothes.   The result is a certainty, without the least doubt. It is a cold fact, beyond all judgment, beyond all hypothesis, hallucination, or suggestion.' It may be remembered that Aristotle said, 'Nothing is known for certain, and even this cannot be positively asserted.' Well, 'Yram' says that this ability to leave his Physical Body and live in a new dimension 'is the only obvious truth that I claim as being true without the least doubt'. Again, 'As soon as we slip out of the physical wrapper this truth strikes us with all its force. We see the familiar furniture of our room just as before. The only difference we notice is a slight phosphorescent glow. Our Physical Body rests inert, like a corpse, on the couch. The impression is striking that instinctively we think we are dead.' In this condition he was able to converse with 'deceased' friends [cf. Statement No. 18].

'Yram' observed the 'silver cord' [cf. Statement No. 19]. In order to inspect its junction with the physical body, experimented at leaving and re-entering the physical body very slowly [cf. Van Eeden and Mrs Gilbert]. In his 'double' he visited a person who lived hundreds of miles away. He took stock of their furniture and its arrangement, etc. and, on returning to physical consciousness, wrote down the details and sent them to his friend and had them confirmed. 'Yram' considered that, 'The principle of self-projection is within the range of science' and stressed the need for preliminary work of a physical, psychological and psychic nature 'because it involves penetrating other worlds, and to enter these without due preparation might well lead to trouble.'

CASE NO. 85—Dr O. A. Ostby

There is no sharp line of demarcation between involuntary and deliberate out-of-the-body experiences. Muldoon's first experience was involuntary and so was that of Dr O. A. Ostby. The latter was first published by Muldoon in his Case for Astral Projection.

Ostby was a Minister for ten years. His first experience of leaving the body had occurred a quarter of a century before the publication of Muldoon's account. He said, 'I awoke one night in full clear consciousness. *I found myself standing in front of the bed looking at my own Physical Body* (cf. Statement No. 17) ... *I thought I had died, but was perfectly happy and had a strong desire to remain in this new state of freedom* [cf. Statement No. 8]. But just then I thought it would be dreadful for my wife to awaken and find my lifeless form beside her. *So I determined that I must try to re-animate my physical form. At that moment ... the spiritual "myself" was lifted right off the floor, laid horizontally and pushed slowly into the physical again* [cf. this return route with those described by Muldoon, Mr H. Dennis, Mrs 'M.A.E.', Miss Peters, etc.] ... Soon after I acquired the ability to go in and out at will. ... I could lie on my couch and my Astral [here = Psychical] Body would go out without my being conscious of the separation. *I would think it was my physical self until I would discover the Physical Body still on the couch.* Then I would go to the window, see the traffic in the street, hear people talk, pass through matter [cf. Statement No. 31] and enter my body again' [cf. Muldoon, etc. The 'dead' often think, at first, that the Psychical Body is the Physical—cf. Statements 17 and 31].

CASE NO. 86—Mr 'H' (Bournemouth)

A letter was received by Muldoon, soon after the publication of The Projection of the Astral Body, from Mr 'H.' who wrote, 'I had a bit of a shock to-day. I was changing my book at the library, when I happened to pick up a copy of your book. I opened it—and what a shock! It was those illustrations. They astonished me! I could only say to myself, "That is I—that is I." When I was about twenty years old I began to have an almost nightly experience of a body coming out of my body, and going sometimes on long trips which were usually delightful. ... They continued for many years. I could float in the air at will. *The floating was exactly as you have pictured it. I always began lying horizontally over my body, floating outwards, then assuming an upright position.* ... I have not yet read your book, not even the Preface, it was the amazement, the shock, of seeing those marvellously accurate illustrations which prompted this letter' [cf. Mrs Roberts's account].

CASE No. 87—*Hermione P. Okeden*

When Ralph Shirley was editing *The Occult Review* he received much correspondence similar to that of Mr 'H.' He cited H. P. Okeden in his *Mystery of the Human Double* (Rider & Co.) as follows. 'I wonder if any of your readers have the power to travel as I do. Whenever I desire to know how and where a friend is, I go and find him. It is done when awake, either sitting quietly in my chair or before going to sleep at night. Perfect quiet is necessary. *I close my eyes, and have a feeling of going over backwards, ... and I find myself going down a long dim tunnel* [cf. Statement No. 9]. ... *At the far end is a tiny speck of light which grows as I approach into a large square and I am "there"* [cf. Mrs Lester, Mrs Tarsikes, Miss Peters, Miss Yeoman, Miss Stables, Miss Bazett, etc.]. I can describe the room my friends are in, the clothes they are wearing, the people to whom they are talking. On several occasions when I have been anxious about a friend who lives in London I have found myself in a strange room among strange people in the country, and there was my friend. *Only once have I been seen and addressed.* ... I have been tested over and over again when I have arranged (beforehand) to go. One friend put on a new evening gown, another moved her bedroom furniture round, which I at once noticed and questioned her about later.'

CASE No. 88—*Mr Staveley Bulford*

Mr Bulford (*Man's Unknown Journey*, Rider & Co. Ltd., 1941) experimented with exteriorization of the 'double' from the Physical Body by means of hypnosis and insisted that the phenomenon is natural to the individual who is developing morally and spiritually. He said, 'Many thousands of experiments have been successfully carried out, and may be repeated at any time by those who will equip themselves for such work.'

Whereas some authors, without explicitly saying so, give the impression that the whole of the non-physical body is exteriorized, Bulford, like Mrs Garrett, Clare, Mrs Tarsikes and others, made an important point: it is that, during physical life, the densest portion is never entirely exteriorized from the Physical Body. (They maintain that complete exteriorization involves death.) *Bulford insisted that in natural out-of-the-body experiences the 'densest counterpart' still remains with the Physical Body (whereas it entirely leaves the Physical Body in natural death).* 'This part,' he said, 'resembles the skin of the Physical Body; it is an outer covering, a shell.' This 'densest counterpart' clearly corresponds to Mrs Garrett's 'surround', to Clare's 'expanding bag', to the 'Bardo Body' of Tibetans, the 'Denser Between Body' of supposed discarnates and the vehicle of vitality or 'body-veil'. Bulford described the 'silver cord', with its cap-like attachment to the Physical and Etheric Bodies, as 'the missing link in the study of psychical research'. He observed, 'With the knowledge of the etheric double [here = Psychical Body—cf. Statement No. 19], and how it is connected with the Physical Body, as well as the ease with which it can be projected, many of the phenomena recorded as dreams, phantasms of the living and of the so-called dead, as well as much hypnotic technique, can be intelligently and scientifically comprehended, and, what is most important, reproduced at will in the most orthodox manner of experimental research by any qualified person.'

Bulford continued, 'The etheric double of another person has been seen by the writer. This was deliberately produced in the presence of others who, seated on each side of him, were able to see the etheric form as clearly as he did. *In this demonstration it was possible for the etheric double to appear with such density and luminosity that the physical sight of everyone present could clearly register this manifestation.*' [If this is true, then, in this case, the 'double' was not a mere body-image but was objective in nature: it was 'real', not imaginary. Compare the evidence based on (a) doubles seen in mirrors (Gerhardi, Miss Peters); (b) 'repercussion' which caused physical effects (under Lind, etc.); and (c) the fact that Mrs Garrett claimed actually to use her exteriorized 'double' as a mirror.]

Bulford described the following experiments which, he considered, proved the existence of the 'double': (1) the exteriorized 'double' of 'G.P.' was seen by Mme 'A.' in hypnotic sleep; (2) Mme 'A.', under hypnosis, was sent to find 'G.P.'s exteriorized 'double' and gave descriptions identical with those of 'G.P.' himself; (3) 'G.P.' and Mme 'A.', hypnotized in different rooms of a house and unaware of each other's presence there, were sent to a particular place (unknown to the hypnotist, in order to eliminate the possibility of telepathy), and, on awakening, gave identical details of the place and were conscious of having met there; (4) 'G.P.' exteriorized his 'double' and observed his Physical Body asleep (cf. Statement No. 17); (5) Mr 'X', a barrister, discovered the whereabouts of Mme 'A', who, unknown to him, was away from London on holiday.

Bulford claimed that any investigator can, with practice, project his 'double', but says difficulty may be experienced by men who are immersed in the senses, or in worldly matters, and those with restricted beliefs as to the nature of man: these can exteriorize under hypnosis [cf. Statement No. 1a]. Bulford's observations as to the conditions and environments contacted by the temporarily exteriorized 'double' agree with those of Yram, Muldoon, Fox, etc., and also with the descriptions of conditions by the supposed dead [cf. Statements Nos. 31 and 39].

Like Gerhardi, Muldoon, Yram, etc., Bulford pointed out that mental harmony is an important pre-requisite to experimenting, since in projecting one is stepping out of the physical into 'next world' conditions where 'thoughts are things' [cf. Statement No. 10]. A man who enters such conditions with harmonious thoughts and feelings contacts a happy and helpful environment, but one who does so with discordant thoughts and feelings contacts an injurious environment. He insists that exteriorization is natural and there is no cause for fear. It is fear, he says, that caused the catalepsy experienced by so many: 'astral' catalepsy is a condition of consciousness but also of paralysis, due to fear and lack of preparation before attempting projection [cf. Mrs Cripps, Messrs Jeffrey, Brown, etc.].

CASE NO. 89—*Mrs Mary Vlasek*

The *National Spiritualist* for April, 1930, carried a report to the effect that Mrs M. C. Vlasek not only exteriorized from her Physical Body during a train-journey, but, in accordance with a pre-arranged plan, 'materialized' to friends who were holding a seance. Details are also given of this claim in a book by A. J. Wills, Ph.D., entitled *Life Now and Forever* (Rider & Co. Ltd., 1942). Although, according to Dr Wills, the results were 'properly checked by all parties', such experiments are not convincing in the absence of suitable reports from scientific investigators with special training for such work. Those who claim that they can deliberately vacate their Physical Bodies should submit to scientific investigation in the interests of truth.

CASE NO. 90—*Mrs Gwen. Cripps*

Mrs Cripps sent the writer the contents of an address she had given to a study group in 1952: she stated, '*I have not been able to read any book devoted exclusively to astral projection—only articles in psychic papers.*' The address, extracts from which follow, was based entirely on her personal experiences.

'*The spontaneous projection of the Astral* [here = Psychical] *Body is not so rare as one might suppose* [cf. Dr Leaf, Mrs Garrett, Muldoon, etc.]. *The bringing back to physical consciousness the memory of astral travels is rare. Owing to ignorance of their nature, projections, when realized, cause fear, but ... they are often closely allied to normal sleep. Many* people experience projection by waking to find themselves in a state of catalepsy. Others experience a mental swaying to and fro, the Physical Body itself being rigid. ... If the Physical Body is kept relaxed and the mind composed, recovery is speedy, with no unpleasant reactions [cf. Bulford, Brown, etc.]. If, on the other hand, one fights, the heart may palpitate.

'In the course of the development of mediumship, catalepsy is liable to occur in some cases at any time during the "sitting". There is reason to assume that all aspects of mediumship involve some modification of the relationship between the Psychical and Physical Bodies. *Very often the projection is only partial, consciousness still remaining in the Physical Body. In this state the Physical Body feels very unstable—a feeling of being "in air", of being "here and there"* [cf. Muldoon, Leaf, etc.]. *In complete projection, consciousness functions in the Psychical Body* [cf. Hartmann's account]. *Sometimes there is an awareness of a connection or attachment to the Physical Body, but sometimes there is not* [cf. Statement No. 19].

'At the moment of complete projection, one is erect, and can turn and view the Physical Body. Being always horizontal when starting a projection, *I have always seen my Physical Body* on the bed, lying asleep [cf. Statement No. 17]. One notices a connecting-force between the two bodies, and, as far as I can judge, the line of force is between the two heads. *This connecting link, or cord, is of an etheric quality and luminous* [cf. Gerhardi, etc.]. It looks *like a shaft of sunlight* that has penetrated a hole in a blind, passing into a darkened room. [This symbol is used by several others, *e.g.*, Dr Hout.] The connecting cord stretches as one wanders, maintaining contact between the two bodies.

'Somehow, when pausing to look back, one loses interest in the Physical Body, and the mind is deeply interested in exploring further afield. *During the processes of changing from one body to another, there seem to occur lapses of consciousness, almost as, when in the Physical Body, one fainted* [= shed the physical body—cf. Statement No. 9], recovered consciousness, and fainted again [= shed 'body-veil': cf. (1) the account of *shedding*, first the Physical Body and then the 'body-veil' with that given by an Australian, namely, Percy Coles, of *re-assuming* those same bodies by others; (2) the description of a momentary loss of consciousness as each of the various bodies is shed, in accounts of the act of dying by supposed discarnates—Statement No. 1b]. But the more one practises, the longer degree of consciousness one seems to hold. Continuity is better: the memory brought back into the Physical Body on return is less confused.

'*Now, as to returning to the physical state. One seems to take on tremendous accelerations of speed. The sensation is of being shot out of space into greater space. ... In the half-way condition of return* [= while temporarily conscious in the 'body-veil': cf. for example the accounts of Mrs Joy, Dr

Wood and Mme d'Espérance].*one realizes how true it is that the body has a life of its own and yet without the power to act without the mind* [cf. Statements of discarnates that memories are imprinted on the 'body-veil'— Statements No. 1b, 34]. The memories of the Physical Body are of the earth, relations, homes, jobs, etc., but they are distasteful to the mind.

'*I always found that as I was trying to unite with my Physical Body, at a certain stage of the process, I became aware of my bedroom. It was always deeply misty* [= 'Hades' conditions—cf. Hives, Mme d'Espérance, Gerhardi, Ogston, de la Mare, Miss Johnson, Miss Brooks, and Mrs Joy, also Statements No. 10 and 41]. *Penetrating the mist, however, were cloud-like white and red lights which somehow guided me back to my body. At the impact of joining the Physical Body there is a feeling of being jerked* [the 'repercussion'—cf. Muldoon, Gerhardi, Brown, Hout, Mrs Leslie, Mrs Boorman, etc.] *and a heaviness* [cf. Mrs 'X'; conversely, Miss Kaeyer described *shedding* her body as 'letting go something dense and heavy']. *The jerkiness passes off, however, with practice. It is with regret that one returns, movement in the Astral Body being so light and unconfined* [cf. Statement No. 8]. Walking and floating are common, though I have found myself in another place without being conscious of any form of locomotion. I simply willed, and nothing, no obstacles, intervened.

'Now where do I go? One cannot give physical names to places on non-physical spheres. ... It is possible to travel in the Psychical Body (1) round certain areas of the physical world, (2) to places, both lower and higher, in the "astral" spheres, (3) to my father in the Spiritual World, (4) to an animal plane, and (5) to a spiritual healing-plane. *The last mentioned was completely dark to me; I felt I was somewhere; I knew I was "in the being", but was not conscious of any body of expression.*' [Compare the 'partial awakening'—Statement No. 25.]

Mrs Cripps said that astral projection assures one of survival, demonstrates the reality of thoughts, shows that the Psychical Body is the 'power-house' for the energy that animates the Physical Body and that prayer is most important to those who are out of the body [cf. Statement No. 29]. The link made by prayer with higher sources gives power and obviates 'repercussion' in the return to the Physical Body. Mrs Cripps, like Muldoon, Yram, Bulford, etc. said, 'One can get into difficulties and with uncongenial companions on the astral. Protection is there but it must be asked for...' Again, 'Oft-times in astral travelling one cannot find a like set of experiences on which to base one's actions [Muldoon and Fox also made this observation]. One is non-plussed, since our experiences are mainly of the physical world. When perplexed on the astral, prayer brings help "on the wings of the wind". *One's spiritual perceptions are more quickened in this state—a veil is drawn over our perceptions while we are in the Physical Body* [cf. the conception of 'blinkers' and the *kenosis*].

Astral experiences far transcend those of material life and it is borne very forcibly on one's mind that the Great Mind that conceived the processes involved in the evolution of life is Love, protecting, secure and satisfying. I think that was what St John meant, in Revelation, when he cried, "And he carried me away in the Spirit to a great and high mountain, and shewed me that great city, the Holy Jerusalem. And the gates of it shall not be shut at all by day, for there be no night there" [Rev. xxi, 25]. *Astral travelling is an education for the life-to-come'* [cf. Statement No. 1b]. Mrs Cripps warns those who would enjoy such experiences to seek them under the right conditions—'Purity of motive must be the foundation of the experience'.

CASE NO. 91—*Mrs H. D. Williams*

Mrs Hilda D. Williams had not read any books about out-of-the-body experiences before having one herself. She wrote [in litt.] *as follows.* 'The incident occurred fifteen years ago, but is still very clear to me. One night I went to sleep. My next recollection is of standing in my room; the furniture and other details were quite clear. Although the room must *have been pitch dark, there was a soft, evenly distributed, pale, yet clear light* [cf. Geddes, Gerhardi, Huntley, Oxenham, etc.]. I walked over to the door, opened it [= habit] and went down stairs to the front door. This I opened, went down the flight of stone steps, through the gate and along the drive. I went along the road but at about two hundred yards from the house I wanted to return.

'*On turning round, I saw a shining white cord, two or three inches wide, composed of four or five loosely woven strands, stretching from my body, as far as I could see, back to the house* [cf. Statement No. 19]. *The next thing I knew, I was standing at the side of my bed and saw my Physical Body* [cf. Statement No. 17]. The cord was attached to the head of my Psychical Body and to the centre of my Physical Body. I thought, "I must get in", slipped into bed, and awoke. I had not been aware of leaving the body [cf. Statement No. 9] but *re-entering it felt like slipping the hand into an easy-fitting glove.'* [The symbol of a glove, here used by Mrs Williams—who had read nothing about these matters—for *re-entering* the body, was independently employed by Miss Yeoman—who also was ignorant of things psychic—for *shedding* the body. Similarly, while Miss Addison said that *shedding* the body was like getting out of 'a tight rubber bathing-suit', Miss Johnson described *re-entering* the body as like getting into 'a tight rubber skin'. These 'doubles' are not mere images!]

CASE NO. 92—*Mr Wm. Dudley Pelley*

Pelley's experience was first described in the *American Magazine*, March, 1929. Later it was published as '*Seven Minutes in Eternity—with their Aftermath'*, 1929. *Prior to his experience, Pelley was a materialist. He had not concerned himself with psychical research, etc.* After the experience he was reluctant to publish the account since it might affect his literary reputation. The Editor of the *American Magazine* persuaded him.

Pelley went to bed. He said, 'About 3 a.m. a ghastly inner shriek seemed to tear through me and I thought, "I'm dying! This is death! My body may lie in this lonely house for days undiscovered." Then two spirits came to his aid, saying, "Don't be alarmed: we are here to help you" ' [cf. Statement No. 3 with regard to 'deliverers']. 'Eventually,' said Mr Pelley, '*I found myself an existing entity in a locality where persons I had always called "dead" were not dead but very much alive* [cf. Statement No. 18]. I pledge my reputation that I talked with these people, identified many of them, called others by their wrong names and was corrected.' *He returned to the Physical Body with reluctance* [cf. Statement No. 8]. *Henceforth he was certain of survival: he was a changed man.*

Pelley was convinced this experience was not a dream: 'We never dream,' he says, 'by the process of first coming awake.' *Although unacquainted with other accounts, his description of what he saw in the 'next' world agrees with those of supposed discarnates, of clairvoyants and of others who claim to have had out-of-the-body experiences.*

Through this experience, also, Pelley found that he had acquired new senses and perceptions. Among these was clairaudience so that, after the experience itself, he was able to continue in touch with the 'spirits' with whom he had conversed during the 'Seven Minutes'. In this way he conversed with them in normal consciousness asking questions and getting 'valuable answers'. He once heard a voice speaking in a language unknown to him. A stenographer wrote the words phonetically. Twelve pages of script were thus obtained. 'I showed them to a philologist who found over a thousand words of Sanskrit in them. It was a message concerning present-day happenings.' He claimed that the message was given in Sanskrit in order that it could not be explained away as a purely 'sub-conscious' production.

We may add that Prof. Bozzano cited Pelley's experience in his *Polyglot Mediumship*, Rider & Co. Ltd., regarding this and similar cases as beyond explanation by the hypothesis of the 'sub-conscious mind' of the 'living' person with super-normal powers of telepathy, clairvoyance, etc. He considered that it constituted evidence of the intervention of 'spirit-entities independent of the medium and those present'. Those (somewhat similar) cases which had been available and analysed by Prof. Richet he agreed to be inconclusive on this question. But Pelley's and certain other cases left him in no doubt. It may further be said that Richet valued all Bozzano's writings and it is stated that he was finally convinced of survival by studying them.

CASE No. 93—*Dr I. K. Funk's doctor-friend*

Dr I. K. Funk the publisher and theologian gave the experience of a physician well known to, and trusted by, him in *The Psychic Riddle*, (Funk and Wagnall's Co.). The doctor went to bed. His feet and legs became 'as cold as those of the dead' [cf. Bertrand, Home, Miss Yeoman, etc.]. The narrator continued, '*All at once ... for an instant I became unconscious* [= shedding the Physical Body—cf. Statement No. 9]. *When I recovered, I seemed to be walking in the air. No words can describe the exhilaration and freedom and clearness of mental vision that I experienced* [cf. Statement No. 26]. I thought of a friend who was a thousand miles distant and seemed to travel with great rapidity through the atmosphere. *Everything was light ... a peculiar light of its own, such as I had never known* [cf. Geddes, Gerhardi, Huntly, Oxenham, etc.]. It could not have been a minute after I thought of my friend before I was standing in a room with him. Suddenly turning and seeing me, he said, "What are you doing here? You were in Florida".' ... He approached the doctor's 'double' and the doctor heard the expression used. He was, however, unable to answer.

The doctor then had an ecstatic experience which he described as follows. '*The consciousness of the things that transpired that night will never be forgotten. I seemed to leave the earth, and everything pertaining to it, and enter a condition of life of which it is impossible to give any thought I had concerning it, because there is no correspondence to anything I had ever heard or seen or known. The wonder and joy of it was unspeakable. I can readily understand what Paul meant when he said, "I knew a man, whether in the body or out of the body I know not, who was caught up into the third 'heaven', and there saw things which it was not possible ['lawful'] to utter." [II Cor. xii, 2.]

'In this latter experience there was neither consciousness of time nor of space. ... Then I thought of the friends on earth and my duties there. ... I found myself looking down upon my own apparently lifeless body propped up in bed. Here I was apart from the body with ... another body to which matter offered no resistance* [cf. Statements No. 17, 31]. After a minute or two I was able to move my body. I got up from the bed and dressed myself.

'I may add here that the friend referred to as having been seen by me that night was distinctly conscious of my presence and he made the exclamation mentioned. We both wrote the next day, relating the experiences of the night. The letters corroborating the incident crossed in the post.'

CASE No. 94—*Mrs H. E. Wheeler*

Mrs H. E. Wheeler, of Woodbridge, told me (*in litt.*) of her two projections. She said, '*I knew nothing of projection until after my first experience; it so impressed me that I read every book I could on the subject.*' Her accounts are as follows.

'Whilst on holiday in 1936, my husband and I returned to the farm at which we were staying to hear the farmer's wife telling someone in the kitchen that a young Australian and a friend had called that evening; they were on a walking-tour and wished to stay a few days. After having had a meal, they had gone out, during which time the youth's mother had telephoned from Australia. Having failed to speak to her son, she had said she would ring up again about 2 a.m. The farmer's wife said that if the young Australian didn't hear the telephone she was not going to answer it. *I was quite worried about it.* About 2 a.m. I awakened to the sound of the telephone. I got up, pushed my feet into my slippers, dashed down the long passage, and knocked loudly. He answered, and I flew back, fearing to be caught in my pyjamas. *I rested both my hands on the bed when, to my horror, I saw myself asleep in bed* [cf. Statement No. 17]. I knew nothing else. In the morning I thought I had dreamed it all, but at breakfast I heard the young man say, "I wish I knew who called me—I'd like to thank them." I kept silent as, on reflection, I realized that I had not, until then, seen the lad, and, what was more important, we had been in the house only two days and had no idea of the layout of the rooms. I did not know which room he occupied.' [If it were not that Mrs Wheeler saw her own Physical Body, this experience might conceivably be an example of a telepathic 'Call' rather than an 'astral projection'.]

'*The second incident occurred about two weeks after my husband's passing in 1945.* I was getting into bed when the thought came into my mind, "I'll see him tonight!" For the first time since he died I slept at once and that *very soundly.* The next thing I knew was that I was standing beside him. He was propped up in bed as usual. As I looked at him he opened his eyes, saw me, put out his arms and said, "Come and give me a kiss!" This I readily did and then he said, "*You know, after that last injection I don't remember anything until now, and I feel fine.*" And indeed he looked as well as he did before his illness. I was very bewildered. I thought, "What is the matter with me, there has been no funeral. I must get the doctor to see him at once." I looked at Eric, and it was then, and then only, that I knew he had passed on [cf. Statement No. 18]. We were going to speak again but I was whipped away. I have not seen him since but sometimes I feel him very near.'

CASE NO. 95—*Miss Cromwell Addison*

This case was given in *Prediction* for June 1936, and by Muldoon in the same year.

'I awoke to find myself floating over my body a few feet from the ceiling. *I could see my Physical Body on the bed* [cf. Statement No. 17]. *I was cataleptic, yet with intensified consciousness.*

'*This was not my first projection, as I had several times been observed by others, in my astral form, many miles away. But this time I awakened while yet over my body. Panic seized me. … I wondered how to get back before any-one discovered my "corpse"! This fear instantly made me recoil into my form with a great shock, and I lay with mighty pulsations passing through my frame* … [cf. Varley, Lind, Sculthorp, Muldoon, Mrs Leonard, Helen Brooks, etc.]. For a few minutes I rested quietly, thinking it over and ·blaming myself for my fear, for I realized the value of the experience I might have gained. Presently the vibrations again increased in intensity and a rocking movement ensued [cf. Muldoon, Sculthorp, Wiltse, Mrs Boorman, etc.]. … I forced myself to be calm and wait for what might occur.

'*Presently there was a strong "pulling" sensation as if from a giant hand, at the top of my head* [cf. Statement No. 13]. *Then I was gradually drawn as if out of a tight rubber bathing-suit, which I knew to be my flesh* [Miss Yeoman said it was like leaving a 'tight glove'; Mrs Boorman and Mrs Williams found that re-*entering* the body was like slipping into a 'coat' and Mrs Parker, a 'bag'].

'Fully conscious, though cataleptic, I thought, "I am in my bedroom at such and such an address; C.A. is my name, my bed is head to the wall adjoining the garden—now my head and shoulders are passing through the wall [cf. Statement No. 31]—now they are over the garden—now I am out to my knees", and still *I could feel the tightness of the flesh below the points which were not free.* "There, now I am out to my ankles; what is going to happen?" [Compare Mrs 'H.F.P.'s account.]

'Then I heard the words "*Let her return now slowly, and next time she will not be afraid.*" [(1) cf. the accounts of Van Eeden and 'Yram', and (2) compare the work of 'deliverers'—Statement No. 3; (3) according to Statement No. 30, those who are morally 'ready' for such experi-ences are aided because of the 'co-operation' they can give in helping the newly-dead, etc.] The whole process was then repeated in reverse, and I glided into my body as slowly as I had withdrawn. *There was a moment of darkness as the head of my Astral* [here = Psychical] *Body slipped into my Physical Body* [cf. Statement No. 9] *but no shock.*

'On another occasion a friend saw me (as she thought) leave my room and the house, even rising to go in search of me. But she returned to find me sound asleep in bed. My "double" was dressed in a red frock which she recognized. Next day I wrote of the incident to an American friend whose letter, also written the same day, crossed mine and arrived two weeks later. She said that she had seen me in the U.S.A. that night, the difference in time being allowed for. I had been followed and seen departing from England, and arriving in the U.S.A. The witnesses were unknown to each other and both mentioned the red dress.

'I have often awakened just prior to entering the body, and am also now well acquainted with the preparatory process of the loosening of the Astral Body, though I have never set myself to attain this object.'

CASE NO. 96—*Mrs F. Collins*

This case followed that just cited, the exteriorization being subsequently corroborated. It reads as follows:

'I have at different times, without any conscious wish, found myself leaving my Physical Body and travelling through space to some scene in which I was present and heard and saw what was taking place at the time. One night … *I found myself leaving my body and floating towards the house of a friend. At that period of my life she was a great deal in my thoughts.* I stopped at her house and wandered around outside, and then suddenly found myself in the scullery where I saw my friend walking up and down in great pain and very ill. I felt very distressed and tried to help her but found I could not do so [cf. Statement No. 28]. *I was so frightened that, with a violent rush, I was back in my body*, shaking violently and suffering from shock [cf. the accounts of Muldoon, Lind, Sculthorp, etc.]. The following day I called upon my friend, and, on being questioned, she admitted that she had been ill in precisely the manner and at the exact time (11.30 p.m.) that I had visited her in my Astral Body.'

CASE NO. 97—*Mrs I. M. Joy*

Mrs Joy, of Fordingbridge, is the daughter of a Methodist Minister. She is not a spiritualist and had attended no seances. She informed me (*in litt.*) that *she had projections before having read any book or article of any kind dealing with these matters.* Mrs Joy said, 'The experience came as a surprise. Astral travelling has happened quite naturally to me for these last few years at any time, day or night. I do not try to get it at all; I just cannot help it happening. During these experiences I am conscious of everything that happens. I seem to wander to a spirit-place where I see and speak to many people that I know to be "dead" [cf. Statement No. 18].

'My first experience followed much activity in my home, such as ornaments changing place and raps [= telekinetic phenomena indicative of a relatively loose vehicle of vitality or 'body-veil']. One morning I sat in a chair and felt very sleepy. Before I realized what had happened, I felt my spirit-body being released from the physical. I could not, just before this, see my hands or feet, and the next thing I knew was that my Astral [here = Psychical] Body was standing up firmly and I started to make towards the door. I passed right through the piano [cf. Statement No. 31], opened the door in the usual way [= habit] and drifted over the back gate, over hedges and up over trees. I cannot remember what happened after that, but when I "came to" I felt rather "heady" and my legs were unsteady. ...'

With regard to other experiences, Mrs Joy further said, 'I was seen by one of my neighbours when I was "out": she saw me enter her cottage—I have done this many times and she thought it was a "vision" of me. ... I also visited my aunt in this way on several occasions. I touched her once and she looked round, worried. She knew who it was, but could not see me. On one of my journeys I visited the house of Sibelius the Finnish composer ...' [The details which Mrs Joy saw in Sibelius's house were said to be confirmed later.] *Until she had these experiences Mrs Joy was not sure of survival. They convinced her of the fact.*

At a later date Mrs Joy wrote to say that in a recent projection she had gone 'towards water'. [Although she cannot swim normally, she 'swam' in it. Mrs Joy added that, 'It was warm and I was tempted to go further, but fear drew me away.' This experience, symbolized by 'water', is to be expected in Mrs Joy's case. It is evident that her 'body-veil' is relatively loose so that she tends to have some awareness of 'earth-veil', or 'Hades' conditions (which are often symbolized by the 'dead' by 'mist', 'fog' or 'water')—cf. Statements No. 10 and 41 and the accounts of Gerhardi, Ogston, Mrs Cripps, Hives, Miss Johnson, Mme d'Espérance, de la Mare, Helen Brooks, etc.]

CASE No. 98—*Mr A. J. Wills*

Mr Wills's first exteriorization, described in Muldoon's *The Case for Astral Projection*, like that of Morrell and Georginus, was caused by pain. Wills was at the dentist's, having a tooth drilled without an anaesthetic. The pain became so acute that he 'lost' himself [= shed the Physical Body, cf. Statement No. 9] and then found himself looking over the dentist's shoulder into his own mouth [cf. Statement No. 17]. Mr Wills's accounts of further experiences are as follows.

'I was with a firm which had a temporary office in an old building. One night I fell asleep to find myself later projected into the old building, going through it, up the stairs, etc. *I was as fully conscious as ever I was in my life.* The light was greyish ... I thought, "It is the middle of the night—what am I doing here?" And with that thought I was returned to my body.

'Three years ago, while travelling on a train, I lay down on the seat and slept. Presently I found that I was propping myself up—physically, I thought [cf. Muldoon, etc.] until I discovered otherwise. I could see the passengers behind me as easily as those in front. Then I saw that it was not my Physical Body in which I was propped up (by my right arm). Looking downwards, *I saw my Physical Body still sleeping on the seat* [cf. Statement No. 17 and the accounts of Van Eeden and Sculthorp]. *For a few moments I admired this new and beautiful body (the astral). It was rosy-pink and glowed like a luminous pearl* [cf. Geddes, Brunton, Gerhardi, etc.]. *Something which looked like an arm* [the 'silver cord'— cf. Statement No. 19] *seemed to run down and merge into the brain of the Physical Body.* Soon I was back in the latter.'

Later, Mr Wills was able to leave his Physical Body voluntarily. Like so many others who made this claim, *he found that to experience strong emotion while 'out' was to cause his return.* He said, 'If I think emotionally of my physical self while "out", I am instantly back into it again.' Also like many others, he found that, while exteriorized, he had abilities of an unexpected nature. With regard to these, he said, 'I have done things while projected which would be physically impossible, such as defying gravity. ... When, while projected at a great height, I realize that there is no physical support under me, I sometimes have a feeling of nausea. ... [Compare the 'Temptation' on the pinnacle of the Temple, Matt. iv, which is said by some to have constituted a test, rather than a temptation.] If this realization of non-support comes slowly, I can overcome it; but if it comes suddenly, I return to the physical body speedily with a shock, causing a jerk of the body. ...' [This corresponds with the 'repercussion' mentioned in so many accounts as occurring when return to the body, on account of the banging of a door or window, etc., is sudden. It also, doubtless, corresponds to the 'repercussion', often of an injurious nature, felt by 'physical' mediums when the exteriorized ectoplasm, part of the 'Denser Between Body', or 'body-veil,' returns suddenly to the Physical Body because, for instance, a bright light has suddenly been flashed on the entranced person. When an ectoplasmic 'materialization' of Mme d'Espérance's was assaulted, her Physical Body was severely injured: she was ill for a considerable time thereafter. The 'repercussion' is similarly observed in certain phenomena in connection with 'witches' (and 'wizards') and with 'black magic' among savage or semi-savage tribes: after the phantom, apparition or 'double' has received an injury (and this was, no doubt, a 'double' highly impregnated with ectoplasm from the 'body-veil', and not a pure hallucination), the Physical Body of the 'witch' or 'black magician' was later found to be injured in the same place and same manner as the 'double'.]

Mr Wills differentiated his experiences from dreams, saying, 'In dreams there is always a sense of confusion and disorder, as if one had nothing fixed or concrete to tie to, and on awakening there is the immediate realization of having been deluded by the somnolent mind.

In projection I find none of this. *At first the sensation of being in different conditions tends to arouse the emotions, which usually cause a return to the physical. But later ... one is never more clear-minded than when projected.'*

CASE NO. 99—*Mr C. L. Banks*

Mr Banks told me (in litt.), '*My first projection happened naturally some time before I understood anything about the occult.*' He continued, 'In 1925 I was walking-out with a young lady who lived at Boston. I used to go over to see her on a motor-cycle. One evening my cycle would not start. I went to bed very disappointed.

'I dreamed that I was standing at her bedroom-door, asking her to come to me. She heard, got up, and followed me downstairs to the living-room, when I stood with my back to a cupboard near the fireplace. She stood in the middle of the room. I beckoned her to come to me and at that point I awoke in the Physical Body. [Compare the experience of Oliver Fox: when out of the body, he tried to touch his sweetheart, and he returned at once. Similarly, the Revd. P. H. Newnham 'returned' when he put his arm round his sweetheart's waist. It is, however, doubtful whether the latter was a case of astral projection or of telepathy and/or clairvoyance.]

'When I did go over to her house, I found the young lady's mother eager to tell me something strange that had happened, but the daughter stopped her, saying that she would tell me herself when we were out walking.

'She would not tell me for some time. After some trouble, to my great surprise, she told me about my dream up to the time when she stood in the middle of the room. It was then that she awoke—in the middle of the living-room. She said that she was so afraid that she stood cataleptic, screaming repeatedly. I asked why, and *she said that she could still see me after she had awakened:* not only so, she could see the cupboard door through me.

'Her father had to go downstairs and console her and get her back to bed. It was this incident that first interested me in occult matters.'

Like several others, Mr Banks said that, on one occasion when he was 'out', he saw *two* of himself (besides his Physical Body). He also claimed to visit the 'Third Sphere' ('Summerland', or 'Paradise') during projections and converse with the 'dead' (cf. Statement No. 18]. He said that things seemed quite real and solid in that condition, but there was one constant difference—the light. He said, '*The light is very bright and clear; there is no light like it here ... it is quite soft, without glare; objects stand out much more against their background, yet there are no shadows.*' The nature of the light enabled him to realize when he was out of his Physical Body.

Mr Banks, like the Countess of Tankerville, Col. Lester and Messrs Brown and Edwards, said that during out-of-the-body experiences he was used in 'rescue work' in the 'lower astral planes' [= the 'earth-veil' or 'Hades'], 'co-operating' with those from the 'Third Sphere' [= 'Paradise', the 'Finer Between Worlds', 'Summerland', etc.] in assisting the 'earthbound' who are said to be the 'spirits in prison' of the Bible [cf. Statement No. 30 and I Peter iii, 19]. The explanation that he gave of the process is that given independently in the com-munications of supposed discarnates. Mr Banks said 'My Guide and I are in coincidence. My Astral Body being straight out of the Physical Body, increases the density of his and so we can be perceptible to the person in need of our help.'

CASE No. 100—Mrs C. H. Smith (née Laura E. Brisson)

Mrs Smith informed me (in litt.) *that she had heard nothing about pro-jection before having the experience. She published her account in* Fate *for Dec., 1950. Details are as follows.*

'In 1918 I received word that my favourite cousin had been killed in a motor accident. I was unable to leave home, and an old friend attended the funeral instead. That night I fell asleep thinking of my cousin. *I awoke to find myself lying in a horizontal position about one foot above my body* [cf. Statement No. 16] *which I could see on the bed below me* [cf. Statement No. 17].

'Suddenly my Astral [here = Psychical] Body turned towards the door and, still in the horizontal position, floated slowly out of the room and down the stairs. Although no door opened, I floated outside [cf. Statement No. 31], then down the porch steps, and turned facing down the street. Then, in a flash, *I found myself standing upright in my cousin's home eighty-six miles from my home.* I was in the dining-room and after-wards described the exact position of a night-lamp on the table. I also saw the foot of my cousin's casket, remembered the colour (a grey velour), and also told the exact place in the living-room where he was laid out. I entered a bedroom where my friend was sleeping, approached her, and, intending to awaken her, pulled her arm. *Then I remembered that I must be dead and it would startle her if she saw me. So I started to turn away from the bed. Suddenly she opened her eyes and saw me.* On the instant I found myself back in my room, lying above my body in the horizontal position. It seemed ages before I could force myself back inside it. There seemed to be an opening in the chest *through which I entered.* [A few others, *e.g.* Mrs Garrett and Mrs Jeffrey left, and returned to the Physical Body by way of the 'chest' instead of by the head—cf. Statement No. 13]. It was a most unpleasant experience, as my body felt cold and rigid.

'When my friend returned from the funeral, she told how she had felt me pull at her arm, awakened, recognized me, and then saw me vanish.'

CASE No. 101—'A.P.H.' of Harrow

Prediction, May 1937, gave this experience as follows. 'During sleep I frequently have the following experience. I suddenly become wide and fully conscious but unable to move my limbs or use my voice [= catalepsy]. This condition is accompanied by a feeling of gasping and a sensation of coolness [? = emission of ectoplasm from the 'body-veil'—cf. Miss Johnson etc.]. Sometimes during these "attacks" I feel that I am revolving through the air at a terrific speed; at other times I hear voices, either terrifying or human. This is not the ordinary type of nightmare. I enjoy good health and am not troubled with indigestion.'

CASE No. 102—'T.S.' (Dorset)

This case was given in Prediction, Sept., 1937. 'Being on the verge of sleep, I suddenly perceived a long object about eighteen inches above my body and parallel with it [cf. Statement No. 16]. It looked like a bolster, rolling over and over very rapidly but keeping in the same position above my body. Then I caught sight of a face on it and it came to rest. Staring at me from it was the image of my own face. Then the vision faded. [Compare Hartmann's narrative: 'T.S.' clearly saw his 'double' from the Physical Body, which is the first stage in 'astral projection'.] Had his consciousness been transferred (by way of the 'silver cord') to the 'double', he would then have seen the Physical Body from the 'double' [cf. Statement No. 17].

CASE No. 103—'N.D.' (Pontypool)

Here is an experience given in Prediction, Nov., 1938. 'I partially awoke to the strange sensation of ascending rapidly. My body was rigid [= catalepsy]. Suddenly I became afraid. Coinciding with this fear, I descended rapidly; a little jerk of the body and I awoke in bed.

'I sank back into a state of semi-slumber and the same thing happened again. Once more I felt frightened and began the descent, apparently in consequence. This occurred three times.'

CASE No. 104—Mr Alfred Gordon Bennett

Mr A. G. Bennett Focus on the Unknown (Rider & Co. Ltd., 1953) described what was almost certainly an out-of-the-body experience (though he did not recognize it as such). There was a side entrance to his father's house which was somewhat peculiar. When he had grown up he 'dreamed' about this door 'most vividly'. He went through it into the house. And, 'here,' he said, 'occurred that curious doubling of the self which Dr Carrington has noted.' [A door, a passage, a tunnel, etc., are among symbols for passing out of the Physical Body. The same symbols are used by certain dying persons: a dying boy said that he could see a 'door' in the corner of the room, adding, 'When that door opens, I shall go through it.' Further, a number of supposed dead communicators described leaving their bodies as passing through a doorway (cf. Statement No. 9).]

Mr Bennett also mentioned an author-friend who, having learned the methods in the East, could enter a state of suspended animation. On awakening from the trance he gave a 'perfectly lucid account of the astral journeys he had undertaken whilst his body was in *samadhi.*' What he said 'appeared to provide abundant proof of the theory concerning the existence of adjoining spheres or super-terrestrial dimensions. But at the same time, it was obvious that he had also travelled extensively in our normal dimensions ...' [cf. Statement No. 26, and the accounts of Mrs Cripps, Mrs Larsen, etc.]. Mr Bennett described successful experiments which he had undertaken in exteriorization. He suggested that his readers should be content at first to leave the body and move only a few feet away from it. Like Bulford, Mr Bennett insisted that it is important, prior to attempting leaving the body, clearly to visualize every detail of what is to be performed and that progress should be slow. Merely leaving the body and walking a few feet should, he considered, be spread over weeks, even months. He said, 'If, at the end of that period all tendency to fear has not been eliminated, and if there is a sensation that the mind is blacking-out and you are losing control over its functioning, then abandon the experiment for good. ... You are not psychically constituted to undertake it.'

Mr Bennett remarked, 'No one can explain why I, who have repeatedly projected without the slightest alarm or discomfort, am unable to climb a high ladder or stand on top of a lofty precipice without wanting to throw myself down.' [But the explanation is obvious. The passing through the 'door'—of the Physical Body—in the 'dream' indicated that Mr Bennett has a relatively loose Psychical Body. The 'Temptation' (Matt. iv; Mark i, 13; Luke iv) 'cast thyself down' (from the pinnacle of the Temple) was in the nature of a test. Mr Bennett's wish to 'cast himself down' represented a 'sub-conscious' desire to exteriorize and so to enter the free and happy conditions known as 'Paradise', of which he, and indeed all of us, are 'sub-' (really 'super-') consciously well aware. But he has yet to overcome habitual thought processes: he instinctively thinks that a fall in the Psychical Body, like one in the Physical Body, would hurt and injure. Until this habitual shrinking from a fall is overcome, the extent of his 'astral journeys' is necessarily limited and that affects his ability, during exteriorizations, to 'co-operate' with discarnates in helping the newly-dead, the 'earth-bound', etc.—cf. Statement No. 30.]

CASE No. 105—*Mrs 'H.F.P.'*

The following is abbreviated from the account given in *Light*, lxxiv, No. 3, 1954. 'At the age of eighteen, while in bed, my left side became numb. *I found myself outside my body, looking down at it on the bed* [cf. Statement No. 17]. I noticed a slight summer rash on my throat which was not known to me, but was found to be there the next morning. *There was an exhilarating sense of happiness and freedom* [cf. Statement No. 26]. I said to myself, "If this is what it feels like to be dead, I shall never be afraid of dying." ...

'*I went through the wall into the next room* [cf. Statement No. 31]. *Looking at my body, I thought, "Must I get back into that?"* [cf. Statement No. 8]. *But I was drawn into it with a rush.* [It will be seen that, whereas many of those who, like Mrs 'H.F.P.', claimed to shed the body *naturally* did so slowly and gently, often, indeed, so gently and naturally that the process passed unnoticed (as it does when we naturally 'fall asleep'). On the other hand, many of these people were conscious of re-entering the body and these are the ones who also describe a rapid and sudden return, and that from considerable ('vibrational') distances (*i.e.*, from the Psychical Body and corresponding 'Paradise' conditions to the Physical Body and earth conditions). When these descriptions are compared with those of people whose shedding of the body was *enforced* (by anaesthetics, etc.), we observe a significant difference: these, who shed the body rapidly and suddenly, are more often conscious of ejection from the body but less often aware of the process of re-entering it. Their return is slow and gradual and from relatively short ('vibrational') distances (*i.e.*, from the 'body-veil' and corresponding 'earth-veil', or 'Hades' conditions to the Physical Body and earth conditions). These matters increase in significance when a comparison is made of the above with what is said by those who claimed to have shed the body permanently, *i.e.*, 'died': the proportion of those who died *naturally* and who were conscious of shedding the body was relatively small compared with that of those whose death was *enforced*. The latter fairly often said they 'felt dizzy', 'fell down', 'went to sleep', 'became unconscious', that 'all went dark', that 'things became black', etc. Being awake and alert at the time of transition, they were aware of something happening. While the Physical and Psychical Bodies were disconnecting, and 'out-of-gear' with each other, consciousness could not operate in either, so that a momentary 'blackout' was produced. Nor is this all. Where 'earthbound' men (who have delayed the shedding of the 'body-veil' and who are consequently delayed in 'Hades' conditions and unaware that they have 'died') are brought to a seance (a 'Rescue Circle') for instruction, they are allowed to enter the Physical Body of a 'medium' (which is vacated in trance for the purpose). Members of the 'circle' can then converse with the 'earthbound' and explain their condition to them. When this work is completed, the 'earthbound' man has to shed the 'medium's body'. Now, when he 'died' he may or may not, have been conscious of shedding his body but he is now conscious, alert, and aware of leaving the medium's body. He experiences death by proxy! It is significant that in this death by proxy, he makes exclamations identical with those cited above—the commonest exclamation is to complain that he is 'falling'. (It is, of course, the 'medium's' Physical Body which is 'falling' away from him.) How can these correspondences be explained unless they refer to something objective?]

'Later someone told me that it was dangerous to leave the body, and I became afraid to do so, and whenever a numbness came over me I shook myself to prevent it. *But I have occasionally been 'half out' and was then simultaneously conscious both of the numbness of my Physical Body and the 'aliveness' of the 'inner' and more vital body'.* [Compare Miss Addison's account. This was a phase of 'dual consciousness'—cf. Statement No. 18.]

Subsequent experiences were then described. In the first, Mrs 'H.F.P.' said, 'I found myself looking down on a railway line where two trains had crashed into one another. ... I was rushing to the help of the injured [cf. Statement No. 30 regarding 'co-operation', and the accounts of Lester, Banks, Edwards, Brown, Mrs Fisher and the Countess of Tankerville]. ... The morning papers next day showed photographs of the accident that had occurred during the night'.

Again, '*I was in a park where the brightness of the trees and the flowers exceeded anything seen in this world* [cf. Statement No. 26]. A friend of my husband's came, one who had died abroad and whom I had never met or even heard described (cf. Statement No. 18]. "Can you help me?" he said, "I want to talk to your husband, but do not want to frighten him"—meaning that my husband would look upon him as dead. My husband joined us and the two friends walked off together. Next day my husband had no remembrance of "going over" in his sleep, but he said that my description of the appearance and mannerisms of his friend was correct in every detail. ... On the "other side" I also saw his widow, whom I had not then met, but when we did meet (after her return to England a few months later) I recognized her. On waking from these experiences I have been conscious of someone whom I felt was a guardian' [cf. Statement No. 3, regarding 'deliverers'].

CASE No. 106—Mrs 'F.B.'

This case was published in *Light*, Jan. 6th, 1912, and in Drayton Thomas's *The Mental Phenomena of Spiritualism* (L.S.A. Publications,

Ltd., 1930). Mrs 'F.B.'s husband left his body. *His 'double' was seen both by his wife and child.*

'We were living in Plymouth. My husband, appointed to a ship in Chatham, had gone there to join it. On July 31st, 1907, he went to Worthing where his father was ill. Arriving there, he found that his father had died and he telegraphed asking me to join him the next day. The following morning I awoke at 6.45 a.m., hearing my husband's whistle, and at the same time my bedroom door opened and he came into the room. *He walked straight to the foot of my bed and leaned over a white-railed cot, which, I must mention, I had moved on the previous day from the night nursery and put in my room. My little girl had been ailing and I wished to have her with me at night. The child awoke, and, seeing her father, sat up and held out her arms to him, saying, "Why, Daddy's come home."*

'I spoke too, but at that moment there was a tap at my bedroom door and, on the maid coming in with the early morning tea, the vision vanished. At midday I went to Worthing and was met at the station by my husband. He began at once telling me of a very curious experience he had had that morning. He said that he woke just before 7 a.m. feeling as if he were fully dressed and that he suddenly saw my room, with me in bed. *The only unusual thing he noticed was that the white cot, which was generally in the nursery, was at the foot of our bed with the child in it.* He whistled to me, and leaned over the cot. The child sat up and spoke and he was turning to come over to me when he heard a tap at the door and the whole thing vanished. He realized that he was in the spare room at Worthing, and that the servant, bringing his shaving water, was knocking at the door. The times were identical and he could not possibly have known that the child's cot was in my room unless he had seen it. I had not told him that the child was ailing. *I mentioned my experience to a friend before going to Worthing.*'

In this case the 'double' was seen collectively and that without any possibility of verbal suggestion. This strongly suggests that the man was actually present in his Psychical Body.

CASE NO. 107—*Mr J. A. Symonds*

This case, from H. F. Brown's *J. A. Symonds, A Biography*, London, 1895, is given by Wm. James in his *The Varieties of Religious Experience* (Longmans Green and Co., 1st ed., 1902, 28th impression, 1917). It is a mystical rather than a psychical experience, one apparently involving the Higher Mental rather than the Psychical Body. Symonds wrote, '*Suddenly ... always when my muscles were at rest, I felt the approach of the mood. Irresistibly it took possession of my mind, lasted what seemed to be an eternity, and disappeared in sensations which re-*

sembled the awakening from an anaesthetic. Space, time, sensation, etc. were obliterated and the underlying, or essential, consciousness acquired intensity. At last nothing remained but a pure, absolute, abstract Self. The universe became without form and void of content. But Self persisted. ... *The return to ordinary consciousness began by my recovering the sense of touch. ... At last I felt myself once more a human being ...'* [cf. the 'partial awakening'—Statement No. 25].

Case No. 108—*Mrs 'H'*

This case was given in *Proc. S.P.R.*, xxxiii, 355. Mrs 'H' 'dreamed' that she was walking in Richmond Park with her husband and a friend, Mr 'J'. She saw, posted on the trees, a notice to the effect that Lady 'R' was giving a garden party. Mr 'H' objected to their attending, since the return to town would be difficult. 'Oh, I will manage that for you,' said Mr 'J'. A carriage then drove up and Mrs 'H' awoke.

Mr 'H' awoke too at that moment and said, 'I have had such a vivid dream. I dreamed that we were walking in Richmond Park and were told that Lady 'R' was giving a garden party. We were invited. I was troubled as to how we should get home, as the party was at ten, and the last train at eleven, when 'J', who was with us, said, "Oh, I will manage that for you".'

This kind of experience is technically called a 'reciprocal dream'. We suggest that Mr 'H', Mrs 'H' and Mr 'J' were all exteriorized from their Physical Bodies. Similar experiences may be common, but they are very rarely remembered. Some reciprocal dreams may, of course, be due to telepathy. Each case calls for individual interpretation.

Case No. 109—*Miss Emma Steele and Mr C. Burgess*

This is another 'reciprocal' case from the files of the *S.P.R.* It concerns Miss Emma Steele and Mr Claude Burgess, a paralytic.

Miss Steele kept a private hotel, and Mr Burgess, one of her boarders, left on Feb. 15. During the night of May 5, Miss Steele awoke to find herself in the middle of her bedroom calling, 'I'm coming!' She had heard the voice of Mr Burgess calling, 'Miss Steele' three times. She put on her dressing gown and lit the gas, and then realized that Mr Burgess no longer lived in the house. It was 3 a.m.

The next morning Miss Steele told the cook of her 'dream'. That afternoon a note was delivered at the house. It was from Mr Burgess and read thus: 'My dear Emma, I had a dream about you last night. I dreamed that you appeared at about 3 a.m. Just a glimpse of you. ...' This experience also may well be a partially-remembered astral projection. The case next cited strongly supports that view.

CASE NO. 110—*Mrs Dreisch*

In the last two cases cited a 'dream' experience was 'shared' by two people. In this one (from *Journ. American S.P.R.*, Feb., 1939) three people were involved. There are obvious indications of 'astral projection'. The account is by Mrs Dreisch, wife of Prof. Hans Dreisch, of Leipzig.

'I went to bed and fell asleep. I dreamed that a fire had broken out in one of the rooms opposite my bedroom. *I felt as if something were pulling me bodily in that direction.* I called "Clara!" (the name of my cook), "Water! Water! Put water on the fire! Oh, Clara!" But I cannot have called out aloud. My husband heard nothing. ... *Never before have I had such a strong dream-impression. It was, in some way, different from other dreams.* I didn't see a picture, but knew that there was danger in connexion with a fire.

'The following morning, I remembered my dream immediately. I felt that it was a dream of the early part of the night. ... When my maid came in with my coffee, she said, "Madam, what a terrible night! *I saw a ghost* [? Mrs Dreisch's exteriorized 'double'—see below], and then something happened to Clara and there was fire and white smoke." Clara and she shared the same room. ... Now she and the cook did not like each other and I was sure that no communication had passed between them in the morning.

'Later, I looked for Clara, told her the maid's story and asked her if anything had happened to her during the night. She said, "Yes—I read a book by candle-light and fell asleep without putting it out. *Suddenly, I felt that you, Madam, were awakening me.* I opened my eyes and saw beside me, on the little table, a huge fire. ... In reality, it was only the candle that had burned down and set off a lot of matches. I took the candle-stick and threw it into the water in the wash-stand. Some hot wax dropped on my arm." Clara showed me the inside of her arm: it was covered with red spots up to the elbow. ...

'I told both girls about my dream and the feeling of a strange power drawing me towards their room, and of my words asking Clara to act. Clara said the fire occurred at exactly 2.30 a.m. ...

'I asked Clara whether she had been frightened upon opening her eyes and seeing the fire? She said, "No, that is the strangest part. *I had the feeling that I was awakened expressly and knew exactly what to do as if I had been told in my sleep!*" [cf. the 'Call'—Statement No. 2].

'The door of my bedroom and that of the two girls close very tightly and my bedroom is separated from theirs by two other doors, so that I could not possibly have seen a light or smelled the smoke of a fire in their room, which could have inspired my dream. ... *All three of us had the feeling that a contact took place between us, though separated by space.* ...'

CASE NO. 111—*Miss Catherine H. Griggs*

This experience is also described in the *Journ. American S.P.R.*, 1923. Catherine Griggs and her mother lived in Waterbury, Conn. They slept in twin beds in one room. One night Catherine lay awake with toothache. Her mother was reading in bed. Shortly before 5 a.m. the daughter fell asleep. Suddenly she felt herself outside her body. Her withdrawal had been so gentle and natural as to pass unnoticed [cf. Statement No. 9]. *She walked round the foot of the bed, observing her own body and her mother* [cf. Statement No. 17]. Her mother's eyes were fixed on her book.

Since Catherine had had previous exteriorizations and (like Fox, Muldoon, Sculthorp, Mrs Peters, etc.) had noted 'incongruities' between the physical and non-physical environments, she walked out of the room and through the half-lighted hall with the object of seeing if the house looked perfectly natural on the present occasion. [She thus, like Gerhardi, Miss Newby, Mrs Leonard, etc., deliberately set out to make critical observations, a characteristic of waking—not of dream-consciousness.] When, however, she was half-way down the stairs, it became 'dark'. She said, '*I timidly went back, got into my body, and awoke.*' *Her descriptions of the process of re-entering the body is interesting: 'I slipped back into myself (body) and then awoke—two separated conditions.*' Glancing at the clock, she saw that it was 5 a.m. The parrot made little sounds and she answered, saying, 'You're a nice little bird!'

Mrs Griggs exteriorized immediately afterwards. [Looseness of the 'double' is known to be hereditary.] Mrs Griggs had observed that her daughter was still awake shortly before 5 a.m. Then she slept, but awoke again exactly at 5 a.m. Mrs Griggs heard Catherine murmur pet words to the parrot and then fell asleep. As on many previous occasions, she 'slipped out easily' from her Physical Body and was aware of a peculiar feeling at the base of the brain. [Compare Muldoon, etc.] Outside her body, she looked at her daughter and heard her murmur to the parrot, 'You're a nice little bird!'—'Nice little nuisance!', Mrs Griggs said. She walked up to the cage and tapped it, but the bird did not seem to hear [cf. Statement No. 28].

Then Mrs Griggs went into the hall to make critical observations. In such 'dreams', if some object appeared unnatural to her, she could usually, by an effort of will, make it resume its natural appearance. [That is, the 'incongruities' are often mental images or 'thought-forms': cf. Statement No. 10.] She went downstairs and into the living-room and noted that the wallpaper was of a different pattern from the actual paper. Although, however, she concentrated on it, her efforts were unavailing on this occasion. Next she saw her daughter's seal-skin coat lying untidily on an arm-chair with the hat perched on top of it.

Mrs Griggs disapproved of the untidiness and also thought, 'Strange—Catherine is not wearing that coat this year—I think it is packed away.' She continued her journey from room to room, finding everything else normal. One room had a low door opening on the porch and she recalled that this door was not to be opened, since, only two days before, Catherine had packed it with cotton-wool to exclude the draught. *But she realized that there was no need to open the door, that, by concentrating on the idea, she could pass right through it. This she did and found herself out on the porch* [cf. Statement No. 31]. There everything was normal, but she could feel that it was colder out of doors than in the house. *She touched the wire screening and felt it give way slightly at first, after which her hand passed through it* [cf. Gerhardi and Mrs Larsen with regard to the electric light switch, also Statement No. 31].

Mrs Griggs returned from the porch to the house, passing through the closed door as before. She then looked into a room that was un-furnished except for her late husband's bureau. *The room actually contained no bed, though she and her daughter had discussed placing one there, and of setting it so that it would face the hall. When Mrs Griggs entered this room in her 'double', she saw that it contained a bed though not in the proposed position. And there, on the bed, reading, lay her husband* [cf. Statement No. 18].

Mrs Griggs wrote, 'I threw myself on my knees and told him about our problems. I asked him if he can see and hear us. He replied, "I always see you. I always can hear you".'

At this point a fear that this might not be her husband entered her mind. [In some of her previous experiences a familiar face had turned into a mocking one—cf. Mme David-Neel's 'monk', a mental image, or 'thought-form' which, apparently, became ensouled by a 'joker' on 'the other side'. Impersonation is well known to occur on the lower psychic levels—(hence the injunction to 'try the spirits whether they are of God'—I John iv, 1]. Her doubts aroused, Mrs Griggs watched her husband's face carefully. It did not change. *Nevertheless her fear caused her re-interiorization: she awoke in the Physical Body.* [The fact that fear, or other strong emotion, caused a return to the Physical Body is noted by many who claimed to have out-of-the-body experiences.]

'Catherine!' Mrs Griggs called to her daughter as soon as she was awake. 'I've been "out"!' 'And I too mother'. They compared experiences and noted that Mrs Griggs, out of the body, had heard the words Catherine said to the parrot and had seen the fur coat left untidily on a chair, etc. With regard to the fur coat, Catherine declared that she had worn that coat for the first time that winter and had flung it on the chair *after* her mother had gone to bed. Next morning it had been removed and put away, yet Mrs Griggs was able correctly to indicate the chair. The research officers of the Society learned that Mrs Griggs and her daughter had had exteriorizations all their lives, but they could not produce them at will.

CASE No. 112—*Mr Stevens*

This case, given among 'clairvoyant dreams' in *The Mystery of Dreams*, by William Oliver Stevens (George Allen & Unwin Ltd., 1950), is probably an example of 'astral projection'.

One morning in 1936, since Mr Stevens's son did not appear at the breakfast table and failed to answer calls, his mother went to see why. She found him sitting up in bed, staring as though shaken by some horror that he had just seen. 'Oh, mother,' he cried, 'I have had the most terrible dream! It seemed so real, I can't get over it.' He related the 'dream' then and there. Coming downstairs, he repeated it to the maid and then told it to his father over the breakfast table. It was as follows.

'I was in a strange place. *I seemed to be in the air about twenty feet above the ground* [cf. Statement No. 16]. I was behind a car, containing a young man and a girl, travelling along a road. Suddenly the machine swerved and smashed against a tall pole. A tall, thin, dark, foreign-looking man got out and lay down on the grass, obviously in pain. He lit a cigarette but could not smoke it. He said something like, "I feel a terrible miasma" (which I took to be a foreign word). The girl stood by, unhurt. The man was fatally injured. *It was all so clear that I am sure it really happened somewhere.* There will be something about it in the paper to-day. Let's watch for it.'

The newspaper arrived in the afternoon. Mrs Stevens brought it into the room with part of the front page exposed. The son started up from his chair, pointed to the picture on the front page, and cried, 'There! that is the very man I saw in my dream!' It was a photograph of a dark young man, the Count of Covadonga. The details described of the accident were exactly as seen in the 'dream' and described eight hours before the paper arrived, except that, according to the young woman, the skid occurred in avoiding a truck. Stevens saw no truck.

CASE No. 113—*Mrs Phyllis Fisher*

Mrs Fisher, of Halesowen, sent me the following (*in litt.*). '*My first out-of-the-body experience occurred when I was young and unaware that such things were possible. I had read no book on the subject.* I was looking into a mirror, preparatory to tidying my hair. I had a strange detached feeling. Some years later, after having been asleep, *I woke with a feeling that I was floating in the air. I relaxed in order not to break this condition. Then I looked down and saw my body on the bed* [cf. Statement No. 17]. I travelled through lovely scenery and saw a crowd of people who were dressed in white [cf. Statement No. 26]. One came forward to welcome me: I think it was my mother [cf. Statement No. 18]. *I returned to my body with regret* [cf. Statement No. 8].

'On a subsequent occasion, I was taken by a guide into the "dark regions" [= the lower 'Hades' conditions]. It was exactly like Dante's *Inferno*—people groped in darkness, scarcely discernible as human beings. I have since done much "Rescue Work" in these regions [cf. Statement No. 30 regarding 'co-operation'; also the narratives of Messrs Banks, Edwards, Brown, Lt.-Col. Lester and the Countess of Tankerville]. In addition to such "astral" travel, I have made earth-visits, obtaining information about rooms, their contents, etc. that later proved to be correct.'

CASE NO. 114—*Mr 'X'*

Richet gave this case (*Thirty Years of Psychical Research*, Collins & Co. Ltd., 1923). Mrs Elgee, staying in Cairo, awoke as though she had been called to see the 'double' of an old friend whom she knew to be in England. The apparition was very life-like and the details of the dress etc. were plainly seen. Mrs Elgee said, 'How did you come here?' The figure came forward and pointed to Mrs Dennys (who slept in the same room). Mrs Dennys awoke and saw the apparition. It then vanished but she was able to describe it exactly, though she did not recognize whom it represented. This was a Mr 'X'. He was not ill. Mrs Elgee met him four years later.

CASE NO. 115—*Mrs 'T.D.'*

This lady 'dreamed' that she floated away from her body. She said, '*I saw myself in bed with a smoky string* [= the 'silver cord'—cf. Statement No. 19] *connecting the two of me. Then I snapped back into my body*'—Fate, Nov., 1954.

CASE NO. 116—*Mrs Elizabeth Bounds*

Mrs Bounds's case was given in *Psychic News*, Oct. 2, 1954. This lady, ninety-four years of age, was pronounced dead by a doctor at the Richard Cusden Home, Streatham. But the matron felt a slight flicker of the pulse and, massaging the heart, restored Mrs Bounds to physical life. Mrs Bounds said, '*I was rushing along a pitch-black tunnel* [cf. Statement No. 9], but a voice said, "Go back, we don't want you yet". I heard Matron's voice calling out of the black tunnel, "Elizabeth, come back". I returned and I opened my eyes.' Shortly after, she was 'up and about'.

CASE No. 117—*Dr Carrington's friend*

Dr Hereward Carrington gave this account, by an acquaintance for whose sincerity he vouched. It was published in *Psychic Oddities* (Rider & Co. Ltd., 1952).

'*My experiences have left an indelible impression on my mind, convincing me that certain happenings of the kind are genuine.* Nothing that anyone can say will shake that conviction. ... Chief among these are the three occasions when I seemingly left my Physical Body and roamed freely about in space in some astral or etheric vehicle. *These experiences were not dreams. I retained full waking consciousness. I could look about me, see my body asleep on the bed and note its position* [cf. Statement No. 17]. I was functioning outside my material body, which I could then realize was not the real "me", but a mere shell. It was merely something I used during my normal waking hours. ... We are not limited to the activities of the physical brain.

'*The first emotion is one of panic. The subject thinks that he has died. It comes as a shock. This emotion often tends to end the projection: there is a sudden "drawing" sensation at the back of the head* [cf. Muldoon, etc. and Statement No. 13]. *A moment of blackness* [= re-entering the Physical Body—cf. Statement No. 9 in reverse] *and the subject finds himself back in the body again.* If instead of panicking, he had kept cool and "willed" to project further, he would have had a never-to-be-forgotten experience—that of living outside his body! Most people have a spontaneous experience before they become interested; then they begin to study the subject. That is what happened to me.

'*My first experience occurred in 1932, when I had never heard of astral projection.* I had been asleep and suddenly found myself "awake", in full possession of my consciousness. I was rigid, unable to move the "body" I was inhabiting [= catalepsy], yet my mind was perfectly clear. *As yet, I could see nothing* (cf. the 'partial awakening'—Statement No. 25]. *Then, after perhaps thirty seconds, I saw the room and my own body lying upon the bed* [cf. Statement No. 17]. The room seemed to be flooded with a silvery, unearthly light: it was not a steady glow—the atmosphere seemed to be shimmering and scintillating [cf. Geddes, Gerhardi, Huntley, Oxenham, Banks, etc.]. I stood at the foot of my bed. A tall benign Figure was beside me. Despite this, I had a sudden panic, thinking I had died. This emotion increased and I felt a peculiar "drawing" sensation at the back of my head [cf. Statement No. 13]. *I reached out my hand to touch my body: the hand passed completely through it* [cf. Statement No. 31]. *This was an added shock. More intense fear shot through me—and then I was back in the Physical Body.*

'Until this time I had been a sceptic of all things psychic, but I went next day to the library and there found *The Projection of the Astral Body*

by Muldoon and Carrington. I read it and tried again, controlling my
fear. I had learned that desire facilitates projection. All that day I ate
large quantities of salt and would not drink water. I went to bed with
a terrific thirst, and slept. My second experience started in a dream and
I had no sensation of leaving the body. [He had done this on going to
sleep.] I found myself in the street of a small town, looking for something—water. I saw a man who seemed normal except that his head
appeared to be composed of yellowish gas. This dream-like character
struck me and I said, "This is a dream!" [He was noting 'incongruities'
between two different environments, namely, normal physical objects
and the mental images, or 'thought-forms' of the dream-world—
cf. Fox, Muldoon, Sculthorp, Miss Peters, Mrs Griggs, etc. and Statement No. 10.] As soon as I did this, I became fully conscious and found
myself "projected". The dream had changed into reality! I now realized that I was in Wentchee, Wash. My body was in Los Angeles.
Walking down the main street, I noted everything. *I said to myself,
"Now, I must not forget this"* [cf. Gerhardi, Mrs Leonard, Mrs Griggs,
Miss Newby, etc., who similarly made deliberate observations]. I was
as fully awake as ever I was in my life. ... I walked along for a couple of
blocks. Then I began to feel that drawing sensation at the back of my
head. ... I found myself being whizzed through space at terrific speed.
[Like Mrs 'H.F.P.', etc., this man exteriorized slowly but returned
rapidly. This is characteristic of *natural* exteriorizations. On the other
hand, rapid ejection and unconsciousness of return characterizes *enforced*
exteriorizations.] I passed through the roof of my house and entered
my room—and my body—without losing consciousness for a single
instant. ... Having divested myself of fear, my return had been normal.
    'The difference between astral projection and death is that the
"cord" binding together the two bodies is intact in the one case and
broken in the other [cf. Statement No. 20]. *Astral projection proves that
there is nothing to fear in death.*'

CASE No. 118—*The 'Prodigal'*

The following experiences are given in *The Prodigal* (J. M. Watkins,
1921). The first is of a 'mystical' nature, the second a more typical
'astral projection' [cf. the Symonds case].
    'I stood looking across the hills. Suddenly, I was surrounded by a
great light or white cloud which blotted out all the surroundings. The
cloud pricked, and I said to myself, "It is an electric cloud." ... Then
there began to pour into me an indescribably great vitality which filled
me from the feet up, gently and slowly. As it rose higher, I felt the
sensation of being freed from the law of gravity—I was a free spirit.
The Power rose in me until it reached the crown of my head (cf. State-

ment No. 13] and immediately the barrier between God and me came down. ... Then the vivid whiteness melted away and I saw everything as before. But I was filled with wonder and peace.

'One night I composed myself for sleep, but *I did not sleep, nor was my wakefulness the usual wakefulness. I did not dream. I could not move* [catalepsy]. My consciousness was alight with a new energy and extended to an infinite distance beyond my body. *Yet it remained connected with my body* [by the 'silver cord'—cf. Statement No. 19]. I lived a life in which none of my senses was used yet which was a thousand times as vivid [cf. Statement No. 26]. ... *My soul was projected and travelled for incalculable distances beyond my body. ... It was, by some de-insulation, aware of the spirit-life as it will be when free from the flesh.'* [Note the symbol of an insulator for the Physical Body: supposed discarnates also use that analogy, as well as those of 'blinkers', 'blankets', 'brakes', etc.]

CASE NO. 119—*Anonymous*

This case is mentioned in W. Whately Smith's *A Theory of the Mechanism of Survival* (Kegan Paul, Trench, Trübner & Co. Ltd., 1920), where it was said to be derived from *Death: its Causes and Phenomena*, by Hereward Carrington and John R. Meader (Rider & Co. Ltd., 1911).

The narrator describes how, as he lay in bed, he felt a cold sensation creeping up his legs from the feet and gradually extending throughout his body [cf. the accounts of Miss Blakeley, Bertrand, Miss Yeoman, etc.]. After some time, he became momentarily unconscious [= while shedding the Physical Body—cf. Statement No. 9]. On regaining consciousness, he was free from the body and 'seemed to walk on air'. He thought of a friend who was some hundreds of miles distant and at once found himself in the presence of his friend, who spoke to him. But he thought that he ought to return to his body and immediately *he found himself looking at his apparently dead body propped up in bed* [cf. Statement No. 17]. He tried to control it and eventually re-entered it. Smith said, 'The credentials of this case are good, and it is important to note that *the friend to whom he referred wrote spontaneously to say that he had seen the narrator at the time and in the circumstances described.* For this reason it can hardly be dismissed as a mere hallucination or dream. ... The narrator, apparently embodied all the time in a vehicle of some sort, saw his own body from outside.'

B.—Enforced Out-of-the-Body Experiences

(1) FIRST-HAND ACCOUNTS

a. Caused by Anaesthetics, etc.

CASE NO. 120—*Dr George Wyld*

WYLD (*Christo-Theosophy*, Kegan Paul, Trench, Trübner & Co. Ltd.) inhaled chloroform to relieve pain. He said, 'Suddenly, *I found my soul, clothed and in the form of my body, standing two yards outside my body which lay motionless on the bed*' [cf. Statement No. 17]. He noted Sir Humphry Davy's experience under nitrous oxide. The latter 'lost all connexion with physical things' and 'existed in a world of newly-connected and newly-modified ideas', exclaiming, on returning to the body, 'Nothing exists but thoughts. The universe is composed of impressions, ideas, pleasures and pains' [cf. Ouspensky, etc.]. Davy's experience transformed that scientist into an idealist [cf. the effect of out-of-the-body experiences on many others, and the statements of Anna Maria Roos, etc.].

Wyld also cited the following. *Mrs Arnot died at 11 a.m. Her daughter was being given chloroform at 12 noon. On recovering consciousness she told those around her that her mother had died, for she had seen her* [cf. Statement No. 8]. Tidings of the mother's death did not reach that house for another four hours.

CASE NO. 121—*Mr F. Cromwell Varley*, F.R.S.

Varley used an acid in certain experiments. The fumes affected his throat and he obtained relief by using ether. Later he used chloroform. He said, 'One night I rolled on my back retaining the chloroform-saturated sponge, which remained in my mouth. Mrs Varley was in the room above. After a little time, I became conscious. *I saw myself on my back with the sponge to my mouth* [cf. Statement No. 17], *but was powerless to move my body. I willed an impression on my wife's brain that I was in danger* [cf. the telepathic 'Call', Statement No. 2]. Thus aroused, she came down and removed the sponge. I then used my body to speak to my wife. I said, "I shall forget all about this, and how it came to pass, unless you remind me in the morning. Be sure to tell me what made you come down and then I shall be able to recall the circumstances".'

When morning arrived, Mrs Varley told her husband what had happened and he eventually remembered the whole experience.

It may be added that Varley not only described both his wife's sister and his wife as having out-of-the-body experiences, but *on one occasion Mrs Varley (like Varley himself in the case just cited), though outside her body in trance, made it speak in a manner similar to that said to be used by the 'control' of a medium.* Mrs Varley said, 'It is not the spirits that now speak, it is myself. I make use of my body the same as spirits do when they speak through me.'

CASE No. 122—Miss 'M.A.B.'

Another case in which a telepathic 'Call' [Statement No. 2] *seems to have occurred* was given by H. F. Prevost Battersby (*Man Outside Himself,* Rider & Co. Ltd.). The lady was given ether. She said, 'I had recently lost a brother, and almost at once I had the idea, "This is what my brother felt like when he died. I won't die, I won't".' She struggled against the effects of the ether, then, 'I heard screaming. *I was up in the air, looking down on the bed over which the nurses and doctor were bending.* I noticed the white crosses on the nurses' backs, where the bands of their uniforms crossed. I heard them say, "Miss B., don't scream; you are frightening the other patients". I was quite apart from my screaming body and unable to stop it. *I said to myself, "If only they would send for 'E'* [a friend, waiting below], *she could stop it". At my thought, that was exactly what they did.* A nurse rushed downstairs and begged "E" to come up. She touched my body, speaking to me. Immediately the screaming ceased. I was physically conscious again.'

CASE No. 123—Mrs E. Hatfield

Mrs Hatfield, a Methodist, wrote (*in litt.*), 'In 1927, I was given ether. *I seemed to float down a dark tunnel* [cf. Mrs Leslie, Mrs Tarsikes, Miss Peters, Miss Yeoman, Miss Stables, Miss Bazett, etc., and Statement No. 9], *moving towards a half-moon of light that was miles away.* I heard the sound of music and smelled the scent as of an old-fashioned bouquet. Then my flight down the tunnel was halted: although there was no obstruction, I could not go further. I staged a rebellion. I wanted to go on. A voice said, "Go back and live." Then I found myself back in the body. *I am convinced that I was dead to this world but wholly alive in another.*'

CASE No. 124—Dr Enid S. Smith

Muldoon and Carrington published this experience, which was also printed in *Psychic News,* July 3, 1954. Dr Smith, Professor of English at Bethel College, was freed from the body by chloroform. 'A radiant angel stood guard at my head,' she said, 'and another at my feet [cf.

Statement No. 3 regarding 'deliverers']. I was free from all pain and limitation. *I tried to tell those who were anxious about me, because my breath, heart and pulse had stopped, that I was out of my body and above it, perfectly natural and safe* [cf. Statement No. 17]. I tried to tell them that I was in no hurry to return. ... Leaving my physical shell lying in the hospital, I took various journeys, guided by spiritual beings. ... There were beautiful vibrant colours, many times more varied and brilliant than our brightest colours. I had seen that kind of beauty and radiance before when at the point of death in a sanatorium. On that occasion also *I had passed out of my body, as I supposed, in death, seeming to sink momentarily into some dark river* [separating the physical from the 'Paradise' world] *that I was crossing* [= the 'earth-veil', 'Denser Between Worlds', 'Hades', etc.—cf. the accounts of Hives, Mme d'Espérance, Mrs Joy, Miss Roos, de la Mare, etc. and those of the supposed dead mentioned in Statement No. 41]. *Were I to die a thousand deaths each would be like the calm, joyous stepping from one room in a happy household to another. ... I am certain that guardian angels will be at my side ...*'

Dr Smith further said, 'Before I returned to my body I visited two friends in Los Angeles, one a renowned artist. Although the artist and his wife, to whom I appeared, did not know that I was undergoing an operation in hospital in New York, *I had awakened and appeared to them in California at exactly the time of my passing out of my body. ...*' (This statement was verified by the friends concerned.)

CASE NO. 125—*Mr M. L. Hymans*

Hymans told Richet the following and he published the account in the *Revue Métapsychique*, 1930. 'I was given chloroform. *I awoke to find myself floating in the air near the ceiling, whence, to my astonishment, I saw the dentist at work on my teeth* [cf. Statement No. 17]. By his side was the anaesthetist. ... I lost consciousness again [while re-entering the body— cf. Statement No. 9] and found myself in the chair, awake and vividly remembering what had occurred.'

CASE NO. 126—*Mr Percy Cole*

The following details are taken from an account of an exteriorization by Mr Cole of N. Balwyn, Melbourne, Australia. Mr Cole is the author of a number of papers on psychology, etc. The full account, which was sent to the present writer *in litt.*, includes evidence that a supposed discarnate Italian lady was what she claimed to be. Mr Cole published some account of this lady in *Light* (Nov. 25, 1937). The case was also reported by Muldoon and Carrington in 1951.

Mr Cole needed to have some teeth extracted. He dreamed that he was warned that he had heart trouble. However, a Dr Costello, who had called to see him on business, arranged to give the anaesthetic.

Meanwhile, Mrs Cole also had a warning dream, though she did not tell her husband about it until after the operation. Mrs Cole dreamed that she saw her husband lying with a towel round his neck. On his cheek was a streak of blood which ran from the corner of the mouth and then at right angles up the cheek. She could not understand how the blood could run up the face. While Mrs Cole lay awake, Mr Cole came from the bathroom saying, 'I will have my teeth out after the holidays.' His wife connected this with her dream and told two members of Mr Cole's staff—this at a later date, but prior to the event itself.

Mr Cole was given the anaesthetic. His further account is as follows. 'The doctor pulled open my eye and said, "He's gone!" but I could see his face and the lamp-shade, so I tried to say, "I'm not gone!" My words, however, were unheard and I let myself go. When I regained consciousness, *I was outside my body, standing behind my own bed* [cf. Statement No. 17]. *My feeling of elation was indescribable.* I was between the doctor and the dentist. They were talking about a house that was for sale and mentioned the price that was asked for it. I looked round the room and found that I was not alone. Other people were there, the nearest to me being the (deceased) Italian lady of whom I had a sketch by the clairvoyant Ronald Bailey and a full description by Mrs Hester Dowden [cf. Statement No. 18].

'The lady said, "We warned you about this, you know," and went on to say that there was some obscure heart trouble. *Then I could see that the doctor had some doubt about my condition. I had stopped breathing. I heard him shout, "Breathe! breathe! Mr Cole!"* Somehow, although I was outside my body, I managed to make my lungs start breathing again. [Cf. the cases of Varley, the army officer and Mrs 'Prothero', who all claimed that, though outside the body, they were able to control it in some way. Note also Mr Coles's observation, given below, with regard to the 'silver cord'.]

'The Italian lady said, "We are just keeping you alive by the vitality drawn from the doctor—we sent him to you." *I could see the doctor's thoughts:* he was afraid I might slip through his fingers. I went round to the other side of my body and saw that the dentist had removed all my teeth except seven in the lower jaw. The doctor pointed to them and said, "What about these?" "He doesn't want them out," answered the dentist. I looked round the room. *The walls were curiously transparent: I could see into the passage, although the door was closed.* Then I saw the table behind my body and, seeing the ether-bottle almost empty, thought, "What a lot they have used." The Italian lady said, "You must go back: you must make a fight for it. Never again have a general anaesthetic."

'*So I turned away from the bright light* [= 'Paradise' conditions] *which shone on my left and entered a gloomy tunnel* [= the Physical Body—this is Statement No. 9 in reverse]. *I fought my way back to a tiny light in the distance* [= 'normal' consciousness in the physical world] *against a stream of shadows which passed all around me* [= 'earth-veil', 'Denser Between Worlds' or 'Hades' conditions—cf. the accounts of Gerhardi, Ogston, de la Mare, Hives, Mme d'Espérance, Mrs Cripps, Mrs Joy, Miss Brooks and Miss Johnson]. *When I got to the light, I found myself in bed.* [This description of *returning*, first to the 'body-veil', and the environment corresponding to it, and then to the Physical Body, and physical world, is identical with the account which Mrs Cripps gave of *shedding* those two 'bodies'.]

'While I was still unconscious my wife had brought a member of the staff to see me, so that he could see that I was lying exactly as she had dreamed. The curious streak of blood, which she had seen in the dream had been caused by my cheek pressing against the pillow. The blood had trickled out of the corner of my mouth and then, when my head had flopped over to the opposite side, the dried blood ran up my cheek at an angle, as she had seen.

'I was too intent watching the little drama being played in the bedroom to make any observations about the psychic cord. [Several others explained their failure to observe the 'silver cord' by the fact that their attention was fully occupied elsewhere. However, some of them felt, if they did not see, the cord. In this connexion, Mr Cole's further observation is interesting.] *I was certainly attached by something, otherwise I could not have made my body breathe when it had stopped.*

'I checked up with the doctor next day, when he rang up to see how I was. He said that what I had heard of the conversation was correct. This was confirmed by the dentist. The latter also made a voluntary statement about the enormous amount of ether they had given me. ... The doctor was a big man, of immense vitality, and I am sure that the end might have been different had I gone to someone else ...'

Case No. 127—*Mr Walter de la Mare*

In his *Behold this Dreamer* (Faber and Faber Ltd., 1939), de la Mare said, 'Only twice have I brought back any clear glimpse of the beyond when under the influence of an anaesthetic: once, of a bare patch of gravel brilliant with sunshine, and again of the shelving sandy banks of *a slow-moving river* [= 'Hades' conditions—cf. Dr Enid Smith, Ogston, Gerhardi, Mrs Joy, Miss Roos, etc. and Statement No. 41]. *The experiences were unusually vivid and appeared to be fragments (as in waking there are many memories) of an impressive experience otherwise lost.* That of the river was suffused with an intense feeling of home-sickness. I grieved at having to come away. The dentist's gas may have accounted for the tears that were on my cheeks, but hardly for my *acute regret at being called back* [cf. Statement No. 8]. *Though it may be merely a deceit of the senses, this coming back certainly suggests a definite journey ...*' [cf. Mrs Wilmot, Mrs Garrett, Hives and Dr van Eeden].

CASE No. 128—*Mr J. A. Symonds*

An account of Symonds's mystical (rather than psychical) states is given on an earlier page. This enforced experience (due to chloroform) was also given in H. F. Brown's biography of Symonds and subsequently in James's *The Varieties of Religious Experience*. *The difference which may occur in the content of consciousness, as between a natural and an enforced exteriorization, is noteworthy.* (It is also shown in the case of Dr Enid Smith.) The fact that this man had mystical states of natural origin suggests that his Higher Mental (or Causal) Body was in relatively loose association with the Psychical Body: hence, when his 'higher bodies' were forced 'out of gear' with the Physical Body, his consciousness operated on a 'plane' that was 'higher' than with average people.

Symonds said, '*I seemed at first in a state of utter blankness* [= shedding the Physical Body, cf. Statement No. 9]. Then came flashes of intense light alternating with blackness, with a keen vision of what was going on in the room around me, but no sensation of touch [= the 'partial awakening'—cf. Statement No. 25]. I thought I was near death. Suddenly my soul became aware of God who was manifestly dealing with me in an intense present personal reality [= the Psychical Body had been shed (= 'third death' or unveiling) and he was conscious in the Higher Mental Body]. *I felt Him streaming like light upon me.* Then, as I gradually awoke from the influence of the anaesthetic, the old sense of my relation to the world began to return and the new sense of my relation to God began to fade [cf. the *kenosis*]. I shrieked, "It is too horrible!" meaning that I could not bear this disillusionment. Then I flung myself on the ground and awoke, calling to the surgeons, "*Why did you not let me die?*" ' [cf. Statement No. 8].

CASE No. 129—'*A Gifted Woman*'

Wm. James published the case of 'a gifted woman' who had been given ether and who had a 'most vivid and real' experience. She said, 'I understood for a moment things that I have now forgotten, things that no one could remember while retaining sanity [cf. de la Mare, Dr Wm. Wilson, Sir Humphry Davy, etc.]. The angle was an obtuse angle. As I awoke I thought that had the Being who had charge of me made it an acute angle, I should have suffered and "seen" still more—

and should probably have died. He went on, however, and I came to. *In that moment the whole of my life passed before me, including each meaningless piece of distress.* I understood then: this was what it had all meant, this was the piece of work it had all been contributing to do.' [The lady's experience during temporary exteriorization corresponds, of course, to the 'Judgment' in the accounts from the supposed dead— cf. Statement No. 34 and remarks under Cases No. 1, 133.]

CASE NO. 130—*Dr Wm. Wilson's observations*

Commenting on 'anaesthetic revelation' in his book *After Life*, Wilson remarked that the similarity in the descriptions of the experience showed '*how identical is the revelation to all. It is not a mere subjective phantasy, as a dream may be, but something very definite.* ... The nature of the "revelation" is such that the failure of verbal expression is comparable to the ludicrous failure of words to describe music itself.'

Dr Wilson was referring particularly to the mystical experiences of more or less 'advanced' people (*e.g.*, Sir Humphry Davy), but he also noted the following case of simple exteriorization from the Physical Body: '*I suddenly had the impression that my Spiritual* [here = Psychical] *Body stood regarding the deserted frame lying on the bed*' [cf. Statement No. 17]. Dr Wilson commented thus: 'Similar externalization of the inner shape seems too commonplace in severe illness, especially when the percipient has been near the borderland of life and death. *It is curious that experiences on the border of death and under anaesthesis should be so similar.*' (The similarity between the two sets of experiences, as described, is not at all curious if, as we maintain, the narratives are closely related to fact. Otherwise, it is inexplicable.)

CASE NO. 131—*Mr Ernest Thompson Seton*

Seton gave his experience in his *Trail of an Artist-Naturalist* (Hodder and Stoughton, 1951). He was given an anaesthetic. He said, 'I was floating among the spheres and other worlds with bright streaming *spirals* that exploded at the end of each wind-up. I knew nothing of time or life.'

CASE NO. 132—*Dr Frederic H. Wood, MUS.DOC.*

Dr Wood described his experiences in *Through the Psychic Door* (Spiritualist Press Ltd., 1954). He quoted communications from the 'dead' to the effect that *many discarnates are 'in a grey, misty land or state* [= 'Hades'] *between the physical earth and the full state of living* [= 'Paradise'], *a kind of half-and-half state, a borderline plane.*' He said that though mortals pass through this state during sleep or under the influence of anaesthetics, the experience is seldom remembered. He himself remembered an experience under ether: '*I recall the soft radiance, pure streams and green foliage which seemed to be more alive than ours*' [= 'Paradise' conditions—cf. Statement No. 26]. In this state Dr Wood met his (deceased) brother [cf. Statement No. 18]. *He was reluctant to return to the Physical Body* [cf. Statement No. 8].

CASE NO. 133—*Miss Beryl Hinton*

Miss Hinton's experience under chloroform was given by J. Arthur Hill (*Man is a Spirit*, Cassell & Co. Ltd., 1918). It is as follows.

'I was above my body [cf. Statement No. 17]. Round it were the doctors, dentist and my mother. I wondered why I was not being judged, since I was obviously dead [cf. Statement No. 11]. *I had been brought up as a strict Roman Catholic and taught that individual judgment follows death. I had never read any psychical books or experiences.* [N.B. The 'gifted woman' who represents our Case No. 129 did experience the 'Judgment', *i.e.*, her 'unveiling' had proceeded further than Miss Hinton's—it had included the denser (emotional) portion of the Psychical Body, whereas Miss Hinton's stopped short at the vehicle of vitality and memory, the 'body-veil'. This difference between what was expected and what was experienced indicates that the experience was not merely due to suggestion. The same conclusion is indicated by the fact that Gerhardi and Miss Yeoman expected to find themselves bodiless and were surprised that they had, in fact, a Psychical Body.]

'I was afterwards told that my condition caused alarm, as I would not regain consciousness. *I have never forgotten that "dream".* Had it been a dream, it would have been coloured by the accepted orthodox idea of what the after-death condition would be. But nothing of the sort. *There was I, above my body, around which were gathered the various people. I could not talk to them* [cf. Statement No. 128]. *I do not doubt that I was out of my body.*

'When given chloroform thirty years later, I was anxious to see if anything of the same sort happened again. But it did not: I had no "dream". So it looks as if the soul *had* lifted from the body on the previous occasion. *That experience has gone further to prove survival to me than all the religious books I have read. It has remained a vivid memory.*'

CASE NO. 134—*Mrs 'X'*

This case was given by H. Prevost Battersby (*Man Outside Himself,* Rider & Co. Ltd.) and by Muldoon (*The Case for Astral Projection*). Mrs 'X' was given ether. She said, 'To my surprise, I found myself standing in company with the doctors and nurses. *I noticed every detail of my surroundings—my Physical Body lying limp on the table, the instruments, bottles, etc.* [cf. Statement No. 17]. After coming round, my body, especially the hands, seemed very heavy. [Others said this, while Miss Kaeyer, etc. gave the converse—they said that *shedding the body was like dropping a heavy load.*] *The experience was very pleasant. If that is how one feels after death, I have no fear of dying.'*

CASE NO. 135—*Mr J. C. Edgerton*

Muldoon (*The Case for Astral Projection*) took this case from J. A. Edgerton's *Invading the Invisible*. His son, given an anaesthetic said, 'My senses suddenly seemed to shift into a body other than the physical. Without mental lapse, I was conscious that I was sitting up and my eyes had X-ray qualities which reduced the Physical Body to a mere shadow. ... *I saw another, brilliantly glistening, body within the shell of the Physical Body* [cf. Statement No. 17]. As I watched this new body (of which I seemed to be a part, and which was more objective to me than my Physical Body had ever been), I slid out of my fleshly envelope with rapidly increasing acceleration. I experienced a soul-shaking wrench that seemed to extend to every cell of my body ... and heard a voice saying, "You are now suffering the pangs of violent death. You are in the hands of friends and everything will be all right" [cf. Statement No. 3 with regard to 'deliverers']. I did not lose consciousness until I was entirely separate from the Physical Body. *This experience convinced me of a future life.'*

CASE NO. 136—*A lady of Dallas (Texas)*

This also was given by Muldoon. It first appeared in *Ghost Stories Magazine.* The lady was given ether. She said, 'I lost consciousness [= shed the Physical Body—cf. Statement No. 9]. Then suddenly I found myself walking up Bryan Street towards my home. I came to our house and went inside. Mother was there. I said, "Mamma, I am so cold!" Then I realized that there were other people present—my baby brother who had died at birth and my grandmother.' (cf. Statement No. 18]. Told to return to her body, she awoke in hospital.

CASE NO. 137—*Mr J. M. Stuart-Young*

This experience, first published in *Two Worlds*, and also in Muldoon's *Case for Astral Projection*, was caused by an overdose of arsenic and quinine. Stuart-Young said, 'I reeled like a drunken man. Deafness, coupled with dimness of sight, gave me the impression that my body did not belong to me. *I thought I was dying, for I seemed to be hovering outside my body.* I thought, "If I see someone whom I know to be dead, I shall realize that I also am dead [cf. Statement No. 31]. I will then break the thread [= the 'silver cord'—cf. Statement No. 19] that holds me to life" [cf. Statement No. 20]. This did not happen. *My confidence in survival has been greatly strengthened by this incident. There was nothing to fear in the act of "passing".*'

CASE No. 138—*Mr B. Landa*

This was published by Muldoon and Carrington (*The Phenomena of Astral Projection*, Rider & Co. Ltd., 1951). Landa had been given an anaesthetic. He felt as if being 'torn apart', after which 'calmness came'. He said, '*Hovering free above my Physical Body, I looked down and saw it on the operating table* [cf. Statement No. 17]. I saw the wound of the operation, etc. Then it vanished. *The experience will never be forgotten.*'

CASE No. 139—*Mrs J. Porter*

Another experience recounted in the same work concerned Mrs Porter. It was originally reported by Prof. Hyslop. Mrs Porter had an anaesthetic. She said, '*I found myself free in the room ... outside my body which was stretched out below me on the bed* [cf. Statement No. 17]. In the room were my sisters and mother. *I had no wish to re-enter my body, but was forced to do so* [cf. Statement No. 8]. The most remarkable thing was this: while hardly awake, I asked, "Where is Mrs 'K'?" Mrs "K", in fact, had not been present when I went to sleep. In answer to a question by my mother, I said, "I saw Mrs 'K' standing there." *The experience made it easy to believe in survival.*'

CASE No. 140—*Mrs D. Parker*

This also was reported by Muldoon and Carrington. Mrs Parker was given gas. She said, 'I found myself passing out of my body, out of the building and out into space. *Soon I encountered a tunnel or passageway, through dark clouds* [= vehicle of vitality or 'body-veil'] *at the end of which I could see light* [cf. Statement No. 9]. *Then I saw my husband who had died the year before* [cf. Statement No. 18]. I was elated but something stopped my advance and drew me backwards. *I felt as if a bag were being pulled down over my head and onwards to my feet.* [This symbol for *re-entering* the body is the reverse of that given independently by others, *e.g.*, Mrs Palmer, for *leaving* the body: some use the identical symbol of a bag, others those of a glove, a skin, a rubber bathing-suit, a coat, a jacket, etc.] *I knew what it meant—that I was rejoining my Physical Body and would awaken when the sensation reached my toes* [cf. other accounts and note that this is the reverse of descriptions of the process of dying]. I heard a voice: "Speak to me! Can't you hear me?" I tried to cry out but in doing so awoke. The dentist said that I had nearly died.'

On another occasion, during anaesthesia, Mrs Parker noted the *spiral* spin of her Psychical Body as it was being forced out of the Physical Body [cf. Rebell, Sculthorp, Hout, Einarsson, Thompson, etc.]. She said, 'It began with a wheel spinning. Then I moved upwards and outwards, through the walls of the place [cf. Statement No. 31]. I thought, "This is death!" '

Case No. 141—*Mr F. Ludlow*

Ludlow (*The Hasheesh Eater*) took the drug called Indian Hemp and found that 'the soul left the physical self'. He said, '*From where I was, hovering in the air, I looked down on my former container*' [cf. Statement No. 17]. Fully conscious and in possession of his faculties, he was yet independent of the Physical Body. He continued, '*I was visible and tangible to myself and yet knew that no physical eye could see me* [cf. Statement No. 28]. *I could go through the walls of the room and return again* [cf. Statement No. 31]. ... Then a voice said, "The time is not yet," and I returned.'

Case No. 142—*Dr Franz Hartmann*

Hartmann's experience under chloroform, first published in *The Occult Review*, 1908, illustrates the fact that, so long as an exteriorized person is within a few feet of his Physical Body, consciousness can alternate between the Physical and Psychical Bodies, giving '*dual*', *or* '*alternate*' *consciousness*, awareness of both this physical world and the 'next'. (This condition is often described by the 'dead' as obtaining during the brief period which *may* intervene between the shedding of the Physical Body and the 'loosening' of the 'silver cord'—cf. Statement No. 18.] Hartmann said that, under the anaesthetic, 'I found myself standing behind the armchair in which my body reclined. *I saw my body and everything about me and heard what was said* [cf. Statement No. 17]. *When I tried to touch the instruments, etc., my fingers passed through them*' [cf. Statement No. 31]. Later, Hartmann noted the transference of consciousness from his Physical to his Psychical Body. He said, 'When in the condition in which the "doubling" [= exteriorizing] happened, the conscious faculties continued to reside in the [Physical] Body [and] I saw my phantom [= 'double' or Psychical Body] in front of me. On the other hand, when the conscious faculties were concentrated in the phantom body, I saw my Physical Body lying on the bed. ... *The facts convinced me that man has an Astral* [here = Psychical] *Body capable of existing independently of the Physical Body.*'

CASE No. 143—*Another Anonymous Lady*

According to an anonymous lady's '*Experiences*' published by J. M. Watkins, 1926, she had a number of typical exteriorizations. *This lady was clearly ignorant of psychic matters.* Her record of her first experience was prefaced thus: 'The following experience is only recorded because years after, the writer read of experiments with a medium in America which confirmed her belief that the idea she had received might be an actual truth'. She continued, 'Under an anaesthetic, she found herself apparently disembodied, in space [= the 'partial awakening'—cf. Statement No. 25]. She was exceedingly happy, scorning the idea of returning to the limitations of earth [cf. Statement No. 8], when *she discovered that she was not wholly free, but was connected to her body by something that looked like a beam of light* [= the 'silver cord'—cf. Statement No. 19] *by which she began to be drawn back to earth* ...' On a second occasion she 'wished very much' to visit a friend in company with her little boy. Being prevented, she went next day instead: but both she and her son had been 'seen' on the previous day and their (quite unusual) garments were accurately described. On a third occasion she heard sounds that she thought ought to be investigated, but was too tired to do this. (In Muldoon's phrase, she had a wish which the 'incapacitated' Physical Body was unable to gratify but which the loosened Psychical Body was able to do). The narrative continued, 'She found herself at the head of the stairs, listening, feeling perfectly normal. *Then she realized, with fear, that she was out of her body, and she returned instantly.*' [Compare, Muldoon, Fox, Lind, Sculthorp, etc., who all found that, while they were out of their physical bodies, emotions caused immediate interiorization. This indicates objective, not subjective, 'doubles'.]

In some of these journeys this lady's critical faculties were operating [cf. Muldoon, Gerhardi, Hives, etc.]. During the war her son went abroad. She 'dreamed' that she entered a club-like building and asked for him. Then she suddenly realized that she could not, in the Physical Body, have made such a journey in so short a time. She made an inspection of the club-like building and its courtyard, awaking convinced that her son was not in the country for which he had sailed. 'In due time the news came that he was held up for some months in another quarter of the world, and in a town whose club offered him hospitality. The club was noted for its pleasant courtyard.'

CASE No. 144—*Mr J. C. Wheeler*

This account was originally published in the *Psychic Observer* and later in Muldoon and Carrington's *Phenomena of Astral Projection*.

Wheeler, almost drowned and pronounced dead, recovered the next day. He said, '*While I was apparently dead, I never was so much alive in my life* [cf. Statement No. 26]. *But I was apart from my body.* I could tell the persons around me everything that had happened when I was enabled to return. ... Being dead is delightful; of that I am sure. After I had been engulfed in the waters, I seemed to float away from my body, and soared above the waters of the lake. *I looked down and could see my body* [cf. Statement No. 17]. I watched the rescuers find it and place it on the bank. Then I floated back to it and became part of it. *Thought of returning to life was repugnant* [cf. Statement No. 8]. Up to the time of that experience I had been an agnostic ... but *I never since have had a shadow of doubt with regard to a spiritual state of existence.*'

CASE No. 145—*Mr G. Costa*

Costa almost died from suffocation. His experience was first published in the book, *Di là della Vita*, and later by his friend Prof. E. Bozzano. *He knew nothing whatever of psychic and kindred matters.*

Costa retired to rest, tired and half fainting, when an accidental movement of his arm upset an oil-lamp. The lamp fell to the floor and continued to burn, giving off volumes of smoke. *Then Costa became conscious he was out of his body and in the middle of the room. He saw not only his Physical Body* [Statement No. 17] but also 'the network of nerves and veins in a state of luminous vibration.' [This is precisely as described, by clairvoyant vision, by A. J. Davis, as well as by D. D. Home while separated from the body.] 'The room itself,' said Costa, 'was almost dark. In spite of this, I noted the objects around me or rather their contours, glowing in phosphorescent luminosity. These gradually melted away as I watched them, and even the walls of the room themselves, so that I found myself able to perceive, in the same manner, the objects in the adjoining apartments' [= clairvoyance].

The body in which he functioned, the Psychical Body, was light and free but it could not affect physical objects [cf. Statement No. 27]. *Fear for his Physical Body* now turned his attention to his mother, who slept in the next room. 'I saw her,' he said, 'through the wall, sleeping tranquilly in her bed.' But her Body, unlike his, emitted a 'phosphorescent radiance'. [This is an evidential feature: 'light', 'phosphorescence', or 'radio-activity', is said to come from the 'double' or Psychical Body when, as in this case, it is at some distance from its physical counterpart. Compare the observations made in connexion with Mrs Leonard's account.] *Costa's intense desire to arouse his mother had the desired effect* [cf. 'the Call'—Statement No. 2]. 'I saw her,' he said, 'hurriedly get out of bed, run to the window, throw it open, then go out of the door into the passage, grope her way to my room and stand over my body. Her contact seemed to make my psychic self re-enter its physical form. I awoke. ....'

b. Caused by Suffocation

CASE NO. 146—*Mrs R. Ivy 'Prothero'*

Mrs 'Prothero' informed me (in litt.) that she had not read any books on this subject before having the experience. It occurred in 1926, some years before Muldoon published his account.

'One night, being very cold, I snuggled down in bed, tucked the clothes well in and covered my head to warm up with my breath. I fell asleep and was almost suffocated. *I found myself out of my body, suspended horizontally above the bed. I was attached by a cord* [cf. Statement No. 19], *much the same as a barrage balloon in the war* [cf. Bertrand, Lind, Gerhardi, Helen Brooks, etc.]. *I looked down on the figure on the bed* [cf. Statement No. 17]. I realized what was happening and thought, "I must get my arms out and get some air." Then I made a more vigorous effort. As I saw my hands appearing, I slipped back into my body, gasping for breath. It was not a dream. *It was extremely pleasant and I was not afraid* [cf. Statement No. 7]. *The experience convinced me that I have a soul as well as a body.'*

CASE NO. 147—*The Hotel Guest*

Wm. Oliver Stevens gave this case in his *Unbidden Guests* (George Allen & Unwin, Ltd., 1949). A lady-guest in an hotel was almost asphyxiated by a defective gas-jet. While unconscious, she felt herself leave her body and immediately found herself in her husband's bed-room, at home, many miles distant from the hotel. A man, a friend and neighbour, was asleep in the same room as her husband. Leaning against the head of the bed was a stout cudgel which had some bark still attached. The room itself was in great disorder. She stroked her husband's face and tried to awaken his friend. But she remained unobserved by them [cf. Statement No. 31]. Then she thought, 'I must get back to my body.' With that, she found herself where her body was in the hotel. *After a 'blank space'* [= the momentary coma while re-entering the Physical Body, *i.e.*, Statement No. 9 in reverse] *she recovered consciousness.*

The doctor told her that she had been given up as dead. She described her experience. The doctor checked up with the story and every detail was verified. It turned out that her husband's friend had come to spend the evening at the house. During his visit a rat ran across the floor. They hunted it with a club which had part of the bark on. They upset furniture in doing so. The friend stayed the night, the club being left handy in case the rat returned during the night.

c. Caused by Falling

CASE NO. 148—*Mr F. S. Smythe*

Smythe, the distinguished mountaineer, described an experience when he fell over a precipice (*The Spirit of the Hills*, Hodder and Stoughton Ltd., 1937). The rope held when he had fallen some twenty feet. He said, 'When I heard Robert shout, my body instinctively braced itself to receive a shock. Half of my brain must have known subconsciously that twenty feet of rope separated me from the belay ... the other half told me that I was certain to be killed. ... *A curious rigidity gripped my whole being* [= catalepsy]. ... *It swamped all pain and fear* [cf. Statement No. 7] *and rendered me insensible to bumps and blows* [cf. Georginus and Morrell cases]. It was as though I were undergoing the change called death. ...

'For how long I experienced this I cannot say. Time no longer existed as time. *Then suddenly this feeling was superseded by one of complete indifference and detachment ... I seemed to stand aside from my body. I was not falling, for the reason that I was not in a dimension where it was possible to fall. I, that is, my consciousness, was apart from my body, and not in the least concerned with what was befalling it. ... Had the tenant already departed, in anticipation of the wreck that was to follow?* [cf. Statement No. 6]. *The experience convinced me that consciousness survives the grave.*'

CASE NO. 149—*Lt. C. F. Callan*

Lt. Callan, of Hillford rd., Liverpool, described (*Liverpool Echo*, June 9, 1954) an enforced exteriorization that occurred when he was injured by a motor-car. He said, 'I saw myself leave my body and go slowly upwards. *I hovered about four feet above my body* [cf. Statement No. 16]. *I could see it lying on the ground* [cf. Statement No. 17]. I became scared and suddenly felt myself coming down again [Muldoon, Lind, Sculthorp, Varley, etc. all found that strong emotion, such as fear, caused re-interiorization]. *I felt content.*' [Callan was *not* reluctant to return to physical life. Whereas many who exteriorized naturally (and typically into 'Paradise' conditions) were reluctant to return to earth, only two (Mrs Porter and de la Mare) whose exteriorization was enforced (and who either remained on earth or did not get beyond 'Hades' conditions) said this. Two other 'enforced' cases (Dr Wood and Symonds) mentioned reluctance to return and these entered conditions higher than those of 'Hades'—Dr Wood 'Paradise' and Symonds 'Heaven' conditions.] Callan's account ended, '*I had a creepy sensation as I re-entered the body.* I opened my eyes to find myself in hospital.'

CASE NO. 150—*An Officer*

This officer published his experience in *Journ. S.P.R.* xxxiv, 1948. In August, 1944, his car received a direct hit from an anti-tank gun and he was thrown a distance of twenty feet. His further statement is given below.

'I was conscious of being two persons—one lying on the ground, on fire, waving my limbs about wildly and gibbering with fear—I was conscious of both making these sounds and at the same time hearing them as though coming from another person.

'*The other "me" was floating up in the air, about twenty feet from the ground, from which position I could see not only my other self on the ground* [cf. Statement No. 17], *but also the hedge, the road and the burning car. I told myself, "It's no use gibbering: roll over and over to put the flames out." This my ground-body did. The flames went out and I suddenly became one person again ...*'

CASE NO. 151—*A Soldier*

G. B. Crabbe gave the experience of a soldier (cited by J. Arthur Hill in his *Man Is a Spirit*) who was blown up in an explosion, as follows: 'He said that *he was up in the air, looking down at his own body which lay on the ground at some distance from him* [cf. Statement No. 17]. *He seemed to be yet connected with the body by a slender cord of clear silvery appearance* [cf. Statement No. 19]. While he looked on, two surgeons came by, and, after looking at the body, remarked that he was dead. ... Stretcher bearers came along and carried him to the rear.' He continued, '*I came down that silver cord and returned to the old body.*' [*Exactly the same phrase was used by Mrs Piper in U.S.A. when returning to her Physical Body after being exteriorized from it in trance.* An objective 'double' is clearly indicated.]

CASE NO. 152—'*Bill*'

In his Autobiography (*World Within World*, 1951), Stephen Spender mentioned a man named Bill. The latter received an injury and nearly died. Spender described how Bill very seriously told how he had 'felt his soul leave his body'. He said 'that it had hovered about the ceiling, floated to a corner of the room, and then returned to his body.'

(2) ACCOUNTS BY OTHERS

a. Caused by Anaesthetics, etc.

CASE NO. 153—Dr R. B. Hout

COMPLEMENTARY to first-hand descriptions of out-of-the-body experiences are accounts by doctors, nurses, etc. who have seen exteriorizations of patients. The latter described the same features as those given by the patients themselves. Moreover, both agree with the narratives of clairvoyants who have recorded their observations of the process of dying. Finally, all three independent sets of accounts agree with a fourth set, namely, the statements of the supposed dead (Appendix V).

A typical case, by Dr Hout, originally appeared in *Prediction* (June, 1936). It was also cited in Muldoon and Carrington's *The Phenomena of Astral Projection.*

Hout, in a hospital, saw three patients who, under anaesthetics, were exteriorized from the Physical Body. He said, 'I became aware of this when the first patient was wheeled into the operating room, partially under the influence of the anaesthetic. *Above, and near the patient, who lay swathed in sterile sheets on the cart, there hovered in mid-air a vague misty outline, having the general contour of the human body. ... I saw the Spirit-body of the patient floating free in space above the operating table.* It rested inert. ... As the Physical Body became more relaxed the freedom of the Spirit-body became greater. ... Now I could see the outlines more clearly. *The patient was an elderly lady, as I could see from the features presented by the spirit-face* [cf. Mrs Garrett's use of her own 'double', or 'Spirit-body', in place of a mirror, another observation which indicates its objectivity]. ... At the end of the operation the Spirit-body came close to the physical but had not yet re-entered it when the patient was wheeled away. ...'

Hout said that in the case of each of these three patients, '*I saw the astral cord that united the Spirit-body with the physical* [cf. Statement No. 19]. *This appeared as a silvery shaft of light.* [Note that Mrs Cripps also described the 'silver cord' as 'like a shaft of sunlight']. It wound around through the room much as a curl of smoke drifts indifferently in still air. *When the magnetic force drew the spirit close to the Physical Body, this cord was more apparent, as though more concentrated. At other times it could not be seen.*' ... [This description of the 'cord' as relatively thick and easily seen when the 'double' was near the Physical Body and as thin when the 'double' was at some distance from the body agrees with

134

those given independently by Muldoon, Fox and Bulford. The fact that the 'cord' was so thin as to be invisible when the Psychical and Physical Bodies were far apart is one of the factors that accounts for some who described having out-of-the-body experiences not mentioning that feature. Other factors, already noted, are that the exteriorized person may not turn round, and so may fail to see the 'cord'. Again, the attention may be so fully occupied with making other observations that this inconspicuous feature may be overlooked.] It is also note-- worthy that statements about the 'cord' similar to those of Hout, etc. are given by supposed discarnates [Appendix V, Statements No. 1b, 19-21]. Hout further said, 'Besides the earthly doctors, other persons, working in the invisible, looked on ...' [cf. Statements No. 3 and 18].

b. Caused by Hypnosis

The same stages, or levels, of consciousness that are recognizable in communications from the 'dead' are found in those of psychics, those of mystics, those who claim to have had out-of-the-body experiences and those who have been subjected to hypnosis: they are 'sub-normal' (or dream) consciousness, 'super-normal' consciousness (with telepathic, clairvoyant, and pre-cognitive abilities) and 'mystical', 'cosmic' or 'spiritual' consciousness (beyond time, space and form of any kind and involving a sense of identity of the observer with the observed).

i. In Ancient Times

We have already noted that out-of-the-body experiences were regarded as genuine from early times in Tibet and China. The same applies to Egypt. Anna Maria Roos (*The Possibility of Miracles*, Rider & Co. Ltd.) referred to a work of the second century that contains references to such experiences in trance-states ('somnambulism'). The philosopher Apuleius went to be initiated into the Mysteries of Isis, the ancient Egyptian deity. The preparations included fasting (a procedure which tends to cause exteriorization). On returning to 'normal', or physical, consciousness he said, '*Approaching the borderland of death, I stepped over the threshold and was conducted through the "elements". Although it was midnight, the light was brilliant. I stepped into the presence of the gods* [= spirits] *of the underworld* [= 'Hades'] *and the gods* [= spirits] *of the upper world*' [= 'Paradise'].

Similarly, Miss Roos found that, when questioned about their experiences during deep trance, the answers given by 'somnambulists' may be summed up as follows. '*First, during the actual passing over, there is a region of darkness through which the soul must pass* [= the momentary coma during the shedding of the Physical Body—cf. the accounts of Funk's friend, Hives, 'M.D.', etc. and Statement No. 9], *then a roaring river which has to be crossed, i.e., the element of WATER* [= 'Hades'— cf. the accounts of Dr Smith, Ogston, Gerhardi, Mrs Joy, de la Mare, etc. and Statement No. 41], *a brilliant light eventually encircles the soul, i.e., the "brilliant light" of Apuleius, the element of FIRE* [= 'Paradise'— cf. the accounts of Gerhardi, Dr Funk's friend, Banks, Mme d'Espér- ance, etc.]: *through the AIR they seem to float, leaving the EARTH beneath their feet'* [cf. Statement No. 26].

'*Thus,*' said Miss Roos, '*the aim of the Mysteries was a state of trance in which the aspirant saw into another world.*' [In other words, with the exteriorization of the Psychical Body from the physical, 'normal' consciousness (of the physical world) was replaced by a brief, 'sub- normal' consciousness and that by 'super-normal' consciousness in 'Paradise' conditions.] Miss Roos concluded, '*We understand why the initiated affirm their certainty of a life after death, a certainty which nothing could ever shake. All who have had any experience of deep somnambulism* [= 'super-consciousness' during 'trance'] *are certain that what they saw was real and no dream or vision.*' This conclusion accords not only with that of so many who claim to have had out-of-the-body experiences but also with the observation of Deleuze that, 'No somnambulist is materialistic or atheistical', with that of Victor Hugo, who said, 'There are no atheistical spirits' and with that of Freud who noted that the 'Unconsciousness' (*sic*) of every person is convinced of immortality. All our doubts about survival and immortality come from our 'intel- lect' or 'reason', from the limited 'normal' consciousness: they are examples of the operation of the *kenosis*. 'We feel that we are greater than we know.'

A claim similar to the above was made by Edward G. Collinge (*Life's Hidden Secrets*, Rider & Co. Ltd., 1952). Collinge maintained that the object of initiation by the Priests of Osiris (husband of Isis) was 'the exteriorization of the subject in the Astral [here = Psychical] Body in full consciousness, so that he passed through the gates of [physical] death.' The methods included hypnosis, rituals and ceremonies. Collinge added, 'Certain experiences in the astral sub-planes would follow, and certain 'tests' of the candidates' courage and control would take place [cf. the 'Temptation'—Matt. iv, 1-2]. Memory of these experiences would remain with the neophyte for the rest of his life, affecting his conduct and outlook from thenceforth. He would know, from personal experience, that death was only a gateway. *The motive of initiation was proof, instead of blind faith, proof at the first Initiation being the evidence of survival, the existence of the Astral* [here = Psychical] *Body and of astral* [here = 'Paradise'] *conditions.*'

ii. *In More Recent Times*

According to Dr Nandor Fodor [*Encyclopedia of Psychic Science,* Arthurs Press, Ltd., 1933) the first-known instance of apparent travelling during magnetic trance was recorded in a letter written to the Marquis de Pujsegur in 1785 from Nantes: a girl was able to 'follow' her 'magnetizer' into the town and correctly to describe what was transpiring there. Similar cases were reported from Germany at about that date. The first claims of this nature to be the subject of serious investigation were French—those of Adolphe Didier and Adèle Maginot. President Seguier called upon the first-named without disclosing his identity: Didier 'visited' the President's room, describing a bell on the table. Although Seguier rejected this description as incorrect, it turned out that a bell had, in fact, been placed there without his knowledge. The two Didier brothers were subjected to experiments in England, accounts being given in Dr Edwin Lee's *Animal Magnetism.* Alphonse was investigated by H. G. Atkinson. Adèle Maginot's 'journeys' were recorded by Cahagnet (whose lost relative she found). While 'travelling' in the tropics, Adèle asked to be awakened since she feared the wild beasts which she 'saw' (cf. the effect of fear in causing the re-interiorization of those who claimed to leave their bodies naturally). In one instance this lady is said to have suffered actual physical injury through an 'astral' journey. She (in the 'astral' body) had 'sunstroke' which turned one side of her (physical) face a bluish-red, the effect being visible for 24 hours. (*This later observation, which resembles that of 'Yram', is important if true, since it is usually difficult, if indeed possible, to decide whether 'visits' and 'journeys' like these are pure clairvoyance and/or telepathy (apart from any question of a 'double') or are genuine experiences and journeys in an exteriorized Psychical Body, or 'double'. In many cases it is impossible to say, but the effect noted above is clearly a 'repercussion' such as occurs in 'materializations' (and consequently is to be noted in certain cases of 'witchcraft'), the stimulus that is applied to the 'double' (probably in such cases a particularly dense and near-physical one) being transmitted (presumably by way of the 'silver cord') to the Physical Body.* It may be said that Mme d'Espérance received physical injuries when 'Yoland', a 'materialization' of hers, was seized by a man at a seance. Again, according to statements of the supposed dead, in some cases there is a brief period between the shedding of the Physical Body and the 'loosening' of the 'silver cord', in which cases injury done to the Physical Body may, in some measure, be felt by the survivor, since impressions are carried in both directions by the 'silver cord'. (Hence, they warn against cremation, etc. until the onset of decomposition indicates that the 'cord' is severed.) If the latter is true it is, of course, the converse of what was said to occur in the case of Adèle Maginot and in certain cases of witch-craft. *Our present point is that Adèle's experience strongly suggests that she did, in fact, exteriorize a 'double' in which she made 'journeys' and by means of which she made observations. It was an objective 'double'.*

iii. *In Modern Times*

The chief experimenters in the exteriorization of the 'double' during hypnosis in recent times have been Dr Baraduc, Col. Albert de Rochas (*Ann. Psychical Science*, 1905), Charles Lancelin, Hector Durville, Dr Alex Erskine and Stavely Bulford. Examples of the phenomena given in Erskine's *Hypnotist's Case Book* (Rider & Co. Ltd.) are often cited in books on psychic subjects. Durville (*Le Fantôme des Vivants*) described the 'silver cord'. *According to him* (*as according to the 'dead', to clairvoyants, to those who have out-of-the-body experiences, Yogins, etc.*), *the 'cord' conveys impressions in both directions and vitality in one. Like them, also, he described it as usually cylindrical but sometimes ribbon-like. He experimented with the 'doubles' of two subjects separated from their Physical Bodies.* He also placed screens coated with calcium sulphide at some distance from the subject and told the subject exteriorized in the 'double' to approach first one and then another screen: the appropriate screen glowed with extra brilliance, suggesting the proximity of an invisible, yet radio-active, non-physical body. Like Fox and Muldoon, he also claimed that, in some cases, it was possible to move physical objects and cause raps, that is, to produce 'semi-physical' or telekinetic, phenomena similar to those that are said to occur at seances in the presence of 'physical' mediums. Durville claimed that he had demon-strated experimentally the separation of the 'double' from the Physical Body. He considered that the vital force is independent of physical matter and that man consists of (a) the Physical Body, (b) the soul, personality or intelligence [which uses the Psychical Body] and (c) a vital link between them, namely, the 'double' or 'astral body' [here = vehicle of vitality = 'body-veil']. Finally, he expressed the view that, since the 'double' can exist and function independently of the Physical Body, there is reason to believe it survives the death of the Physical Body.

Lancelin (*Méthode de Déboulement Personnel des Vivants*) concluded that the separation of the 'double' from the Physical Body was essen-tially a separation from the Physical Body of nervous force and 'sensi-bility'. It occurred most easily among men of nervous temperament and the best conditions were found among men who were physically robust, emotionally calm and mentally clear and determined.

Recent experiments in the exteriorization of the 'double', made in the United States, are described in Stewart Edward White's books

(*The Betty Book*, Psychic Press Ltd. and *The Road I Know*, Robert Hale, Ltd.). White calls the 'double', or Psychical Body, the 'Beta Body'. *He describes himself and his co-experimenters as 'singularly innocent of organized research'. Nevertheless, their results are the same as the systematic French investigators mentioned above.* Vouching for the accuracy of his descriptions, White says, 'the reader is at liberty to question anything but the absolute and entire good faith of the experimenters'. *When 'Betty', their subject, returned from an exteriorization she said it was with 'a peevish kind of resentment'* [cf. Statement No. 8]. The route which her 'Beta Body' took in the course of returning was *'oblique'*—she said, 'I am coming down like a leaf—zig-zag' [cf. Rebell, Sculthorp, Hout, Einarsson, Thompson, Mrs Parker, etc.].

Professor Hornell Hart (*Tomorrow*, vol. ii) cited three well-authenticated cases of 'extra-sensory travel' produced by hypnosis. Baron von Rosen hypnotized Alma Radberg, Reid hypnotized John Park and Cornillier hypnotized 'Reine'. In each case the subject was sent on a 'journey' and veridical information obtained which could not have come through the physical senses. Although, however, these hypnotized persons *may* obtain the supernormal information by the use of a 'double' which was exteriorized from the Physical Body, no evidence is adduced that this was the fact: their results, like those of Erskine's subjects, might have been obtained *either* by the use of a 'double' *or* by purely telepathic and/or clairvoyant processes. Since the possibility of the latter is generally conceded, additional evidence must be adduced for these cases to be interpreted as exteriorizations of 'doubles'. Such additional evidence includes 'repercussions', as in the Maginot case. Similarly, it is suggested in the case of 'Jane' (whose 'travels'—described in *Proc. S.P.R.*, vii—enabled her to bring back veridical information). She showed great dislike, when exteriorized, to being among crowds, having the impression of being jostled. This, however, like the fear of falling, might result from habitual thought, from experience in physical life. The indirect evidence, given in the above pages, seems inexplicable unless man is, as claimed, equipped with a 'double' consisting of a series of several non-physical bodies which can, on occasion, be 'exteriorized' from, or thrown 'out of gear' with, the Physical Body. The fact that the statements made by those who are supposed to have left their bodies permanently are identical with the depositions made by those who claim to leave them temporarily leaves little, if any, doubt that both are substantially true.

Conclusions

MEN and women of many, perhaps of most, nationalities and of all stages of culture, throughout human history, have claimed to have out-of-the-body experiences. The fact that so many people independently give identical accounts—especially in connexion with shedding the Physical Body and re-entering it—indicates that *these are not mere dreams but actual experiences in a non-physical body, an objective double of the Physical Body.*

While there are all gradations between people who have 'died', those who nearly died, the very ill, people who are merely exhausted and those who are quite well, representatives of all five groups describe one and the same succession of experiences as having followed the shedding of the Physical Body. (*Our analyses show that the supposed dead and people who claimed temporarily to have left their Physical Bodies had the same experiences, the same 'levels' of consciousness, the same bodily constitution and the same series of environments, or conditions.*)

Four out of every five of our cases of temporary exteriorization concern people who were not ill or troubled in any way but who, on the contrary, were normal and well. This proportion is the more remarkable in view of the fact that illness and pain are among the causes of exteriorization. *It is therefore evident that leaving the Physical Body is a natural, and not an abnormal, process.* (Correlated with this conclusion is the Statement [No. 7], made by the 'dead', that survival of bodily death is natural, automatic and universal and is independent of religious beliefs, etc.)

According to communications from the 'dead', those who died (*i.e.,* shed their bodies *permanently*) in the *natural* course of events, typically awoke in '*Paradise*' conditions (feeling 'alive', 'alert', 'secure', 'peaceful', 'happy', etc. in an environment which, though 'earth-like', was more beautiful, and with 'super-normal' consciousness—including telepathic, clairvoyant and precognitive experiences). On the other hand, those whose transition was *enforced in the prime of life* were typically first aware of *earth or 'Hades'* conditions (in the latter case feeling 'confused' and 'bewildered' in an environment which was more or less enshrouded, sometimes 'misty' or 'foggy', with 'sub-normal', or dream consciousness). According to the independent testimony of people who left their bodies *temporarily*, those who did so *naturally* similarly typically entered '*Paradise*' conditions, while those whose exteriorization was *enforced* were typically at first aware of *earth or 'Hades'* conditions.

This agreement, observable in numerous independent accounts, points to the conclusion that both sets of narratives describe genuine experiences.

Many statements, made in numerous independent communications from the 'dead', seem to be quite unbelievable—until they are considered in the light of the whole basic philosophy advanced. One of these is that our 'dead' loved ones (who seem to be 'lost', 'departed', etc.) are actually 'nearer' to us than when they were beside us in the flesh—that the Physical Body, had to some extent, 'veiled' them from our deeper sight. This statement is understandable in view of the after-death bodily constitution that is described. It is, moreover, supported by a number of the narratives of temporary exteriorization cited above: Lord Geddes's doctor-friend was aware of the thoughts, unexpressed in words, of those around him, etc. A second almost incredible statement, commonly made in communications from the 'dead', is that many people do not at first realize that they have died, *i.e.*, that they have permanently shed the body. This also is supported by accounts of temporary exteriorizations—many (like the 'dead') said that, at first, they thought they were still in physical embodiment and only later found that they possessed a non-physical body, a 'double' of the body of flesh. Again, those of the 'dead' who had been brought back, by injections, etc., from the gates of death, so far from expressing pleasure and gratitude, were most reluctant to return to physical life: one man 'damned!' his well-intentioned doctor. In view of the tenacity with which we all —young and old—cling to physical life, this statement in communications seems incredible. Yet it is supported by the fact that many who temporarily left their bodies also expressed reluctance to return to them. *Both the communications from those who left their bodies permanently and the testimonies of those who left them temporarily contain apparently unbelievable statements which, nevertheless, are quite understandable in a wider context.*

In *permanent* exteriorization (*i.e.*, death), *all* the vehicle of vitality, or 'body-veil', is said to leave the Physical Body along with the Psychical, or Soul, Body: (a) a man who dies *naturally* in old age tends to be mentally fatigued and tends to 'sleep' (and dream) until (after an average period of three to four days) the enshrouding vehicle of vitality is shed from the Soul Body—then he 'awakens' in 'Paradise' conditions; (b) a man whose death is *enforced* tends to be awake at the time but, though awake, his Soul Body also is enshrouded by the vehicle of vitality—hence he has *either* only 'normal' consciousness and contacts the earth environment, *or* 'sub-normal' (dream) consciousness in 'Hades' conditions (depending on how long the 'silver cord', uniting him to his Physical Body, remains 'unloosed'). Once the 'silver cord' is severed and the 'body-veil' shed, he is in the same state as a person whose transition occurred naturally.

We suggest that in those *temporary* exteriorizations which occur *naturally* only a little of the vehicle of vitality, or 'body-veil', goes out with the Psychical, or Soul, Body. Nevertheless, this 'little' is important, since it prevents any 'living' person from entering into the full 'super-normal' consciousness and 'Paradise' conditions of the natural after-death state—see the cases of Kelly, Mrs Leonard, Gerhardi, Dr R. B. Hout, etc.

We suggest that in those *temporary* exteriorizations which are *enforced*, much of the 'body-veil' is ejected from the body and it more or less effectively enshrouds the Psychical, or Soul, Body. Hence, those who are forced out of their bodies by anaesthetics, etc. typically *either* remain in earth *or* enter 'Hades' (dream) conditions. The interpretation indicated above agrees with what is described in our Case Histories and with the general underlying proposition, implicit in psychic communications, to the effect that the various states of consciousness (namely, 'normal', 'sub-normal', 'super-normal' and 'Spiritual') and the various environments or conditions contacted ('earth', 'Hades', 'Paradise' and the true 'Heavens', or Nirvana, respectively) are determined by the bodily constitution at the time (See Table, p. 228).

Certain apparently exceptional cases must be considered. There are a few people who, on leaving the Physical Body naturally, experienced 'Hades' conditions before entering the typical 'Paradise' state. This was doubtless due to the fact that, with them, the vehicle of vitality, or 'body-veil', was in loose association with the Physical Body. In several such cases (*e.g.*, that of Mme d'Espérance) there is independent evidence of a relatively 'loose' vehicle of vitality. Conversely, there are a few people who, on being forced out of the body, contacted 'Paradise' conditions: with these there is usually independent evidence that the Psychical, or Soul, Body was relatively loosely associated with the Physical Body. Thus the apparent exceptions to our generalization (that natural exteriorization typically brings 'super-normal' consciousness in 'Paradise' conditions, while enforced exteriorization typically brings either 'normal' or 'sub-normal' consciousness and either earth or 'Hades' conditions) are comprehensible. The few exceptions 'prove' the rule to be a valid one.

Finally—and this represents an important corroboration of our generalization—we have found *six cases in which one and the same person, on different occasions, underwent both natural and enforced 'projections'*. When Dr Enid Smith's 'double' left the body naturally she entered 'Paradise' conditions; when forced out, she merely experienced 'sinking momentarily into some dark river' (*i.e.*, entering 'Hades' conditions). Lilla Lavender, George Sandwith and Louis Henderson (whose cases will be included in a forthcoming book by the present writer) entered 'Paradise' conditions when they went out naturally and

'Hades' when ejected. Symonds had a 'higher' (a 'mystical', 'spiritual' or 'cosmic') experience when he left the body naturally than when forced out. No one claimed to attain 'higher' conditions when forced out of the body than when they left it naturally. One, namely, Varley saw the earth environment only under both conditions of exteriorization. *Thus, five of the six available cases afford positive support for our interpretation, while the sixth is not antagonistic but neutral.*

Other authors have tried to prove the reality of 'astral projection' on the evidence that the 'double' was undoubtedly seen at some place distant from its physical counterpart and that the person concerned had acquired super-normal knowledge of the place which his 'double' visited. Still others rely on the experimental production of the phenomena. The present writer, however, does not think that such evidence will ever prove the case—it might (or might not) indicate telepathy and/or clairvoyance, whereas we have to demonstrate (in addition) the presence of *an objective double, a non-physical body, an 'astral body'*. Even if a double is seen collectively, is photographed, performs some physical act, such as breaking a glass, it does not necessarily follow that the phenomena are inevitably due to an *objective* double—a 'materialized' 'thought-form', or mental image, could presumably produce these effects. Like survival, astral projection is undoubtedly true but exceedingly difficult to prove. Indirect, rather than direct, evidence provides the basis of proof. It should be remembered that the atom (in spite of its name) was splittable from the dawn of creation, yet it is only in recent years that the fact has been demonstrated.

Features in accounts that indicate a 'double' that is objective in nature (and not a mere body-image) include: (1) the characteristic sensations when it leaves (and re-enters) the body; (2) the presence of the extension which is likened to a 'silver cord'; (3) repercussion-effects; (4) the characteristic differences, brought out above, between exteriorizations that took place *naturally* and those that were *enforced*. People who interpret *all* 'doubles' as mental images cannot explain these features: we who interpret *some* as objective 'astral bodies' have no difficulty in doing so. We therefore invoke the principle of economy of hypothesis. Nevertheless, in many individual cases it is impossible, on account of the lack of such features in the descriptions, definitely to decide as between a subjective and imaginary 'double', i.e., a mere mental image, and an objective and 'real' double, i.e., an 'astral *body*'. But the main case, namely, the existence of true astral projection, seems to be established beyond reasonable doubt.

Astral projection assures us of survival and indicates the mechanism involved in the process. It also provides definite information, though of a general nature, as to the conditions and environments of the successive after-death states. It points to still 'higher' experiences, those called 'Spiritual'. The information obtained accords with that revealed in our Scriptures, but it is fuller, more coherent and it is independent of authority. *In view of these studies, we are, in an increasing measure, 'ready to give a REASON of the HOPE that is in us'* (I Peter iii, 15).

'Are we returning, therefore, to doctrines enunciated 7,000 years ago? Yes and No. Yes, in the sense that the ancients knew more about these things than is generally supposed. No, in the sense that present scientific methods have brought practical confirmation and the beginning of an explanation.'—Prof. C. Flammarion, 1923.

'By annihilating the necessities of the body we may loosen the bonds of the Spirit and enable it to manifest some of its inherent endowments. Ascetics and saints have frequently done this voluntarily, and disease or a peculiar constitution sometimes do it for us involuntarily. While it is undesirable that we should seek to produce such a state, it is extremely desirable that we should avail ourselves of the instruction to be gained by the knowledge that such phenomena exist and that thereby our connexion with the Spiritual World may become a demonstrated fact.'—Catherine Crowe, 1848.

Appendix I

HISTORY OF THE SUBJECT

A. Early Accounts of Experiences

ASTRAL projections have been described in Egypt, India, China and Tibet from pre-historic times. In Tibet the phenomena were so frequent that those who produced them were given a special name—*delogs*—meaning 'those who return from the Beyond'.

St Paul tells us that he experienced something in the nature of an astral projection, while Philip, 'caught away' from Gaza, 'was found at Azotus' (Acts viii, 39). The latter event must have occurred a few years before A.D. 60. The Initiations into the Mysteries clearly included the deliberate production of astral projection (with specially selected and specially prepared candidates). Yet de Vesme suggested that Initiations contained 'no secret'. Plato's 'Vision of Er' and Plutarch's 'Vision of Aridæus' (the latter written about A.D. 79) describe only partially satisfactory projections—by men who had not undergone initiation. That of Aridæus was the result of a fall. Sopater of Apamena mentioned a man who, having seen the 'Mysteries' in a 'dream', had to be initiated in order to ensure secrecy. This statement is highly significant.

The famous 'dream' of King Gontran (A.D. 561–592), of Burgundy, was obviously a projection.

In 1726, Thomas Say, the well-known Quaker Minister, had an out-of-the-body experience which was described in *The Life and Writings of Thomas Say* (Philadelphia, 1796) and subsequently quoted by Dr J. W. Graham (*Psychical Experiences of Quaker Ministers*, Friends' Historical Society, 1933). Graham also cited Sarah Birkbeck's experience in 1840.

Experiences similar to those described in this book are not only said, by the Roman Catholic Church, to have occurred to many Catholic 'Saints', but are claimed to be better attested than those of modern psychical research. It is said, for example, that, in the thirteenth century, St Anthony of Padua, while preaching in Limoges, suddenly remembered that he had undertaken to conduct a service in a monastery at the other end of the town. He drew his hood over his head and knelt in apparent prayer while the congregation reverently waited. At that moment the Saint was said to have been seen by the assembled monks to appear and heard to read the appointed passage in the Office. He then disappeared. Similar statements are made concerning St Severns of Ravenna, St Ambrose and St Clement of Rome. In 1774, Alphonse de Lignori, imprisoned at Arezzo, fasted for five days and, on awakening on the morning that ended the fast, stated that he had been present at the death-bed of Pope Clement XIV. Those present at the bedside of the dying Pope are said to have confirmed his statement, declaring that they had seen him.

While some claim that psychical and mystical experiences are essentially distinct from each other, others hold that they are basically similar, depending upon the exteriorization of the 'soul' from the body. It was a primitive belief in Germany and many other countries that when a person goes to sleep, the 'soul' (or 'soul-body') leaves by way of the mouth and that failure to return would mean death. As with the ancient Egyptians, since the soul-body is independent of gravity and can 'fly', it was conceived as a bird. (A puny, weak and ineffectual soul was symbolized as a mouse.) Now supposed discarnate communicators say that the soul-body leaves the Physical Body temporarily in sleep and permanently at death, usually leaving chiefly by the head and all the pores, but that when, in violent death, it is suddenly forced to go, it leaves by the largest 'pore', namely, the mouth. The aborigines of Australia, the Eskimos, Arabs, Zulus and many others held the same doctrines about a 'soul-body' and its exteriorization from the Physical Body, temporarily during sleep, permanently at death. Anna Robeson Burr (*Religious Confessions and Confessants*) is quoted by Mr Walter de la Mare *Behold the Dreamer* (Faber & Faber Ltd., 1939) as follows: 'The early mystic is impregnated with this conviction of a wandering soul; it underlies his experience; it is the real basis of his belief in mysticism. If we turn to the great passages upon which mysticism is founded, what do we find? Richard of St Victor's famous statement is, on close analysis, seen to be only this—that he believes his soul could be "away". Augustin's reliance is, after all, but upon that great "if" the soul might be "away". The texts cited by Dante serve to show his appreciation of the fact that the soul can be "away". "It seems to the ecstatic," writes Teresa, "that he is transported to a region wholly different from that where we find ourselves ordinarily." The frequent failure of the mystic to remember details of the "wholly different region", and his inability to describe the experience except by means of symbols, are readily explained and need not be regarded as indicating that both "region" and consciousness of it were imaginary.'

The conclusion of Mr G. C. Barnard (*The Superphysical*, Rider & Co. Ltd., 1953), Dr R. C. Johnson (*The Imprisoned Splendour*, Hodder & Stoughton, Ltd., 1953) and Prof. C. D. Broad (*The Mind and its Place in Nature*, Kegan Paul, Trench, Trübner & Co. Ltd., 1923) that mystical experiences contain elements in common with each other that can be explained only by admitting their genuineness, seems inescapable. They seem to be out-of-the-body experiences which typically occur at relatively 'high' levels, that is, because consciousness in these cases is operating through bodies of relatively subtle nature. There seems, in fact, to be three fairly well-defined levels of out-of-the-body experiences in general: (1) those with 'sub-normal', or 'dream', consciousness, when the 'body-veil' is outermost, (2) those with 'supernormal' consciousness, when the Psychical Body is outermost and (3) those with 'mystical', 'cosmic' or 'spiritual' consciousness, when the Spiritual (= Higher Mental, or Causal) Body is employed. In the present book we are primarily concerned with the two 'lower' levels, but the same person can have a psychical experience at one time and a mystical one at another, according to circumstances (or, rather, according to which body is outermost at that time).

B. More Recent Accounts

It is about a century since Robert Dale Owen, in his *Footfalls on the Boundary of Another World* (Light Pub. Co. Ltd.) published narratives of out-of-the-body experiences. Some were claimed to be of 'unquestionable' authenticity and 'with strong presumptive evidence against hallucination'.

Frau Hauffe's experience, first published in 1829 by her medical adviser, Dr J. Kerner, was translated into English in 1845 by Mrs Catherine Crowe under the title *The Seeress of Prevorst* (T. C. Newby). Frau Hauffe, when ill in bed and her physical body cataleptic, saw her 'double' seated in a nearby chair. The figure rose, approached, and finally merged with her body. The union caused an electric-like shock. (Compare the 'repercussion' described (a) by Muldoon, etc. when returning suddenly to the physical body, (b) that observed in cases of 'materializations' and (c) that described in certain cases of 'witchcraft'). Frau Hauffe, who thus regained the ability to move and speak, told Kerner of her experience. Although the doctor had not seen the exteriorization of his patient's 'double' from the physical body, he had observed the effect of its return.

After giving a number of other narratives, Owen made the following observations. 'This phenomenon is evidently the same as that which, under the name of *wraith*, has for centuries formed one of the chief items in what are usually considered the superstitions of Scotland. In that country it is popularly regarded as a forewarning of death. This, doubtless, *is* a superstition; and one may rationally conjecture how it is originated. The indications are—that during a dream or a trance, partial or complete, the counterpart of a living person may show itself at a greater or less distance from where that person actually is. And that, as a general rule, with probable exceptions, this counterpart appears where the thoughts or affections, strongly excited, may be supposed to be.'

The idea that for a person's 'double' to be seen indicates his impending death is not entirely superstitious. The idea no doubt arose because people observed a number of correlations between apparitions and subsequent death: it was a generalization. But the sequence was not invariable, because illness is not the only factor that loosens the 'double' from its physical counterpart. In some people the 'double' is naturally 'loose', while it may be loosened by drugs, anaesthetics, etc.

In an appendix to Owen's book, Angus McArthur said, 'The ravages of malignant diseases, like lupus and cancer, the gnawing of consumption, and even the physical waste which accompanies starvation, have no effect on the psychic form. ... *Only when the return to earth, in a materialized form, is made within a comparatively short time of the 'passing over' is the spirit compelled again to resume its contact with these physical conditions of its own material body which existed when death took place.* The man who has died of hunger again feels its pangs when he materializes, and he whose fatal illness was bronchitis comes fighting for breath into the circle. Strange, indeed, these things sound, but they are only part of the ordinary experience of investigators. ... The psychic form, however, is not affected by these conditions. Away from all material ills, free from all material requirements and obligations *one looks back at physical life as at a dream. ...*'

To return to the consideration of out-of-the-body experiences proper: soon after publishing her translation of Kerner's book, Mrs Crowe published *The Night Side of Nature* (T. C. Newby, 1848). She agreed with the teachings given through the Seerest of Prevorst (and, indeed, given by St Paul and by hundreds of other psychics and by some philosophers, *e.g.*, Dr Joad) that man is a triune being, consisting of body, soul and spirit. The soul was considered to be clothed with an ethereal body ('Nervengeist' = 'body-veil') which continues to carry out the vital processes of those whose body is unconscious in trance, etc., while their souls 'travel' in non-physical environments. Death consists in this ethereal body withdrawing, along with the soul, from the Physical Body: after a period (which is somewhat variable), the 'ethereal body' (= 'body-veil') disintegrates releasing the soul (in the Psychical Body). Mrs Crowe accepted the view that apparations of the 'double' may be due to the 'body-veil' having separated from the body. Her statement may be thus quoted. 'According to this theory, this nerve-spirit, which seems to be an embodiment of—or rather, a body constructed out of the nervous fluid or ether—in short, the spiritual body of St Paul, is the bond of union between the body and the soul, or spirit; and has the plastic force of raising up an aerial form. ... When this body is cast off, it follows [= accompanies] the soul (in the Psy-chical Body); and as, during life, it is the means by which the soul acts upon the body, and is thus enabled to communicate with the external world, so when the spirit is disembodied, it is through this nerve-spirit that it can make itself visible, and even exercise mechanical powers.' The 'nerve-spirit' or 'body-veil' is a vehicle of vitality.

Mrs Crowe considered that not only 'somnambules' (clairvoyants in trance) but ordinary sick people occasionally have experiences that suggest this view. She pointed out that when Peter was miraculously released from prison and a girl opened the door of the believer's house, insisting that he was there, they said, 'It is his angel'. Mrs Crowe said, 'What did they mean by this? The expression is not *an* angel, but *his* angel. Now is it not a little remarkable that in the East to this day a "double" is called a man's angel, or messenger?'

Hugh Miller (*My Schools and Schoolmasters,* 1852) described a 'dream' which was identical in content with that described some thirteen hun-dred years before as experienced by King Gontran in Burgundy. Such 'dreams' are obviously 'projections'.

The Life of Isaac Hopper, 1853, included an astral projection experi-enced during an illness. In 1876, in *Hafed, Prince of Persia,* communica-tions received through David Duguid (W. Foulsham & Co., London, Hay Nesbit & Co., Glasgow) mention is made of a man who, though in a normal condition, 'saw an exact counterpart of himself' standing before him. There was some corroboration of this experience, since the 'double' was said to be seen by another person who was present.

In 1887, Adolphe d'Assier, a Positivist, claimed to have discovered the explanation of 'spiritualist' phenomena (*Posthumous Humanity,* George Redway). After giving many examples of astral projection, he maintained that 'living' men have a double of the Physical Body and this, infused with 'mesmeric ether', or vitality, gives a natural explana-tion of apparitions of the 'living' and also of the 'dead'—that it is merely a portion of the total body which survives death (correspond-ing, of course, to the 'astral shells' of others). Thus, he considered that phantoms of the dead never represent surviving personalities but 'belong to the natural order'. He even envisaged 'an invisible vascular plexus' which, during earth-life, united the 'double' to the Physical Body, that is, the 'silver cord'. If this student had had certain cases at his disposal, namely, those which exhibit the transference of the con-sciousness from the Physical Body to the exteriorized 'double', he would have realized that he had been amassing evidence in favour of, and not against, survival.

In 1889 'Nizida' (*The Astral Light,* Theosophical Publishing Co. Ltd.), writing on occultism, with some remarks on spiritism, referred to the 'double' and its role in mediumship.

C. Modern Accounts

The Theosophists have long claimed knowledge of 'astral projection'. Mrs Annie Besant, as early as 1895 (*Borderland*, II, p. 216) said that she could 'leave the body at will' and thus 'reach and learn from living human teachers.' Two years later (*The Ancient Wisdom*, Theosophical Publishing House Ltd.) she gave a general account of the matter which was further enlarged in *Man and his Bodies* (*ibid.* 1900). C. W. Leadbeater (*The Inner Life*, i, 1910, *Invisible Helpers*, 1911, *The Life After Death*, 1912, etc., Theosophical Publishing House Ltd.) made similar observations and, in general, they agree with the experiences subsequently described by people who have never heard of those authors (or of Theosophy).

These supposed experiences, long known as 'travelling clairvoyance', 'trance clairvoyance', 'doubling' and 'bilocation', were called 'self-projection' by F. W. H. Myers (*Human Personality*) but to-day are commonly described as 'astral projection', 'astral travel' or 'E.S.P. travel'. Myers considered that Mrs Piper's fragmentary utterances when returning from trance to the waking state, Stainton Moses's accounts of his journeys in the 'spirit world' and Home's trances, 'all suggest actual excursions of an incarnate spirit from its organism'. Although agreeing with Gurney that apparitions are not of a physical nature, he maintained that collective cases (at least) occupy space. He suggested that such apparitions could affect space without necessarily affecting matter, that is, that space somehow belongs to the 'metethereal', as well as to the physical world (whereas matter does not). His suggestion that certain people have a special kind of make-up, or constitution, that renders their 'double' liable to separate from the total personality and therefore to be seen by others accords with the statements of 'astral projectors' and the 'dead' that some people have loose 'body-veils' (vehicles of vitality) and others loose Psychical Bodies. Myers called this peculiar make-up 'psychorrhagic diathesis', meaning the breaking loose of the soul. He did not think that 'the whole vital principle' was thus exteriorized, but a 'psychical element' and noted that it was 'probably of very varying character' (compare accounts of Mrs Garrett, etc. regarding the variations in the density of the 'double' exteriorized under different conditions). Myers said, 'I hold that this phantasmogenetic effect may be produced either on the mind, and consequently on the brain of another person—in which case he may discern the phantasm somewhere in his vicinity, according to his own mental habit or prepossession—or else directly on a portion of space, 'out in the open', in which case several persons may simultaneously discern the phantasm in that actual spot'.

In 1923, Prof. Charles Richet (*Thirty Years of Psychical Research*, translated by Stanley de Brath, Collins & Co. Ltd.) expressed his opinion that 'travelling clairvoyance' or 'astral projection' are not genuine supernormal phenomena. He said: 'external autoscopy has no metaphysical significance'.

The *Essays* of Prentice Mulford, first published in the United States of America in the White Cross Library and in 1913 by G. Bell and Sons Ltd., included one entitled 'You Travel While You Sleep'.

With the popularization of 'occult' subjects in the last fifty years or so, the number of people who have published descriptions of apparent out-of-the-body experiences has increased very greatly and we now know that they are by no means uncommon (whatever their interpretation may be).

The individual accounts of these experiences are naturally difficult, even when possible, to corroborate. They can seldom be accorded that degree of probability which we attach to those supernormal experiences that, after careful investigation, are published by the Society for Psychical Research. But there is no need, on that account, to neglect them entirely. It seems highly probable that they have great significance in relation to communications from the so-called dead and to the theory of survival.

Until quite recently, those who claimed to have occasional, involuntary out-of-the-body experiences did not study them in order to determine their causes and conditions and so to produce them at will. The French hypnotist Lancelin seems to have been the first to publish brief directions for their production. In England, in 1903 (and again in 1909), Vincent Turvey described what he called 'travelling' in his 'mental body', but he could not do so at will.

In 1920 Oliver Fox published in the *Occult Review*, and also in his book *Astral Projection* (Rider & Co. Ltd.), an account of the methods he had developed in order deliberately to leave his Physical Body. In the same year, A. Zymonidas (*Normal and Abnormal Evolution*, The Spiritual Ray Publications) issued warnings against the 'artificial' acquisition of this ability as 'a step that leads directly away from Spiritual evolution'. In 1923, Dr E. Osty (*Supernormal Faculties in Man*, Methuen & Co. Ltd.) reviewed the work of Drs Sollier, Comar and Buvat on these matters and accepted their view that the term 'autoscopy' included hysterical and purely mental phenomena only. The term 'external autoscopy' was used for 'seeing' either the Physical Body or the 'double', and the term 'internal autoscopy' for seeing the internal organs [cf. the cases of Dr Wiltse and Mr Costa]. The latter phenomenon was attributed to 'the transformation of tactile into visual impressions'.

In 1928, H. Ernest Hunt published some descriptions of 'projection' in his *Why We Survive* (Rider & Co. Ltd.), and others were given by

Mrs F. E. Leaning in the May issue of *The British Journal of Psychical Research*.

About the same time, Dr Hereward Carrington, in his *Modern Psychical Development*, summarized all the information he could find on this subject. In 1927 he was surprised to receive a letter from a young man, Sylvan Muldoon, to say that he had been experimenting on these matters for twelve years and could supply important details that were undescribed by the recognized authorities on whom Carrington relied. In particular, Muldoon had discovered methods by which, he claimed, almost anyone could obtain the experiences for themselves. Too much credit can scarcely be accorded to Muldoon in this matter: he said, 'I determined the causes' then 'produced the phenomena at will, before I even read one word on the subject'. Carrington thereupon directed Muldoon's further experiments and he also is deserving of our warmest thanks. He eventually published, in collaboration with Muldoon, the book *The Projection of the Astral Body* (Rider & Co. Ltd., 1929). In the Introduction to this book. Carrington said. 'It would be impossible for Mr Muldoon to have written what he has without in some sense experiencing what he claims. His reading upon the subject has been very scant; he lives in an obscure village: his knowledge has been gained at first-hand.' Muldoon said, 'I had heard that we live after death, but that was the sum-total of my knowledge on the subject.' Meanwhile, Oliver Fox, in England, unknown to either Carrington or Muldoon, had published the methods that he had developed to produce voluntary and conscious out-of-the-body experiences. A second book by Muldoon, *The Case for Astral Projection* (Aries Press Ltd.), contained numerous accounts of the experiences of others.

In 1935, Sax Rohmer published an article on projection in Nash's *Pall Mall*, No. 508, xcv, in which he referred to various examples of the phenomena and gave instructions for the production of the experience. Rohmer is said (in *Fate*, Nov., 1953) to have given detailed instructions for producing voluntary experiences 'in the now defunct *Forum* over a quarter of a century ago'. This must have appeared in the 1920's. The writer has not seen either of these accounts.

In 1936 (March) and 1939 (January) Wm. Gerhardi gave narratives of his own experience in *Prediction*. This he also published in his novel *Resurrection. Prediction* for 1936 (July and October) also contained extracts from Dr Nandor Fodor's *Encyclopedia of Psychic Science* (Arthurs Press, Ltd.), while the October and December numbers included articles by Muldoon. Dr R. B. Hout published in that Journal in June, 1936 and W. F. Lovatt in August, 1938.

In 1938, Prof. E. Bozzano (*Discarnate Influence in Human Life*, J. M. Watkins and Co. Ltd.) gave a valuable discussion of this subject under the heading: 'The Phenomena of Bilocation'.

Meanwhile, Carrington had kept in touch with this aspect of psychical research. In his *Psychic World* (Kegan Paul, Trench, Trübner & Co. Ltd., 1938) he referred to *The Tibetan Book of the Dead*. He said, 'It is of no little significance that statements made by Tibetan priests a thousand or more years ago have been quite independently verified by a young man living in a small western town in U.S.A.! It seems incredible indeed that all this should be mere coincidence, and leads us to a belief in the actuality of the astral body, which has been believed in by primitive peoples in all times and is an integral part of their magical doctrines and ceremonies'. [He might have added that statements similar to those of the Tibetans (and of Muldoon) were transmitted orally in China and in Egypt from early times.] In 1939, after 39 years of psychical research, Carrington recorded his considered opinion that the doctrine of the 'astral body' is 'so nearly established as to constitute virtual proof'. In 1951, in conjunction with Muldoon, he published *The Phenomena of Astral Projection* (Rider & Co. Ltd.).

Prediction for March, 1940, carried an article on 'astral travel' by J. R. Gregg. It gave his own experiences and included hints for would-be 'projectors'.

Miss L. M. Bazett (*Beyond the Five Senses*, Basil Blackwell, 1946), who had a number of these experiences, like Gerhardi, apparently knew nothing of those of others. She stated that she had not only been outside her own body, but had observed other people while outside theirs. Miss Bazett said, 'To some people this may seem an impossibility, yet the "living" are sometimes seen at a distance from where they are physically at the time of the vision'. After giving an instance of this from her personal experience, she explained it as follows. 'If, as many believe, the psychic or spiritual body is one that co-exists in this life with the physical, and is freed from it at death, then in all probability, it vacates the physical from time to time during life; many cases of the "living" being thus seen are on record.'

Stewart Edward White (*Across the Unknown*, Robert Hale Ltd.) stated that his wife was able to leave her Physical Body at will.

In 1950, William Oliver Stevens (*The Mystery of Dreams*, George Allen & Unwin Ltd.) considered that, 'There is an ever-increasing volume of evidence to support the belief that there is such a thing as astral projection. ...' He gave instances from among his personal friends (mentioned above). He commented, 'If all this is true, it follows that thought, memory, powers of observation and even communication are not dependent on the cerebral cortex. Hence, human personality is independent of the Physical Body, and survival of death becomes a hypothesis buttressed by still another formidable body of evidence.'

The late G. N. M. Tyrrell (*Apparitions*, the Seventh F. W. H. Myers

Memorial Lecture, S.P.R., 1942—edited by Mr Edward Osborn and re-published in book form, with a Preface by Prof. H. H. Price, by Gerald Duckworth & Co. Ltd., 1953), after reviewing several cases of 'travelling clairvoyance', said, 'There seems to be nothing in these cases which compels us to assume that the clairvoyant "travels" or is consciously present at a point of observation in space, as Myers supposed. I am not even sure that the statement that a consciousness is present at a particular point in space has any meaning. ... How can a consciousness be so many inches away from, say, the corner of the table? ...' Several points may be made in this connexion. The first is that Tyrrell assumes that consciousness is 'subjective' and a table 'objective' and 'never the twain shall meet'—yet there must be something wrong with the definitions since, in point of fact, they do 'meet'! Secondly, ingenious and valuable as are Tyrrell's theories of apparitions in general, so far as cases of 'astral projection' (or 'travelling clairvoyance') are concerned, they completely fail to explain two matters: (a) the similarities in the accounts of the process of shedding (and of re-entering) the Physical Body, the existence of a 'silver cord', etc., and (b) the fact that the same features occur independently in accounts from the 'dead'. Thirdly, Tyrrell's idea that consciousness can operate without a body (of some sort) is pure assumption, in support of which there can be no evidence of a direct nature. Fourthly, as against making such an assumption, we have the statement of both 'astral projectors' and the 'dead' that they do use a body of some kind, and if this is true it completely disposes of Tyrrell's argument that, since consciousness has no relation to space it could not cognize objects as from particular points in space: the effect of the supposed body would be to limit the operation of consciousness to certain points in space. Fifthly, if a body of a 'semi-physical' nature were used, the space-relationships might not be greatly different from our physical space-relationships, though when a 'super-physical' (= Psychical) body, or a still subtler Spiritual Body, was employed such would not be the case. Yet even so, our physical space-relationships may well be imposed on the experience by force of habit—just as 'astral projectors' say that at first they do many things from sheer habit (e.g., trying to turn the handle of a door, trying to turn on an electric switch, speaking in words, walking step by step—and note that these same activities are attributed to the newly-dead). The fact is that Tyrrell failed to make out his case in relation to those apparitions that are 'astral projections'.

Fate for Nov., 1953 carried an article entitled 'Astral Journeys' by Roy M. Frisen, formerly editor of various newspapers. Six cases were cited. Dr T. P. Hyatt was said to make an exteriorization under hypnosis and, on returning, to have received a warning letter about such practices. No supporting evidence was, however, adduced, either of the 'journey' or the letter. Bill Sabin, 'Dean of Hawaiian newspaper-men', was described as making an 'astral journey' from Hawaii to Brooklyn (some 5,000 miles) and to have obtained veridical information of the fact, correctly describing a house he had never seen in the flesh, together with its surroundings and contents. These represented natural exteriorizations. An enforced projection, by a woman probation-officer, was then mentioned: she remained conscious when ejected from her body by an anaesthetic. Following this enforced experience, the woman practised leaving her body voluntarily until she could do so 'at any time or place', though she confined her excursions to 'short distances'. Sax Rohmer was next quoted, and Mr Frisen's article closed with instructions for 'astral projection' given by Dr Maneck Anklesaria, 'boyhood friend of Ghandi and friend of Nehru'. The accounts are of a popular nature and, although what are described may have been true out-of-the-body experiences, no evidence to that effect is adduced.

Gertrude Ogden Tubby, B.S., former Secretary to the American Society for Psychical Research, in a manual for the scientific study of psychical phenomena (*Psychics and Mediums*, Rider & Co. Ltd.), written after twenty-six years of professional work, said, 'Astral travelling, according to the testimony and observation of those who have had this super-normal experience, is closely related to hypnotism and its operations, but the physical body remains quiet while the consciousness travels about under auto-suggestion. *However, the consciousness is aware of having a secondary body—as it were a counterpart of the physical body, but of less solid substance.* ... It is not limited by matter in the physical sense, can move freely regardless of walls and floors and physical barriers, and can go where its attention takes it, maintaining its connection with the physical body by a cord or thread. ... This thread, in some cases, is seen as light by those who are clairvoyant and by those who are conscious of their own astral travels. This fact coincides very prettily with the fact that psychic individuals are often termed "lights" by those who claim to communicate through them in the non-material sense.'

H. F. Prevost Battersby in two books (*Psychic Certainties* and *Man Outside Himself*, Rider & Co., Ltd.) gave an interesting résumé of astral projection, but he included some cases which are probably, and others that are almost certainly, of a nature entirely different from the projection of the human 'double'.

G. C. Barnard (1933), discussing 'travelling clairvoyance', thought that, in spite of the evidence suggested by the experiments of de Rochas, the possession of a 'double' is very improbable. He regarded 'out-of-the-body experiences' as due to clairvoyance and/or telepathy, 'sometimes,' he said, 'with the essentially irrelevant projection of an ectoplasmic phantom, which is mistaken by the patient, and often by his investigator, for a permanent vehicle of the soul.' Barnard's book is most interesting, but he failed to state on what grounds he concluded that the 'ectoplasmic phantom' was irrelevant. This is the point at issue. Others claim the reverse—that the 'ectoplasmic phantom' [= the 'body-veil' = vehicle of vitality] is the densest part of the total non-physical 'vehicle of the soul'. This is the crux of our problem. No one seems satisfactorily to have separated purely telepathic and/or clairvoyant experiences of physically-embodied people from experiences said to occur in a non-physical body.

Accounts of projection are also given in Frank Lind's *My Occult Case Book* (Rider & Co. Ltd., 1953) and in Dr R. C. Johnson's *The Imprisoned Splendour* (Hodder & Stoughton, 1953). The latter examined the Wilmot case (our No. 55) in the light of the theories of apparitions that were put forward by G. N. M. Tyrrell (*see* above). He decided that Tyrrell's theories were unsatisfactory as applied to that case, and that it included evidence for astral projection. Like Catherine Crowe, Prof. Bozzano and many others, Dr Johnson insisted that astral projection has 'profound significance for an understanding of the structure of the human self'. This conclusion was reached because those who describe out-of-the-body experiences commonly attribute them to shock or anxiety, describe them as painless, very pleasant and very vivid. In addition, the Physical Body was seen from outside and several cases included supernormal (telepathic and clairvoyant) activities.

Dr Horace Leaf, PH.D., F.R.G.S. published an article entitled *Extrusion of the Psychic Double* in *Chimes*, Sept. 1954. One observation is reminiscent of Varley's account: 'I have personally been out of my Physical Body and on one occasion made my body speak to me.' He pointed out that Durville, who induced the extrusion of the 'double' by means of magnetic passes, found that it occasionally became semi-solid and humid to the touch. He regarded psychic photography as providing much evidence for the 'double': the first photograph taken by Mumler (the first 'spirit photographer') was that of a 'living' man. 'Later,' said Leaf, 'while Mumler took photographs of one of his clients, the man passed into a trance [= exteriorized his Psychical Body], and the subsequent picture represented him standing beside his own body!' He also referred to the difficulty of remembering experiences, especially those which involved the complete separation of the Psychical from the Physical Body. In this connexion he cited the case of Stainton Moses, given in *Phantasms of the Living*. Moses resolved to appear, while asleep, to a distant friend, without informing him of his intention. Next morning he was unaware whether he had failed or succeeded—yet his friend had seen him. Dr Leaf agreed with Muldoon that unconscious projection nearly always occurs in the dream state, but added that it also often occurs while people are awake 'and functioning consciously else-where'. He maintained that analyses of dreams will show that 'a good percentage of them' are symbolized forms of out-of-the-body experiences (a conclusion with which we would agree—see Appendix VI). He also envisaged a plurality of non-physical bodies: he said, 'From personal experience I know that extrusion can occur in several different ways, and that more than one super-physical body may be involved. The real etheric body [here = 'body-veil'] belongs in some way to the physical world. Theosophists are right in insisting that, while the physical body is made up of four denser degrees of matter, the etheric body is made up of three finer degrees. ... According to them, one dies out of the etheric body just as one dies out of the ordinary physical body' [= the 'second death' of communicators]. Dr Leaf also realized that the different points of attachment of the 'silver cord' (head or solar plexus) are to be correlated with the different ways of leaving the Physical Body. He said, 'This contradiction of locality (of the cord) fits well in with the different ways in which extrusion is experienced. There seems to be no law governing the matter, but a general rule. Thus, some people extrude immediately and whole, as it were; others move outward through the head; others through the feet, while some claim to have dissolved and then re-formed over the physical body.' He added, 'It is much the same regarding the different ways in which they return. In my case I always entered at the head, gradually obtaining control of the physical organism slowly downwards, as if the etheric body settled slowly into the physical body.' Like Mrs Cripps etc., Leaf found that the first experience of extrusion can be very disturbing. He said, 'With me, this was because I awoke before obtaining full control of the Physical Body. ... I discovered that by remaining perfectly calm and relaxed, readjustment proceeded normally. The use of the will not only retarded control but resulted in fear.'

Telepathy and clairvoyance, together with occasional ectoplasmic phantoms, cannot, we claim, explain the concordance between the accounts of 'astral projectors' and those of the supposed dead (which latter we claim not only to be mutually concordant and coherent, but to be supported by a large number of independent considerations, and especially regarding descriptions of the non-physical body itself, the sensations described as experienced on leaving the Physical Body, the reviews of the past earth-life and the 'silver cord'). This indirect evidence is supported by a considerable body of evidence that, in certain cases at least, is not so convincingly explained by telepathy and clairvoyance as by astral projection.

Apart from these psychological evidences, there is the evidence that the 'ectoplasmic body' which is sometimes seen, heard, felt and even photographed in connexion with 'astral projection', so far from being, as Barnard believed, an occasional and irrelevant factor, is a constant and essential feature. Much could be said in support of this claim, but considerations of space oblige us to refer to two matters only that seem otherwise inexplicable. First, the resemblance of the ectoplasmic phantom seen (and occasionally photographed) in cases of 'astral projection' to (a) that seen (and occasionally photographed) leaving the body of a dying person and (b) to those seen (and often photographed) at 'materialization' seances. Secondly, the connecting 'cords' are seen (and occasionally photographed) joining such phantoms that are derived from men's physical bodies to the 'double' (in a manner similar to the way in which a newly born baby is joined to its mother). The ectoplasmic phantom is the essential feature of a 'materialization'. It has exact parallels in every respect with the phantoms of astral projection, indicating that here also they are essential features. (The fact that no phantom is seen in many cases is readily explained. They are seldom seen in connection with death. Those that are seen and photographed at 'materialization' seances can apparently be as solid as actual flesh at one moment and melt away to invisibility and intangibility at the next).

The exact nature of many published experiences (i.e., whether they represent true 'astral projections' in the 'double' or only clairvoyance and/or telepathy) must remain uncertain for lack of adequate information on which to found a judgment. Most books on this subject include, under true 'astral projections', experiences of both types. They confuse the reader, tending to make him sceptical of the existence of true 'astral projection'.

Prof. H. Hart, Professor of Sociology at Duke University, published an article entitled *Man Outside His Body* in *Tomorrow*, vol. ii, No. 2, p. 81, 1954 in which he reviewed the evidence for the reality of 'astral projection' from the purely scientific standpoint. He recognized that, 'the projection of viewpoint' (including the seeing of one's own Physical Body from without) is an established fact. A questionnaire submitted to University students showed that, 'At least twenty per cent of college-level young people believe that they have experiences of this sort'. Moreover, 'Of those who report a projection of viewpoint, at least seventy per cent remember more than one such experience.' Features of the total experience that he thought required more evidential support include (1) the ESP-travel observation of objects and persons, (2) the ESP traveller as an apparition and (3) encounters between two ESP travellers. On the basis of the evidence in hand, Prof. Hart estimated the likelihood of the genuineness of out-of-the-body experiences as 'fairly high'.

Many books have been written on this subject and the present writer considers that genuine out-of-the-body experiences do occur. But he maintains that the fact has not been demonstrated. Direct evidence is rarely, if ever, possible. Moreover, since an exteriorized person would, presumably, exercise telepathic and clairvoyant powers, the phenomenon is difficult to separate from telepathic and clairvoyant phenomena that occur apart from possible exteriorization. He suggests that the indirect evidence adduced in this book suffices to establish the phenomenon (see also his article in *Light*, LXXVII, 1957, p. 39 and Appendix VIII).

Prof. Hornell Hart also published an article entitled 'ESP Projection: Spontaneous Cases and Experimental Method' in *Journ. A.S.P.R.*, 47 (Oct. 1954), pp. 121-146. In the same year Stephen Hobhouse (*A Discourse on the Life to Come*, Independent Press Ltd.) said that he had been told by a medical man that epileptics sometimes report out-of-the-body experiences (a claim which was made by Muldoon as early as 1929). The doctor considered that this has 'a foundation in reality'.

Prof. K. H. E. de Jong, University of Leyden, also considered that the evidence that 'living' people sometimes temporarily vacate the body is reliable. He said that 'it weighs heavily in the balance in favour of human survival of bodily death'. (*Spiritualisme Moderne*, 1955).

Appendix II

ADDITIONAL DETAILS (NATURAL EXPERIENCES)

THE writer asked in *Two Worlds, Light, Psychic News, Fate, Chimes* and other papers that deal with psychic subjects for personal accounts of supposed out-of-the-body experiences. In doing so, he avoided reference to anything specific, in order to eliminate possible suggestion. After receiving narratives from correspondents, he sent them the following questionnaire.

QUESTIONNAIRE REGARDING 'ASTRAL PROJECTION'

1. What books had you read about projection BEFORE having the experiences? Did you know of these things from others or did they come as a surprise? Did you think you might be dreaming?
2. Did you project of your own ability, or were you aided?
3. Did you 'visit', (a) earth-scenes only, (b) 'astral' only or (c) both?
4. With what emotion did you contemplate return to physical life?
5. When 'out', was consciousness more vivid than normally? Did you note any other differences from normal consciousness?
6. Did you become convinced of survival? Were you doubtful before?
7. Do you remember details when 'out' better than those in normal experiences?
8. Did you, during the experiences ask, 'Am I dreaming?'
9. Were you, during the experiences, conscious of past, future or of distant things, persons and events? (If so, what things, etc.?)
10. Did you, when 'out' make any critical observations? Note any incongruities, inconsistencies? Did anything cause surprise?
11. Had you any unexpected inabilities (*e.g.*, not turn door-handle, not make yourself heard by others?).
12. Any unexpected abilities? (*e.g.*, pass through walls, was this ability present on EVERY occasion?).
13. Did you deliberately contrast 'out' conditions and environments with normal ones? Did you try any EXPERIMENTS? (*e.g.*, repeatedly passing through walls, repeatedly exteriorizing slowly to observe process, noting differences when you were near to (or far from) the Physical Body? How near when you ceased to feel physical 'pull'? Were you aware of both physical and non-physical conditions when within a certain distance of Physical Body? Did you lose awareness of physical things when beyond that distance? What distance? Always same?

14. Did you see your own Physical Body?
15. Did you see your 'silver cord'? (If so, what colour? How thick? (i) when you were near to physical, (ii) when several yards away from physical? Where did it join (a) Physical Body and (b) non-physical body? Did you see non-physical body? What colour? Clothed how?).
16. Did you communicate with 'dead'?
17. Were you surprised or frightened, etc., at anything while 'out'? What effect did the emotion have? Did you seek evidence, *while* 'out' that you *were* 'out'? What was it?
18. Did you experience catalepsy (rigidity)? When? Could you lessen it? How?
19. What did it feel like to (a) leave and (b) re-enter the body?
20. How many times have you been 'out'? Can you go 'out' at will?

We may now give some individual comments from the replies received. Mr Brown finds that the return to the Physical Body is always tinged with the fear of being unable to re-establish contact with it. When 'out' of his body and observing some incongruity he 'frequently' thinks he might be dreaming. 'This,' he says, 'has the effect of increasing consciousness tremendously, facilitating a true projection' (cf. Fox). While 'out' he often seeks evidence of the fact, but only on one or two occasions has he had 'really successful' results. Like some others, he 'often' passes through walls (etc.) 'for the pure pleasure of doing so'.

Mrs Mary Tarsikes said, 'On two occasions when I was near death I was surprised at what I saw and thought. I criticized what I saw. On one occasion I passed through the roof so quickly that I found myself high in the air. In a few minutes I saw myself standing in a bright fog, and was surprised ... I thought I had died.

'*I think I can say that I cease to feel the draw of the physical body when from three to ten feet from it. And it is within ten feet of my body that I am aware of both my physical and spiritual bodies. I lost the awareness of my physical body when farther than ten feet from it.*

'*I have seen my "silver cord". The time I saw it most clearly, it was shining white. ... it was perhaps about half-an-inch in thickness ... I was high in the air and my cord guided me back through the heavy darkness to my physical body. At that particular time, I saw it joined to my spiritual body at the navel. I did not see my Physical Body then—I had left it on the bed. My spiritual body was then clothed in an almost white robe. ...* I communicated with the dead. ...

'I can only go out at will if there is a sufficiently strong reason for doing so.'

Miss Zoila C. M. Stables, in reply to my enquiries, provided many interesting points. The first of these (omitted in so many published accounts, yet of considerable importance as eliminating any possible explanation as due to suggestion) was that, *when she had her first experience she had never heard of such matters.*

Miss Stables seems usually to project without aid, but, she says, 'On one occasion I know I was aided. I was lying still, concentrating on getting "out", when *a voice said quietly, "Move them apart". I knew my hands were meant.* (I generally lie with them clasped together.) I unclasped and moved them about eight inches apart, and instantly floated free. But when I "came to", my physical hands were still clasped together.'

She is not sure whether she visits astral, as well as earthly scenes, saying, 'I like to think they are astral scenes, because I see there unfamiliar flowers; but it might easily be some other part of this earth. *The scenes do not differ from earth scenes, except in so far as they are more vivid, more brilliantly coloured and clearer in every way.* I seldom see the every-day scenes with which I am familiar, though I have done so.'

The experience helped Miss Stables 'tremendously' as regards her belief in survival. She said, 'It helped tremendously; not only intellectually, but in the realization of it ... without which no merely intellectual conviction is complete. I used to hope survival was a fact in ante-projection days, but could never fully believe it to be so: all the evidence seemed to be against it.'

Again 'I have never for a moment believed I was dreaming during a projection; any more than I could believe I am dreaming at the present moment! The experience is far too real for that. I KNOW I am not.'

Miss Stables, while exteriorized, is conscious of past, future and distant things. 'Usually,' she said, 'the events are, so far as I can tell, in the present. I did once, however, see into the future whilst projected ...'

She stated, 'There are no inconsistencies or incongruities in the surroundings, but *I seem, in different projections, to have bodies of varying densities, so that on one occasion I can float through concrete walls, and on another the leafy branches of a tree may bar my progress ...* which actually happened once. Did anything cause surprise? Yes, the foregoing circumstance did. *I was also surprised once, on glancing into a mirror, to see myself reflected as I was in youth.* In physical life I am middle-aged, and my hair is grey. In the projection it was dark.'

Miss Stables continued, 'I do not seem to have unexpected abilities. I usually have the power of going through solid objects, but this is never unexpected. It seems the normal and natural procedure. *On a few occasions I found myself UNABLE to pass through some solid object and THIS occasioned surprise.*

'My "out" periods are, unfortunately, very brief, and I am mainly concerned with trying, by an effort of will, to postpone the inevitable and imminent "coming-back". I have experimented a few times in changing the direction of my course by will-power—quite successfully. (I always seem to float—not walk—and, unless I exert my will, have little control over my movements.) Once I looked down at my bare feet—three blue rays, one long, two short, were fanning out from them. [A similar phenomenon has been recorded by others.] On a subsequent occasion, remembering this, I looked down to see if the blue rays were still there. This time my feet seemed to be wrapped in mist, and only one ray (the long one) was visible through it. *This envelope of mist is a feature I have noticed on several occasions, usually about the lower part of the body.*' [It probably represents ectoplasm, part of the 'body-veil'. Something similar is described by Mrs Jeffrey.]

'I have never communicated with the "dead" whilst projected. But I have, on many occasions, wakened from a dream of "dead" loved ones INTO the projected state. They seem to inhabit a "sphere" that is further away than that I appear to be in, whilst projected. *I have come to regard projection as a stage on my journey back from the places I believe I visit in sleep. Though probably it is not a case of moving through actual distance so much as becoming atuned to different vibrations, and hence to different states of being.*

'*Any emotion aroused during a projection appears to hasten return to the body. I have never been frightened whilst "out". On the contrary there is usually a feeling of confidence, of utter and complete security.*

'The only sensation of which I am conscious in leaving the body is always (after a short period of "willing" to rise) a jolt in the feet, as if that were the last point to separate. ... It seems to be the culminating point in the process, for immediately afterwards I am floating free.' [Miss Stables is evidently one of the relatively few who leave the body by way of the feet. This probably explains the 'rays' which she saw coming from her feet.]

'Re-entering the body is usually just a cessation of the vibratory sensation that always accompanies a projection—in my case at least. My brother, who has also experienced projection aptly describes it as a "Buzzy feeling".

'I find (after re-entering) that if I do not move a muscle (physically) I can often float off again. If I do move, however, be it so much as a finger, the condition is broken and I cannot regain it. Some small physical movement seems to be necessary to effect a complete reunion with the body.

'I have often encountered, whilst projected, the condition Oliver Fox refers to as "astral currents". I may at any moment be swept away willy-nilly, by what appears to be a strong wind; it does actually seem to be a wind, for it bends the astral trees as a storm would bend the trees here. It never takes me far, for I waken.'

Miss Peters gave an important. detail in her reply. When I read the printed account of her experiences, I noted that she feared being at some height over the sea—yet this emotion did not (as is universally said) cause re-interiorization. Without specifically referring to this, however, in her answer to the questions, Miss Peters explains the apparent anomaly, since she says, 'hasty return was prevented by invisible operators'.

The *doctrines and opinions* of the 'dead' often disagree with each other, but the accounts of their *experiences* agree in every essential matter. This difference between the variety in opinions and the concordance in essential experiences (which also, of course, applies to us 'living' people) is sufficiently marked as to be of considerable significance: it very strongly suggests that what are described as the experiences of the newly-dead correspond to fact. This conclusion is reinforced by the fact that the same condition is found when we analyse the communications of those who claim to have out-of-the-body experiences. Few of the latter offer their opinions on why strong emotion tends to cause them to experience a rapid return to their physical bodies, and some of those who do (*e.g.*, Mr Sculthorp) may clearly be in error. But this only serves to emphasize the fact that, while their *opinions* varied and might be of little value, the *experiences* they describe were essentially identical. As with the statements of the 'dead', the suggestion is that the descriptions of *experiences* correspond with objective fact, while the differences in *explanations* indicates the absence of collusion and of 'cooking' of the accounts.

We draw attention to a somewhat similar matter in Lt.-Col. Lester's account of his meeting with his (deceased) wife during an out-of-the-body experience. The fact that Lester was at a loss to explain an apparent anomaly is of value and interest to us.

Mr Edwards's case is noteworthy in two important respects. First, although he knew nothing about psychic matters, like Sigrid Kaeyer and others who were similarly situated, he described the 'silver cord' and his description tallies with those of Muldoon, Gerhardi, etc.: he 'felt' rather than 'saw' the cord; its attachment was to his head and the effect was as though he was pulled towards the physical body by 'stout elastic or rubber'. Secondly, he was clearly 'awake', since he was able to make critical observations. In particular, he noted an incongruity—he was not where he ought to be, namely, in bed. [If we merely dream of being elsewhere than in bed, we do not specifically note the fact.]

Mr J. H. Brown was surprised at an incongruity that he noticed while exteriorized from his Physical Body: he thought he was in 'mist' or 'water' [= 'Hades' conditions] through which it was necessary to move by a process analogous to swimming: but he noted that the 'water' had not the power to wet his clothes.

Before commenting on Mrs Cripps's narrative, I cite some points from her answer to my questionnaire. *The experiences 'assuredly' had a greater and more vivid consciousness than ordinary and 'a greater intensity of being'.* They convinced her of survival more definitely than any other phenomena. *Details of her astral experiences are 'always tenaciously held'.* She says, 'They do not become dimmer, which is more than I can say for the experiences of ordinary life'. While 'out' of her Physical Body she was 'completely conscious of the situation' and could 'reason clearly'. She did not feel a clear demarcation between past, present and future but was conscious of distance 'in the sense of remoteness'. *While exteriorized, she said, 'I looked out for incongruities, for I was wanting to* prove that I was not looking on what is called phantasy in comparison with physical conditions. My observations were centred on light, colour, texture and temperature. *Light appeared uniform: I could never see any shadow* [compare Jas. i, 17]. Colour was clear and intense with a living quality. In the brighter planes texture had a fineness and in the darker planes a coarseness. Colour and texture seemed to be related: the more ethereal the colour, the more fine the texture. Temperature was neither hot nor cold, but always congenial.'

Mrs Cripps further stated, 'In one place it was in half-light to me. I tried to rise above the level of the ground in order to get an aerial view, but was not able to hold the position for any length of time. I folded up like a deflated bag and fluttered to ground-level. Always before in bright places I could hold the aerial position and enjoy looking down on the scenes.

'When I travelled in the astral body round my own house I could pass out of a room into another without going through the doorway: but I didn't deliberately go through walls—*I found that habit persists, and I would use a doorway as normally.*

'Touching articles of furniture was possible and I remember opening the oven door and hearing the noise I made in doing so. Also I could hear sounds that other people made as they came into my house and in the same "out" condition as myself.

'I did not deliberately experiment in exteriorization. There are repercussions to the physical body after having done so, a feeling of tiredness. That is why I let the operation take its own course—though I have always an idea beforehand that it is going to happen.

'*I never feel the pull of the "cord" when leaving the body, but feel it when returning to normal. When the two bodies are only slightly disconnected, there is a feeling of instability. Often in this condition I have felt, as it were, a hand under my arm-pits which helps me to adjust myself. When I am "out" and unstable, the environment seems the same too: outlines are confused. It is as if a shimmering veil enveloped all.*

'If, when "out", I was going beyond what I call earthly limits, I would lose awareness of physical and non-physical conditions at a short distance, say the extent of the bedroom. But I would keep awareness if only travelling round my own home.

'*I saw the "silver cord". It appeared to be luminous and of a greyish-blue tint. I could see the vitality in it, a pulsation. The greater the distance between the two bodies becomes, the thinner the cord, but there is no change in colour. I have not noticed beyond two or three yards. But the "thinning out" process was apparent. It appeared to be connected between the two heads of the bodies.*

'*I saw my Physical Body asleep on the bed. I also looked on my non-physical body, and well remember glancing at it in a mirror in which it was reflected.* The two bodies look alike. The non-physical was clothed as I would normally clothe myself. But the clothes seemed to be more 'one' with the body, not appearing as detachable, as on the physical body, but more as though they had "grown on". One seems to retain the same style of clothes as one wore before the act of exteriorization. Only on one occasion have I been conscious in the "out" state of having on a dress that I had never seen in my life. I was quite able to decide whether I liked it or not. The colour of the "out" clothes is consistent with the colour of the normal-state clothes.

'*I saw and communicated with my own "dead" and with others. One seems to be able to project thought to another person without language*, though one could be conscious of speech.

'I was definitely surprised when I first exteriorized. This wears off with later experience. But delight and enthusiasm never stale. The emotions experienced made me want to force the situation. But at this point a greater power, which I feel to be external to myself, forces me back to the normal state. It is as if a greater wisdom says, "So far and no further yet".

'The "other-side" people are always anxious to teach one: they would say, "This is reality". The Door-keeper Guide who was with me in the "out" state appeared in countenance the same as I have seen him clairvoyantly in the normal physical state. I would meet him as a normal person would meet a friend on earth. He always looked as substantial as myself—there was no "ghost-look" about him. We would converse. I never knew this man but, believe me, he is as real in spirit as my father (who is also in spirit) is to me.'

So much for Mrs Cripps's replies to my questionnaire. Although she had read no books on the subject, *the experiences which she describes exhibit numerous points of similarity with those of Muldoon.* We note the following: (1) Mrs Cripps refers to the state of physical catalepsy that is also described by Muldoon (and which Staveley Bulford considers is avoidable). (2) She discovered for herself, by experience, what Muldoon noted in connexion with the return to physical embodiment (and the 'jump' or 'repercussion' that may occur) and Bulford noted regarding catalepsy, namely, that deliberate relaxation of mind and body obviates these unpleasant, even alarming, features. (3) She described the condition of partial exteriorization exactly as does Muldoon: there is a feeling of instability, of being 'in the air', of being 'here and there'. Muldoon describes as 'elementary states' in astral projection as indicated by 'the adhered, or glued-down sensation, the sensation of floating, of whirling, of zig-zagging, of uprising, 'jumps' (repercussion) in the hypnagogic state (just before sleep), breath-taking sensation at pit of stomach, a feeling as if one's consciousness were getting out of one's head' (nota bene). He says, 'These same things may have happened to you many times' and been put down vaguely as 'nerves'. (4) Like Muldoon, Mrs Cripps saw her own 'silver cord' and her description of the feature and of its function agrees exactly with that of Muldoon: it was (like the astral body) said to be 'luminous' by both: 'whitish-grey' by Muldoon, 'grey-blue' by Mrs Cripps and both said that vitality was visibly pulsating through it. In both accounts it seemed to be attached at the *head* of both the physical and the non-physical body. It was 'elastic' to Muldoon, while Mrs Cripps said it 'has the capacity to stretch'. Both noted that their cords became thinner the further they got away from their Physical Bodies and Mrs Cripps failed to notice her cord after she was beyond two or three yards from the Physical Body. She said it looked like 'a shaft of sunlight', a descriptive phrase which is used by Gerhardi. (5) Mrs Cripps describes 'lapses of consciousness' that she observed 'during the process of changing from one body to another', she likens these to faints when in the Physical Body. Similarly, Muldoon says, 'Just as the astral body leaves the physical, the consciousness grows dim for an instant; then comes back again.' This clearly corresponds with the 'momentary unconsciousness' described by supposed discarnates as they shed the Physical Body, an unconsciousness which tends to be prolonged to an average period of from three to four days in cases of death in old age but which may itself pass unnoticed in an alert person who is killed suddenly in the prime of life. (6) Reluctance to return from the exteriorized state to interiorization and physical life is expressed in many of these experiences (and in communications of so-called dead): Mrs Cripps is no exception— return was 'distasteful'. (7) The 'misty' condition described 'at a certain point' in return is interesting. In view of our analyses of psychic communications generally, it would be interpreted as indicating consciousness in 'Hades' conditions. Muldoon speaks of 'a foggish' light everywhere ... a diffused light ... none too bright, yet not too dim' and this is highly suggestive when we consider that Mrs Cripps experiences two momentary periods of unconsciousness [= shed two 'bodies'], misty conditions being encountered in the first and brilliant Light in the second, and she claimed to visit both earth-scenes and non-physical realms: similarly, Mr Coles left 'bright' conditions, passed through a 'tunnel', then a 'stream of shadows' and awoke in the Physical Body. Muldoon, on the other hand, described only one 'momentary unconsciousness', his environment was 'foggy' and he did not claim to visit any sphere other than the earth: 'I have never seen any but earthly things'. (8) Mrs Cripps describes return to the Physical Body as accompanied by 'a feeling of being jerked', while Muldoon speaks of 'repercussion' that may occasionally be so severe as to 'give the feeling of being split through the centre of the body'. He says the latter is rare because an exteriorized person seldom returns from a very considerable 'distance' at very great speed: average returns are described, as by Mrs Cripps, as 'jumps'. (It may be added that similar phenomena are described in connexion with 'materialization'.) Many others who have described their out-of-the-body experiences include this shock of sudden return. (9) In describing return to the Physical Body, Mrs Cripps also said it was a return to 'a heaviness'. This phrase is not, I think, used by Muldoon, but it is used by Mrs Piper and others in describing their return to their Physical Bodies after being exteriorized in trance. (10) The various movements possible in the astral body, as described by Mrs Cripps, are identical with those given by Muldoon. There is walking 'due to habit', floating, and willed transportation without any knowledge of intermediate space and objects: 'One finds oneself in another place,' says Mrs Cripps, 'without being conscious of any form of locomotion. Simply willed and nothing intervening (no obstacles).' The same methods of locomotion are described by Muldoon and others. (11) Mrs Cripps seems to describe the equivalent of what we call the 'partial awakening' in the accounts of supposed discarnates: in one state of consciousness she merely felt she was 'somewhere', was conscious of her existence but of nothing else—not of 'any body of expression' or an environment that would correspond to such a body. (12) Exteriorization taught Mrs Cripps that the personality survives bodily death: Muldoon concludes his first book, 'had no one else in the whole world ever suspected "life after death", I should still believe implicitly that I am immortal—for I have experienced the projection of the astral body'. Wishful thinking on his part? By no means. He also says, 'I wish death would bring one long and dreamless sleep. But alas, my experiences have proved conclusively to me that "dust thou art, to dust returneth"—was *not* written of the Soul'. (13) Mrs Cripps found that when she was apart from the Physical Body 'thought is a very real thing': Muldoon says 'It seems that on the astral the mind *creates* its own environment—yet the environment is *real*! Hence the common term, the "Plane of Illusion".' (14) Mrs Cripps found that 'The astral body is the power-house from which is transmitted the power that animates the physical body', and she described how she observed vitality pulsating in the cords that unites the astral to the Physical Body. Muldoon described the 'etheric body' as 'a condenser of cosmic, omnipresent energy' and said that 'the more energy that is condensed in the astral body, the tighter will that body be bound to the physical counterpart'. He said that when we sleep 'our astral bodies move slightly out of coincidence for the purpose of becoming charged with cosmic energy'. He similarly described 'a regular pulsating action' in the cord which, he says, 'is an outward manifestation of a subtle, vital process'. The similarities of these independent descriptions is remarkable. Identical statements are made by the 'dead'. (15) Mrs Cripps insisted on the value of prayer while in astral conditions, as do most of those who claim to have exteriorizations. Muldoon, Gerhardi and others put the matter slightly differently, insisting on the need for 'right thinking'. She said, 'One can get into trouble on the astral, the outcome of one's ignorance of law: one can get into difficulties and with uncongenial companions'. Muldoon described a meeting with a man whom he hated, who had died, and who 'meant revenge'. (16) A noteworthy remark made by Mrs Cripps is as follows: 'Oft times in travelling one cannot find a like set of experiences on which to base one's actions. One is nonplussed. ...' Compare this with the following extracts from Muldoon. 'Some will tell you that they can see vast distances when projected and conscious in the astral body. This, like everything else, is not always true. In fact, one can scarcely answer one single question concerning the astral plane without saying, "sometimes this is true, and sometimes it is not true. One might project and encounter one condition, interiorize again, and think he knew all about the astral; yet he would know only about that particular condition which he experienced. Because of these innumerable conditions, many stories concerning the astral world are contradictory. ..." Again we are reminded of the common term, the 'Plane of Illusion'. (17) 'One's spiritual perceptions are more awakened in this state. A veil is drawn over the perceptions on the earth-plane', says Mrs Cripps. Muldoon says, 'You may think that you can think and act with rapidity; but once you have become conscious in the astral body, you will realize at what a snail's pace the conscious mind moves in comparison. ...' Other similarities between the independent testimonies of Mrs Cripps and Muldoon might be indicated, but those mentioned above will suffice for our purpose. If astral projection is a fact, these similarities are readily understood: but on what other hypothesis can we account for them? And how shall we explain—on grounds other than the survival hypothesis—the obvious similarities between the content of both of these accounts and the content of narratives by the supposed dead?

The fact that the essential content of all these accounts is the same is a strong argument in favour of the reality of the experiences. The fact that in certain cases the experience includes some additional feature (*e.g.*, the review of the past life in the case of Elizabeth Blakeley) does not in the least weaken this conclusion: it represents support for a further statement in the communications generally, namely, the statement that the total non-physical body is complex, consisting, as it were, of several layers (which may equally truly be described as distinct 'bodies') and, whereas in many cases only one layer—that next to the Physical Body—may be utilized by consciousness (a single layer being shed), in other cases a second, or even a third layer may be used by consciousness (two or three 'bodies' being shed respectively), producing different experiences and contacting different environments, worlds, realms, spheres, planes or conditions. This conclusion also receives support from three other considerations. First, one and the same person (*e.g.*, Mr Edwards) claims usually to contact astral environments when 'out' of the Physical Body, but occasionally he finds that he is not on the astral but on earth; conversely, others usually 'visit' earth conditions, but occasionally contact the astral plane; finally a few, like Muldoon, seem to be confined to earth conditions. Secondly, it is said in several communications that the shedding of a 'body' causes a momentary unconsciousness and it is to be noted that those who claimed to contact two levels of environment (*e.g.*, Mrs Cripps) had not one, but two of these periods of momentary unconsciousness. The third point is concerned with the preliminary 'misty' condition so often described not only in temporary exteriorization but also in enforced death in the prime of life (and in many psychic experiences): this we interpret as 'sub-normal' consciousness in the layer immediately next to the Physical Body, namely, the electro-magnetic or ectoplasmic layer, the vehicle of vitality or 'body-veil'. All this constitutes indirect evidence in support of the statement that man has a non-physical body that consists of several interpenetrating 'layers', or alternatively, that he has several progressively subtler non-physical bodies. The misty conditions [= 'Hades' or 'the Denser Between Worlds'] may be followed by bright ['Paradise'] conditions and these by the conditions of brilliant Light of mystical experiences. Everything, in fact, tends to support the statements of both supposed discarnates and many who claim to have temporary exteriorizations, that man is provided with a series of progressively subtler 'bodies' that are derived from (and can therefore be used as media of consciousness in) a corresponding series of progressively subtler environments, 'worlds', 'spheres,' 'realms,' 'planes' — the 'many mansions' mentioned by Jesus (John xiv, 2).

I asked Mrs Cripps how she accounted for the fact that she could, when 'out' of her Physical Body, pass through walls and yet open an oven door? (There are, of course, several possible answers.) She replied that the two phenomena did not occur on the same occasion and continued, '*I have noticed that when I had the capacity to pass through a wall, I also seemed to have the capacity to travel further away (or should I say "further extend my consciousness"?) than when only able to travel round my own home*, as during the oven-door incident. I wonder whether the difference is connected with the quality of the substance of the astral body. ... It would seem that one's [non-physical] body, in its various modes of being, is like one great "apport".'

Mrs Cripps then pointed out that those who have 'passed on' do not always pass through walls. On one occasion her father (who is 'dead') entered the room accompanied by her mother (who is 'alive'), not through the wall, but through the door. The father intimated that his wife would become ill and that that would be the beginning of the end. Mrs Cripps said, 'He linked his arm within hers as a sign of their being united. She appeared equally as animated as he. I was quite able to grasp my father's arm in happiness at this meeting: to my "out" hands he felt quite tangible. The queer thing was that he just disappeared to my "out" eyes before I returned to my Physical Body in the usual way. I can only think my mother did some astral travelling on this occasion.' [The explanation of this seems to be that the 'dead' father entered by the door in deference to the habitual thoughts of the exteriorized mother— had he endeavoured to take her through a wall the shock might have returned her immediately to physical life. Many of the newly-dead are said to go in and out of doors by sheer force of habit, when they could pass directly through the walls. The disappearance of the father is also interesting: he had probably had to reduce his 'vibratory rate' to correspond to that of his wife (with a relatively low rate because of its continued attachment, *via* the cord, to the Physical Body): having accomplished his mission, prepared his daughter for her mother's illness and eventual transition and comforted the latter (who, we note, was 'equally animated'), he resumed his normal condition of higher rate of vibration and so became invisible to his exteriorized daughter (and, no doubt, to his exteriorized wife). He had assumed, or 'built up', a temporary condition.]

The following are points from Mr Wm. E. Edwards's replies to my questionnaire. He says, 'With my first experience, my main and overwhelming emotion was stupefaction at the reality of the experience (with later experiences, one's emotions were governed by knowledge of the facts). Very often there would be a greater sense of freedom, of buoyancy. I have experienced many times floating through space, floating down stairs, willing to float upwards, giving the sensation of a lift when it begins to rise. *All emotions are much increased in the astral state.* I was not immediately convinced of survival by my first experience, since I belonged to a sect that believed that only the "saved" had a future—that there was no natural survival. (Compare effects of erroneous ideas on the 'dead'.) He gives an experience that includes a typical example of an inability during exteriorization. He says, 'One night I was on duty at an A.R.P. depot, some four miles from our bungalow. I awoke in the early hours and was so relaxed that I felt I might be able to project; so I tried, and succeeded. I gently floated out of my body. I glanced round and could see the sleeping forms of the other men. Then I found myself floating up through the concrete roof. I passed through it and continued to float up into the sky until I passed through the clouds. I then said, "I will go home". The "lift" immediately went into reverse, and I floated gently down, passed through the roof of our bungalow and found myself in the living room. I thought, "I must try to awaken Dad", and went towards his bedroom. I put my hand to the door handle and seemed to pass through the door. I found myself standing by his bed calling "Dad, Dad", but he did not hear. Then I knew I must return and was hurtled through space back to my Physical Body in the A.R.P. post. I hovered over it (some way up, so that I could not see it), then felt the two bodies coincide. For a few seconds there was catalepsy, noises as of bells, flapping of wings, etc. I opened my eyes (still fully conscious): it was 3 a.m.' He further said, *'I have not seen my "cord" but I felt its pull when I deliberately prolonged the projection a little longer than was wise. It caused a pain in the centre of the forehead. Occasionally it caused a headache next day. I have many times communicated with the "dead".'*

Mr Sculthorp had read books by Muldoon, Yram and Swedenborg in an attempt to explain the exteriorization-like experiences that he was having. He never felt fear while in 'higher' astral conditions but did so in 'lower' conditions. In the latter, he said, 'one generally has a feeling of disquietude or apprehension ... a sensation I have never felt on earth, even in times of danger.' This he attributed to the malicious thoughts and feelings of those who normally inhabit the 'lower' regions, and he gave examples of their activities. These were 'stunted', 'wizened' and 'smelt' badly. The face of one was 'full of deep cracks', reminiscent of Swedenborg's 'man with a face like the bark of a tree'.

All Mr Sculthorp's exteriorizations were, according to him, carefully planned, for his education, by discarnates. When he returned to the Physical Body a symbol was shown him to signify the experience; at first this symbol consisted in relief carvings in marble on the ceiling; later it was a golden arabesque pattern.

One phrase in Mr Sculthorp's account is reminiscent of that used by Mrs Piper on her return to physical life from exteriorization in trance. He returned from a projection one brilliant June afternoon: but it did not seem bright to one who had been in astral conditions: on the contrary, he thought, 'How dull!'

Mrs Eileen Garrett 'had never heard of astral projection' when she first experienced it. The exteriorization was unaided. She states, 'When I return from trance, I have a sense of having dwelt in deep rich sunlight' and added, 'I can recall this dwelling on dark days and the memory of its vividness is enough to light up my room. The beginnings of trance were at times cataleptic, but now I control the function by breathing. I leave my body, and re-enter it, with great ease and with a great sense of adventure and lightness. In so-called travelling clairvoyance I am not at all certain that I do travel. Being absolutely certain that mind is universal, I imagine myself calling in the experience. This I believe I can do, since knowledge is universal, and since I believe that all inspiration is external, so do I believe that one demands, as in prayer, the knowledge for which one seeks.'

Mrs R. Ivy 'Prothero' gave the following additional details in reply to the questionnaire. 'The quality of the experience was quite different from that of a dream. *I knew I was not dreaming.* I do not recall the act of getting out of my body. The entire experience was enacted within the bedroom. I realized that if I passed over completely, I would not see or mix with my loved ones again. In view of my forthcoming marriage, I suddenly felt active, having everything to live for.

'When "out", I think consciousness was normal. It seemed to be quite a natural state of affairs. *I was completely convinced, from that moment, of survival.* I summed up the situation and then devoted all the forces I could muster to return to the Physical Body. Every detail of it all—it was in 1926, when I was 28 years old—still stands out clearly in my memory. *I knew how it had come about (almost suffocation) and I wanted to get back to living in my Physical Body.*

'When "out", I observed that *my spirit seemed to glow with sufficient light to see all the things in the room, and that I was buoyant, about three feet above my body in bed, attached to it by a slender cord, also slightly luminous.*

'At first I saw the completely covered form on my bed, which I knew was me. Then I saw my hands emerge after fighting my way out of the entangled bedclothes. As I gasped for breath, in a flash I slipped back into my Physical Body.

'The cord looked like a softly-glowing white light, about $\frac{1}{4}$ in. in diameter. It appeared to join both physical and spiritual bodies from the centre of the stomach.

'I became possessed by a sense of urgency when I knew that, if I wanted to live, I had a chance by fighting my way out of bed. I remember imploring my Physical Body to exert every effort [compare Cromwell Varley]. I did not experience catalepsy. I do not remember leaving my body, and my return was a sudden merging, in less than a split second. It seemed like a sudden downward motion into my body.'

Mrs Peggy Roberts, in answer to the question as to whether she contacted earthly scenes, 'astral' scenes, or both (question No. 3) said, 'Both, so far as I can say. What I imagine must be astral scenes are bathed in most beautiful mellow sunshine, and after returning to the normal condition I always had a sort of inner glow and felt at peace with the world.' In answer to the question about the 'silver cord' Mrs Roberts said she had not actually seen this feature, adding, 'but I definitely have the feeling that I am still connected to my Physical Body.' This is in agreement with several other narrators. Similarly, Mrs Roberts experienced the same sensation as Mr Dennis (who also had no previous knowledge of these matters) when leaving the Physical Body. She said, 'I feel a peculiar whirring, as if I am coming out from the top of my head.'

Mrs I. M. Joy gave the following additional details in response to the questionnaire.

(1) Mrs Joy sometimes left her Physical Body at will, sometimes involuntarily. On some occasions she was aided. One man in particular, a discarnate R.A.F. officer, seemed to be a helper.

(2) Mrs Joy did not want to lose the sense of elation and freedom by returning to the Physical Body. *She did not entertain the possibility that she might be dreaming, saying, 'No! I knew I wasn't!'* Mrs Joy was able, after 'earth-travelling' to describe correctly scenes in Southampton Water (including the position of wrecks and of a white rescue boat) and elsewhere. Among the 'dead' whom she saw, and with whom she conversed, were some she had not met in earth-life, including many who were killed in the war.

(3) In answer to my question (No. 10) as to any surprise while 'out', Mrs Joy made a statement which is of great interest in relation to those of a number of others (Mrs Howard W. Jeffrey Sr., etc.). She said, 'Yes, something did surprise me. I saw another likeness of myself projected in front of the astral. *With my Physical Body in the chair as well, there must have been three of me!* (The 'three' would, presumably, be (1) the 'Psychical Body', (2) a portion of the 'body-veil' that had left the physical along with No. 1 [see below] and (2) the Physical Body.)

(4) It may be noted that in her original narrative, Mrs Joy said that, while out of the Physical Body, she 'opened the door in the usual way'. This is in contrast to most accounts: in most cases it is found that they cannot turn door-handles or press electric light switches. But the fact that Mrs Joy experienced certain 'physical' phenomena (the movements of physical objects without contact, raps, etc.) shows that this was not only possible but even probable. Moreover, whereas most who left their Physical Bodies and who tried to draw the attention of their still-embodied friends by touching them, failed to make any impression. Mrs Joy's touch was felt by her aunt. (All these statements suggest that her non-physical body contained considerable elements from the

'body-veil' and this suggestion is supported by her mental condition while 'out', for whereas most who left the body naturally (and were in the 'Psychical Body') had intense and vivid consciousness, with telepathy, pre- and post-cognition, etc. Mrs Joy said (in answer to question 5) that her consciousness was 'about the same' as normal. It is further supported by the answer given to question No. 14 (see paragraph No. 6 below).

In view of these considerations, Mrs Joy's answer to my question No. 11 is interesting. She said, 'I could always turn door handles'. Also, 'People seemed to see me: two girls were frightened when I was earth-travelling: they looked towards me and ran away.'

(5) In answer to question No. 13 Mrs Joy said, 'Yes, I repeatedly passed through limited window-space. I also lifted it up and got out, and I got out quite easily. As soon as I left the Physical Body I had no difficulty in projecting myself when about a few feet away from my bed, as I was always in bed when I passed through the window and projection was quickly performed ... I ceased to feel the "pull" of the Physical Body as I sat up in bed. I lost awareness of the physical immediately I sat up.'

(6) The answer to question No. 14 is also interesting, suggesting some limitation of consciousness due to the impregnation of the 'Psychical Body' by elements which, though belonging to the 'body-veil', had been extruded along with it. Most people who leave the Physical Body naturally, and who are, therefore, in the 'Psychical Body' claim to see their own Physical Bodies. Mrs Joy did not. She said, 'No. Contrary to what most people say. I had deliberately tried to see my Physical Body during my early travels when I sat in my chair, but ... I could only see the chair itself.' She added, 'In normal sight I could always see a counterpart of this chair, built up just around a few inches away from it.'

Replying to question No. 15, Mrs Joy said, 'I saw a cord, but I do not know if it was my own. ... It was lowered "down through the clouds" towards me, ending just above my astral head. ... It was black [compare the account of Sir Alex. Ogston] and about half an inch wide.'

(7) Mrs Joy has left her body many times, sometimes at will.

Synopsis of Replies to Questionnaire

The general results of our questionnaire are briefly as follows. A significantly large proportion of men and women who claimed to have had out-of-the-body experiences did so before they had read or heard of them and all the accounts agree with each other in many respects. The consciousness was typically more intense and vivid than normally in natural cases and the memory of what transpired was correspondingly acute. All those who were either sceptical or doubtful about survival were thereafter convinced that it is a fact. Although a few, at an early stage in the experience, thought they might be dreaming, the great majority insist that they were quite sure that they were not. Many found that, while outside their Physical Bodies, they enjoyed abilities of an unexpected nature: by far the commonest of these abilities was that of being able to pass through walls, etc. About a half of these people exercised their critical faculties in the exteriorized condition. (In part, this would, of course, depend on the original mental make-up of the person concerned. But, in addition, many who said that they did not make critical observations gave, as a reason, the fact that 'everything seemed natural'. On the other hand, those who were forced 'out' did not deliberately experiment, etc.) Most narratives include the statement that the Physical Body was seen from a distant point outside it. About twice as many reported seeing (or feeling) the 'silver cord' as did not: a large proportion of the former had never heard or read of that feature. (It is said that there are several good reasons why some failed to see [or feel] the cord; it is behind them and the attention is focused elsewhere, etc. Moreover, those who had more than one interiorization, *e.g.*, Fox, did not see it on all occasions.) Fear or any other strong emotion almost always caused a return to the Physical Body and, unless there were special circumstances, such as young children to rear, the return was invariably made with great reluctance. Some say that they were aided (by discarnates) in exteriorizing, but two or three times as many say that the phenomenon occurred naturally and spontaneously. A number of 'projectors', claim, when exteriorized, to be aware of 'earth' conditions only, but an approximately equal number claim to visit both 'earth' and 'astral' scenes. A few said they were in 'astral' conditions only.

Appendix III

INCOMPLETE (OR INCOMPLETELY-REMEMBERED) NATURAL EXPERIENCES

WE mortals are well aware that our experiences during physical embodiment are seldom so intense, vivid and 'real' as they might be and that the relatively feeble attention which we give to them accounts for our poor ability to recall them. As St Paul, and many of the supposed dead (as well as many who claim to have had out-of-the-body experiences) maintained, what we regard as 'normal' consciousness is little better than a dream, in comparison with what is possible.

In view of the above, it is not surprising that out-of-the-body experiences include portions that are clearly incomplete (or that are incompletely remembered). When consciousness is operating through the Psychical Body (as is typical in natural exteriorizations) it is characteristically more intense and the details observed are more clearly remembered than normally. Even so, there are diminutions of consciousness and gaps in narratives. When consciousness is restricted by the exteriorized portion of the vehicle of vitality, or 'body-veil' (as is typical in enforced exteriorizations) relatively little is experienced (or remembered). The very brevity of the accounts of enforced experiences, as compared with natural ones, is significant. Varley (who instructed his wife to remind him of what had happened while he was out of his body) was an interesting case. It seems highly probable, as is said independently by clairvoyants, those who claim to have out-of-the-body experiences and the 'dead', that most of us have experiences of this nature, but do not remember (or do not recognize) them. Where exteriorization was enforced (by anaesthetics, drugs, suffocation or falling), little or nothing may be experienced (or remembered) but the 'first review' of the earth-life to date [cf. Statement No. 5]. This was reported by de Quincey (who took opium), Admiral Beaufort (who was almost drowned) and by Prof. Heiron and many others who fell from great heights.

The following cases, on the other hand, seem to owe their incompleteness to what we have called the 'partial awakening' [cf. Statement No. 25], several examples of which occur in the cases cited in our text [Muldoon, Mrs Cripps, Symonds].

CASE NO. 154—*Dr. C. E. Simons*

Simons, whose experience was given in *Journ. S.P.R.*, 1894, found himself incapable of movement (catalepsy), yet fully conscious. He asked himself whether he was dreaming or not. He said, '*I had a sudden consciousness of being divided into two distinct beings. The second of these was free and was able to look at "myself" fastened in my seat. ... There was an elastic force* [= the 'silver cord'—cf. Statement No. 19] *between the two which prevented the bond between them from being broken. When the distance between the two reached a certain limit the elastic force which united them stretched. Beyond this limit—about two yards—no voluntary effort on my part could lengthen the distance between my fluidic body and my Physical Body, and when that limit was reached, I felt a strong sensation of resistance in the two bodies. This phenomenon of "doubling" lasted about five minutes. Then the fusion began, I fought against it, finding that I could hinder it by an effort of will. Finally, curious to know what was happening, I permitted the fusion, which was rapid. ... I had no feeling of dreaming. ... During the period of the "doubling", I never ceased to ask myself what was happening, taking care also to observe what was happening about me.*'

CASE NO. 155—*Mr Basil Crump*

An article by the Editor of *The Occult Review*, lxxii, No. 3, 1945, is here of interest. He points out that Tibetan Yoga practices facilitate the exteriorization of a non-physical 'body' from the physical body. Although in books such as Basil Crump's *Replenishment from the Central Source by a New Method of Raj Yoga*, reference is made to the earlier phenomena only of out-of-the-body experiences, it may well be that this reticence should not be attributed to either incapacity or inexperience. The method is as follows. After meditation (including Yogi postures), the body is completely relaxed (significantly enough, with both the arms and the legs uncrossed) and the mind is emptied of every emotion, thought, desire and volition. Then the 'Spark of Divinity' (*Manas*) is sent out from the Physical Body by a supreme effort of the will. When this operation is successful, the 'soul' can be seen to float away from it. The body is not only free from pain but is full of warmth and vitality. The mind is free and untrammelled.

The Editor pointed out that Mr Crump had described the first stages of 'astral projection' but that the account omitted 'the many planes on which it is possible for the soul to manifest at will—ranging from the physical, through the astral and mental, to the Spiritual, with diversions in the realms where all is colour, art-form, music, drama or literature', and little of 'that stream of invincible "light-power" which seems to sweep through the universe and from which all life appears to draw substance, which can heal, purify and sustain'. He claimed that Yogis tend to exaggerate the means and so lose sight of the end, and said, 'If the end can be attained by short-cuts and without harm to physique or mentality (and nobody can claim that Yogi methods cannot result in harm to both), then why indulge in Yoga? ... It is possible that here, as in many other things, the West does indeed lead the East, after all!'

Although the Editor did not offer an explanation of the absence from the Tibetan Yogi's experience of the succession of 'spheres' usually described by those who temporarily exteriorize from their Physical Bodies by natural process, we venture an explanation. We suggest that it is due to *the 'partial awakening'*. Muldoon himself experienced this: he said, 'If consciousness makes its first meagre appearance in the hypnagogic state, and the sub-conscious Will is under projection-inclination, *the very first conception is that one exists "somewhere". There is, as yet, no awareness of an environment.*' (Muldoon normally passed on from this preliminary and partial stage to awareness of an environment: but the latter was of the earth, and never beyond. Consequently, although the latter were 'complete' experiences for Muldoon, they were 'partial or restricted' experiences compared with those of others who, in addition, contacted 'higher' conditions). All the earth-experiences of all men are necessarily partial experiences [cf. I Cor. xiii, 12; Eph, v, 14].

Case No. 156—*Mrs 'A'*

The case of Mrs 'A' is selected from those given by Robert Dale Owen in his *Footfalls on the Boundary of Another World* (Edited and Revised by Angus McArthur, 'Light' Publishing Co. Ltd.). Mrs 'A', the wife of a colonel, awoke to find herself standing by the side of her bed in her home at Woolwich. *She was looking down on her own Physical Body* and that of her sleeping husband [cf. Statement No. 17]. She thought that she was dead. *Mrs 'A' made three critical observations. First, she noted that, while her husband's face looked fresh, hers was pale and lifeless. Secondly, since (as she thought) she had died, she was pleased at having escaped the physical pain that she imagined necessarily accompanied that process. Thirdly, moving towards the wall, and expecting it to arrest her progress, she discovered that she had a most remarkable ability, namely, that of passing through it without hindrance* [cf. Statement No. 31].

Mrs 'A' then found herself in the room of a friend, a Miss 'L.M.', at Greenwich. They conversed. Then she awoke, saying, 'So I am not dead, after all!' Her husband asked what she meant and she narrated her experience.

Miss 'L.M.' was due to visit the 'A's' two days later. They told her nothing, but when Mrs 'A' said, 'My last bonnet was trimmed with violet, I shall select that colour again', her friend replied, 'Yes, I know that is your colour.' 'How so?' 'Because when you came to me on Wednesday night you were robed in violet.' 'I appeared to you on Wednesday night?' 'Yes, about 3 a.m. We had quite a conversation. Have you no recollection of it?' *Mrs 'A' could remember the fact that they had conversed, but not the details.*

CASE No. 157—'M.D.'

'M.D.' was the signature appended to a letter that appeared in the *Spectator* for Sept., 1952. The writer said that he became unconscious after an operation. He continued, 'Consciousness slowly returned and I felt deliciously peaceful. I strove to make out the figures round my bed. Then, as I slipped back into semi-consciousness, *I realized I was dying; I was floating above the bed, the figures now beneath me* [cf. Statement No. 17]. *I had left my body and felt indescribably free.*'

CASE No. 158—*Mrs Gertrude Snow Palmer*

Mrs Palmer, of Redmond, Oregon, U.S.A., a writer and artist, informed me (*in litt.*) that *she had read no books on, and had no knowledge whatever of, these matters prior to having the experience. Although it was 'totally unexpected', everything that occurred seemed to be 'quite natural'* [cf. Statement No. 9]. Mrs Palmer's description is as follows.

'The experience occurred thirteen years ago, but it was so vivid that my memory of it is as clear as when it happened. I had been very ill and was in constant aching misery. I was lying on a bed-sofa. My husband was still at work.

'*I became aware of an odd sensation that started at my feet and progressed slowly upwards—a sort of dis-association. It crept upwards past my hips and began to affect my abdomen, and I began to understand that I was dying. The thought of dying had heretofore been associated with fear and with ideas of horrible struggles. Now I understood that it was nothing of the kind* [cf. Statement No. 7. Note also that Mrs Palmer's description of *leaving* the body is the converse of Mrs Parker's of *re-entering* it.] *It was kind and gentle,* and there was a feeling of great and wonderful expectation. The sensation travelled swiftly up past my arms and, when it went into my head, *I was suddenly not in my body but above it.*

'*I was even above the roof of the house, which became as if it were not there —it was transparent.* There was no feeling of having a body of any kind. [Compare the 'partial awakening'—Statement No. 25.] I could see, but all-around, as if my mind—which was essentially that 'I' that was the being—had eye-facets all over. I could hear in the same way. *First I noticed my seven-year-old son, playing with blocks. Then my attention was drawn to a far-away brightness that called me mightily.* The atmosphere that

I inhabited in this state was a lovely pink haze. There was also a swelling of beautiful music something like a pipe-organ. I thought it most heavenly. *I was tremendously appreciative of the sense of freedom from my heavy, ungainly body* [cf. Miss Kaeyer and Anon.—Case No. 42. Conversely, Mrs Cripps and Mrs 'X' found the body 'heavy' when it was re-assumed]. I wanted very much to go towards that brightness.

'Then I looked back, or rather, I focussed my mind back into the room below. *I could see my Physical Body lying there.* I thought, "I am too young to leave the earth—it wouldn't be fair to Darrell and my husband". At the same time I saw my husband coming up the walk and I knew he would be terrified if he found my body lifeless down there. *I didn't want to go back, but I knew I must, and then I was back* (cf. Statement No. 8]. There was no feeling of re-entering my body—I was just there, though it took an awful effort to move myself [= catalepsy]. I hadn't quite "made it" in time, for Don thought I was dead when he first looked down.

'I don't know how long it was before I got my eyes opened, but when I did I was satisfied that going back was the only thing I could do. I was not conscious of passing through the roof, either coming out or going back.

'Until this experience I had just hoped that we survive death. *Since then I have had no fear of death—quite the contrary. All seemed very natural.* It was as if some part of me had always known it would be like that— something like a merger with a Higher Self.

'I think it will be wonderful to be free from the limiting body that I now have to carry around, to go on and find what lay at the end of that brightness, to live in the unfettered plane beyond this one. The contrast between being in the body and being out of it was about like that between being confined in a 3-ft. by 5-ft. cage and suddenly being let out of it. The contrast between the light Astral [here = Psychical] Body and the heavy Physical Body was the difference between light and dark ... and the same with the difference between the astral world and the physical world. I was not aware of an astral body, but had a feeling of being round like a ball. I could see in an all-round way, instead of with a single focus, as in the Physical Body. There was a wonderful feeling of harmony in the astral world. *I saw my Physical Body and was only too happy to be out of it. ... I could have left my body as easily as one casts off a garment. The only thing that brought me back was love for my family.*

'My first emotion was tremendous relief in getting clear of my body, which was ill. Then followed a relief that dying had not been the struggle I had always thought it would be. Next came an excitement about the astral world, and a great desire to go towards the glow manifesting on the horizon of the pink mist around me. I had the thought,

"What survives is the mind ... essentially the I AM of being, the Individuality".'

CASE NO. 159—*A tuberculosis patient*

A partial (or partially-remembered) experience is given in *Prediction* for Nov., 1953. It was quoted from *Amrita Bajar Patrika*, of Calcutta. The writer, a tuberculosis patient, said, 'I experienced death and came back to life again. Suddenly I became aware of my existence outside my body. At first I could not realize that it was death. *I was steadily being moved upwards in a lying position. I applied all my strength to come down to my body, but in vain! The outgoing man had the same form as the body he had vacated, but it is doubtful if he had any weight.'*

CASE NO. 160—*Mr S. L. Bensusan*

Mr Bensusan, the author, described an experience when he was ill. It also was given in *Prediction*. He said, 'Lying helpless and inert, *I suddenly found myself above the foot of the bed, looking at my motionless body. I wanted to get away from it, but every now and then the nurse moved it and I became one with the body on the bed'* [cf. Ogston's account]. He continued, 'I was fully satisfied that we are not our bodies, that bodies are no more than the vehicle through which we function. ... When I recovered, on more than one occasion I went in danger of my life. It was not courage that sustained me in difficult hours; it was *the profound consciousness that neither fire nor water, knife nor bomb could touch me. They could shatter the container, but the contents were safe. ... The body is not the self.'*

Appendix IV

CERTAIN 'DREAMS' AS
'INCOMPLETE NATURAL EXPERIENCES'

'DREAMS' that possibly represent partial (or partially-remembered) out-of-the-body experiences, as might be expected if such experiences are natural to mankind, are commonly reported. These are in addition to those that are conditioned by what we call a 'partial awakening'.

James Langham (*More than Meets the Eye*, Evans Bros., 1951) described a recurring dream. He said, 'I would be standing on the grass near the edge of a cliff. There was coldness and mist [= 'Hades' conditions]. The sky was grey and a quiet grey sea was just visible far below. I would find myself propelled forward by some unknown means [compare Muldoon and others], and the next moment I would be moving horizontally through the air out to sea. That would last only for a few moments. I would then begin to "drop", "fall", or perhaps more accurately, to "float" very slowly downwards towards the sea itself. This was accompanied by a feeling of terror. Invariably I awoke just before reaching the surface of the water' [Muldoon described similar 'dreams' and recommends 'letting oneself "go" ']. Langham pointed out that his 'dream' resembled that of the innkeeper's daughter in Cervantes' *Don Quixote*, where it is said, 'I have many times dreamed that I was falling from a tower and never coming to the ground. When I awoke I found myself as weak and shaken as if I had really fallen.'

Havelock Ellis (*The World of Dreams*) described the falling dream as 'the best known and most frequent type', while Miss Mary Monteith (*A Book of True Dreams*, Heath Cranton, 1929) mentioned, 'That fall from a great height, accompanied by a feeling of terror and followed by a jump which awakens the sleeper to a condition of breathlessness and palpitation ...'

Dreams of falling are, of course, related to those of rising, floating and flying. Muldoon (*The Projection of the Astral Body*, Rider & Co., Ltd., 1929, written in collaboration with Dr Hereward Carrington) correlated all three types of dream with out-of-the-body experiences: he showed that they correspond to the route taken by the 'double', or 'astral body' (a) in exteriorizing from the Physical Body when we fall asleep, (b) in taking a journey, and (c) in returning to it when we awaken. This route is as follows: usually, the 'double' rises above the sleeping physical counterpart in a lying-down position (exactly, it should be noted, as is described both by clairvoyant observers of dying persons and by supposed dead persons). It may then do one of two things: in some cases it uprights at once over the Physical Body; in others, while remaining in the lying position, it rises to about four feet above the Physical Body. (Compare the distances given by clairvoyants, by others who temporarily left the body and by the supposed dead, which vary from a foot or two to about four feet.) It then moves off several feet to one side (still lying horizontal), lies there for some time, and returns to the original position above the Physical Body. Muldoon's observations showed that, 'This is as far as many projections progress, and it is in this type of experience that many aviation dreams are instigated.'

The fear which brings the 'dreamer' back to his body with a jump or 'repercussion', is often due to the remembrance of some frightening incident during the preceding day. But it may also be due to some degree of realization of one's position above the physical earth.

Muldoon recognized three types of 'fall' in returning to the Physical Body, correlating them as follows: (a) the 'straight' fall, accompanied by a 'jump' (repercussion), is due to some violent emotion, usually fear; (b) the 'spiral fall' is due to a compromise in consciousness between the tendency of the non-physical body to rise above, and that of the Physical Body to fall to, the earth; (c) the 'slow, vibratory fall' is due to an almost equal balance of the factors involved. Muldoon said, 'You can break a falling dream, merely by "letting yourself go": do not fear hitting the bottom; just let yourself fall ... fear speeds the fall'.

It would appear that if one is conscious of leaving the Physical Body, it will cause a 'dream of rising'; if conscious of moving horizontally ('travelling'), there may be a 'dream' of floating or flying, and if conscious of returning, a 'dream of falling'.

'Communications' from the supposed dead also include the statement that temporary excursions from the Physical Body are common among educated and advanced people but that consciousness in such excursions is mercifully limited until one has, by repeated experiments, overcome all fear of heights. Until then, one is not free of the 'next world' during sleep and one's 'co-operative' ability is necessarily curtailed.

G. Sime (*The Land of Dreams*, The Macmillan Co. of Canada, Toronto, 1940), after reading Maeterlinck's essay on dreams in his *Life of Space*, determined to write down her dreams on awakening, and to avoid reading any accounts of dreams by others. She had 'motion dreams' that included 'flying, springing from the earth into the air, floating among the tree-tops, skimming swiftly along the ground and bouncing like a ball.' She noted that, '*All such dreams bring a sense of physical well-being, frequently amounting to rapture.* My dream-shade is nearly always happy when it realizes that it is in the middle of a motion dream'. Of all such dreams, those of 'bouncing', sometimes to 'amazing heights', were the most delightful. She said to herself, 'This time I shall remember how it is done, and be able to do it when awake'. She recalled 'one dream in which the dream-shade, while it was actually springing up and down in a room, touching the ceiling and then the floor, *deliberately conveying the rationale of movement, as one might say, to my walking consciousness, "Now you won't forget", it proclaimed triumphantly, "see, it is quite easy. Look! Feel! Remember!" But the waking self was too circumscribed to catch the trick.'* [Compare Gerhardi, Miss 'W.S.', etc.]

Miss Sime also said, '*I must fairly often, I fancy, have dreamed of flying without being conscious of the fact, for I remember that on the first occasion of my travelling by air, and of looking down on the landscape, I said to myself, "Why, it's like a dream!" And then it was borne in upon me that I had frequently seen the earth and its cities spread out so in my sleep.*' (This accords with the statement made by many supposed discarnate 'communicators' that we mortals 'visit' the 'next world' nightly while exteriorized from the Physical Body during sleep. While most such experiences do not enter 'normal consciousness' and are 'forgotten', some few filter through—and all will be recovered when we finally 'pass over'. These repeated visits represent one of the reasons why, after death, the 'next world' seems 'natural' and 'familiar'. They mitigate the shock of transition.)

(Assuming that, in these 'dreams', Miss Sime was in a non-physical body, like Mrs Joy, Mrs Jeffrey, Miss Stables, Turvey and others, she was sometimes apart from, and observing, the non-physical body in which she had the experiences: that is, she operated in three distinct non-physical bodies. She said that, in a particular 'dream', 'I was flying downwards between two cliffs and the other 'I', who was standing apparently outside the dream, had the most extraordinary view of myself thus heading downwards ... I foresaw, and prepared for, the wheeling flight which was to carry me in the opposite direction— slantingly upwards.')

Miss Sime also described the common feature of 'astral catalepsy': she was unable to move or speak. As would be expected if illness predisposes to exteriorization, many of her happiest 'dreams' came when her body was ill—'I would find myself wandering in beauty, sometimes in company with winged, strong and beautiful Beings, or flying above plains, cities, etc.' She continued, 'It would seem that there is some spot in us which is impervious to pain, and which retains its placidity, unmoved by whatever suffering of mind or body may be going on at its side [cf. Smythe, Morrell, Georginus, etc.]. I only reach this spot when I am asleep and dreaming: or when I am awake and dreaming too.'

Miss Sime visited the city of Florence so often in 'dreams' that when she eventually went there for the first time in the Physical Body, she knew the city thoroughly (and proved the fact to a friend). She could describe 'with the utmost accuracy', the interior of buildings unvisited in the flesh.

Miss Lilian S. Dawe, formerly Secretary of the D'Oyley Carte Opera Company, gave an account of her 'projection'-like dream in *Psychic News*, Sept., 1954. Miss Dawe had this dream repeatedly since the age of five. It is as follows.

'I am standing in a large room, with a parquet flooring. It is full of people who are strangers to me. With a jerk, I launch myself off the floor with my right foot. This sends me floating over the heads of the people. *It is a most pleasant and exhilarating sensation.* I am free from all hampering weight. *The experience is so vivid: all the next day I feel certain that I really can fly.* I find myself trying to elevate my body as I do in the dream. On a recent occasion I floated out with my feet straight before me, as though I were sitting up in bed. I do not feel any jerk when returning to my body.

'Once, during an illness, *I was conscious of my Physical Body on the bed. I floated above it, looking down at it with a feeling of pity* (cf. Statement No. 17].

Appendix V

STATEMENTS OF THE 'DEAD' REGARDING THEIR EXPERIENCES

THE following statements were obtained by the writer by analysing numerous 'communications' from the supposed dead, as to what they experienced at, and soon after, death. They concerned people of *average* type. (The experiences described by great saints or great sinners are somewhat different.) The 'communications' are cited in *The Supreme Adventure*, James Clarke & Co. Ltd., 1960, to whom thanks are rendered. The value of the statements is there assessed.They are cited here for purposes of comparison with the narratives of people who left their bodies only temporarily.

INTRODUCTORY

Statement No. 1a.—Dominant and habitual thoughts and feelings, including fixed ideas and strong expectations, affect a person's experiences in the immediate hereafter.

Statement No. 1b.—'Communications' agree with the teaching of St Paul (I Cor. xv, 44) that, in addition to his Physical Body, man possesses a physically-invisible and intangible body. *St Paul called the physical the 'carnal' body and, in addition, recognized (a) a 'natural' (Psychical) and (b) a 'Spiritual' Body.* He said that those of the 'dead' who are 'seen' by the 'living' are recognized because the Psychical Body, or 'double' is similar in form to the Physical Body.

'Communications' include statements similar to St Paul's but use such terms as 'astral' (star-like, *i.e.*, luminous) body, 'etheric', 'ethereal', (= light, airy, unearthly, heavenly) body, etc. *Numerous communicators indicate a detail of man's total bodily constitution additional to those given by St Paul.* (The latter made no claim to exhaustive treatment of the subject: he was not describing the succession of after-death states.) They say that the total Physical Body includes (a) the 'dense Physical Body' and (b) an 'ultra-gaseous' portion, a 'magnetic field' or 'Denser Between Body'. This is intermediate between the dense Physical Body and the Psychical Body, or Finer Between Body. Some call it the 'astral body', others the 'etheric body', but still others apply those terms to the Psychical Body. *Many point out that it is not a 'body', since it is not a vehicle of consciousness. It has the form, but neither the tissues nor the sense organs of the Physical Body. Its functions are (a) to receive vital energies (collected by the Psychical Body) and transmit them to the Physical Body i.e., it is a vehicle of vitality, and (b) to bear the impression of every event in its owner's life, i.e., it is a memory-record. From its effect on consciousness, we call this the 'body-veil'.* It interpenetrates and extends beyond the Physical Body. It affects the immediate after-death experiences. A 'communicator' makes a statement very similar to those of the well-known psychics Mrs Eileen J. Garrett and Dr Horace Leaf, thus: 'The denser atoms of the etheric body [here = the vehicle of vitality, 'body-veil' or 'Denser Between Body'] are so akin to the physical that they also disintegrate shortly after death. ... The finer portion [= the Finer Between Body or Psychical Body] its life-essence, lives on.' Dion Fortune said, 'The etheric double [here = the Psychical Body] is primarily a body of magnetic stresses in the framework of whose meshes every cell and fibre of the Physical Body is held as in a rack. But intermediate between this and the dense Physical Body there is what may be called the raw matter [= the 'body-veil'] out of which dense matter is condensed. This was called by the ancients Hylê (First Matter) and by the moderns 'ectoplasm'. It is this projected ectoplasm which produces the phenomena of physical manifestations.' Many communicators describe the 'body-veil', vehicle of vitality, or 'Denser Between Body' as 'semi-physical' in nature.

The Phsycical Body not only has the outline of the Physical Body, it reproduces it cell for cell. It is, in fact, the basis and mould of the Physical Body. It 'vibrates' much more rapidly that the Physical Body and is consequently invisible to mortal eyes. It is much more sensitive than the Physical Body and hence receives impressions that are not received by the Physical Body. It not only interpenetrates the latter but extends some feet (or more) beyond. One 'communicator' described the Psychical Body as 'a magnetic area of creative thought—a vibrating, always circulating system of electric currents flowing up from the solar plexus, crossing behind the neck, and emerging at the feet—a glowing whorl'. Another (who called it the 'Beta Body') said that it has 'the form, shape and all the attributes of the Physical Body intensified'. He insisted that it is 'material' and 'not vapourish'.

Here is the chief cause of confusion in psychic communications and we propose to avoid it by adopting the earlier terms used by St Paul [*plus* the term vehicle of vitality (and memory), or 'body-veil']. Some 'communicators' group the 'body-veil' as part of the *total* Physical Body, others, like Leaf, group it with the *total* Psychical (or Between) Body and still others, like Fortune, treat it as intermediate between, but distinct from, both. In different communications the terms 'astral' and 'etheric' body and 'double' may mean (a) the 'body-veil' or (b) the Psychical Body or (c) a combination of both.

The Spiritual Body interpenetrates, and extends beyond, the Psychical and Physical Bodies. It 'vibrates' more rapidly than the Psychical and is described as 'super-physical' in nature.

In a few—a very few—people some component of the total non-physical body is relatively loosely associated with the adjacent one. If the 'body-veil' is loosely attached to the Physical Body, the person concerned is a potential 'physical' medium: ectoplasm can be exterior-ized, producing 'raps', 'levitations' and other 'semi-physical' pheno-mena. The latter may occur quite apart from spiritualistic seances, though they are facilitated by them. They are occasionally found in association with highly religious people (see Appendix I). Looseness of the 'body-veil' may be natural or it may be induced by prolonged debilitating illness, undue fatigue or fasting, severe shock, the abuse of alcohol or drugs and by seances.

If the junction between the Psychical and the Physical Bodies is relatively loose, the person concerned tends to be a 'mental' medium, with telepathic, clairvoyant and pre-cognitive faculties—that is, with interventions in 'normal' consciousness, from the 'super-normal' con-sciousness. The possession of a relatively loose 'body-veil', with potential 'physical' mediumship, is unrelated to the moral and spiritual nature (so that a 'physical' medium may, or may not, be morally reli-able). The possession of a relatively loose Psychical Body may, or may not, have moral significance. A highly religious person tends to be a 'mental' medium, though there is no guarantee that a 'mental' medium is highly religious.

A mystic has a relatively 'loose' Spiritual Body: 'intimations of immortality' enter his or her 'normal' consciousness from 'spiritual' (not psychical) sources. His consciousness is not limited by time, space or form.

According to 'communicators', man (in the sense of 'Spirit', 'Higher Mind', 'Ego' or 'Over-soul') 'clothes' himself in a series of progressively denser bodies (the physical being the densest) for purposes of experi-ence, expression, development and unfoldment. 'Spirit' is too vast to express and unfold itself otherwise: it is, indeed, limitless. The bodies act as sphincters (comparable to the iris of the eye or to a camera-shutter) or to the 'blinkers' on the headgear of a horse): they limit the amount of awareness that gets through to what can be dealt with at that time. So long as a man is incarnate (that is, operating through the whole series of bodies—super-physical (Spiritual), semi-physical (Psychical) and Physical—the 'vibratory rate' of consciousness is slowed-down to the physical rate. This retardation provides us with opportunities of controlling thought and emotion during our reactions with the physical environment and fellow-men. In proportion as we control our thoughts and emotions, the Psychical and Spiritual Bodies tend to become organized: in so far as they are organized they can be used effectively by consciousness after the Physical Body is shed at death. During earth-life, the Psychical Body acts as a link between the Physical and the Spiritual: it is analogous to a gear. The 'body-veil' is not a vehicle of consciousness, but a vitality-lung and memory-record. When, as with us mortals, consciousness is 'imprisoned' in and limited to the whole series of bodies (including the physical) we regard it as 'normal'. When, as in certain temporary and abnormal conditions, it does not get through to the physical, it is enveiled and enshrouded by the 'body-veil': it is then 'dreamy' and 'sub-normal'. When it operates with little restriction in the Psychical Body, it is 'super-normal'. When the Spiritual Body only is used, restriction is at a minimum and we have 'spiritual', 'cosmic' or 'mystical' consciousness.

We now review the statements of the supposed discarnates with regard to sleep, etc. A man is 'alive', 'awake' to, or conscious of the physical world because his Spiritual, Psychical and Physical Bodies all coincide and are 'in gear' with each other. Limitation of 'vibration-rate' necessarily involves a limitation in the range and intensity of consciousness. Nevertheless, only through such limitation can man (who essentially is 'Spirit', Mind or Consciousness using a Spiritual Body with extremely rapid 'vibrations') become aware of the slowly-'vibrating' physical world, that is, can he receive visual, tactual and other stimuli from the physical world. Only when he experiences physical sensations, based on stimuli from the physical objects, can he interact with the latter, learning about the physical world—and about himself—using it as a means of self-knowledge and self-development. If his ideas of the physical world are erroneous, they are corrected by practical experience. The process of trial-and-error in physical life leads to accurate thought. The farmer knows that he can get out of his land only what he puts into it.

In the light sleep, of average people (in whom the 'body-veil' is very closely knit to the Physical Body), the Psychical Body is partially disengaged from, or 'out of gear' with, the Physical Body. In this condition, the Physical Body no longer primarily transmits stimuli from the physical world—or acts upon the physical world. During sleep the Physical Body recuperates in preparation for the next period of interaction with the physical world. In the light sleep, especially in that of mediumistic people (in whom the 'body-veil' is in loose association with the Physical Body) part of the 'body-veil' accompanies the Psychical Body and there may be some consciousness in (and possibly some remembrance of) 'earth-veil', 'Denser Between Worlds', 'Hades', or 'Sheol' conditions.

In deep sleep the Psychical Body is completely disengaged from ('out of gear' with) the Physical Body. The sleeper usually at first seems to lie from a few inches to a few feet above the Physical Body, in a horizontal position. [The Psychical Body is said to leave the Physical Body by all the pores, but chiefly (as a rule) by the head. In some cases, however, where there is a weak place in the Physical Body, it may leave chiefly by the side, the breast, the feet or the solar plexus.]

Many men are said to spend much of the night lying horizontally over their (separated) Physical Bodies. Meanwhile, the Physical Body is not only being allowed to rest, it is being re-charged with vital energy that is absorbed by the Psychical Body: the vitality is passed to the vehicle of vitality and thence, down a cord-like connection that appears to be described in the Bible (Eccles. xii, 6) as the 'silver cord', to the Physical Body. The term 'cord' (suggesting a definite, unalterable thickness) is deceptive: it is symbolic. The feature is actually more of an 'electric', or 'magnetic' nature. It stretches indefinitely and seems to be composed of many intertwined 'threads'. There is usually one 'cord', passing from head to head, but occasionally two 'cords' are described, differently attached. In addition, there are many minor connecting 'threads'.

During deep sleep the Psychical Body may move along horizontally over the physical feet, eventually standing erect. The movement of this body is unrestricted by physical objects, such as doors and walls. The man may, at times, be more or less conscious of the environment corresponding to the Psychical Body, *i.e.*, to the 'Finer Between Worlds', 'Paradise' or Elysium. Occasionally such experiences are more or less clearly remembered on waking, *i.e.*, he has 'dreams' (often distorted, often symbolic) representing actual events and 'real' surroundings. Clear remembrance of conscious experiences during deep sleep is not possible, however, unless the physical brain has been given special memory-training. Pythagoras, some 600 years B.C., seems to have described such training. It is important to note the difference (from a bodily point of view) between sleep and death: in sleep (and in astral projection), *part of* the 'body-veil' leaves the Physical Body and accompanies the Psychical Body; in death, *the whole* 'body-veil' leaves the Physical Body (and, in addition, its cord-like connexion with the Physical Body soon becomes severed).

(1) NATURAL DEATH IN OLD AGE

Statement No. 2.—As a man who has attained a ripe old age prepares to die to leave his Physical Body (not temporarily as he has done nightly, but permanently) his *thoughts and feelings often go out, possibly more or less unconsciously, to the friends and relatives who have 'gone before'. If so, the latter are aware, by telepathic process, of the fact: to them it represents a 'call'*; knowing that his passing is imminent, they come to aid and

welcome him. Several communicators say that strong affection between the dying man and his discarnate friends represents a particularly
strong 'call', one which is sure to be obeyed. Many 'communicators' say
that, apart from this specific 'call' (to personal friends and relatives), all
who die are met and, so far as is possible, welcomed, helped and
instructed. There are said to be two chief limiting conditions (see
Statements 3 and 4).

Statement No. 3.—This is the converse of Statement No. 2. Several
'communicators' say that the excessively self-centred man, on dying, is
not met by 'departed' *friends*: he has failed to make the necessary 'call'
to them. As already said, such men are, however, met by others
('deliverers') who voluntarily specialize in such duties.

Statement No. 4.—A fixed idea, especially the idea that there is no
after-life, acts like a post-hypnotic suggestion: it naturally prevents the
sending of a 'call' to departed friends. Although men who die under
this disadvantage are not neglected, their mental condition delays their
acceptance of help.

Statement No. 5.—In the early stage of death, *immediately after the
Physical Body is shed, a man reviews his past earth-life*: this (first) review is
typically of an impersonal non-emotional and non-responsible nature:
it is a mechanical process.

Statement No. 6.—Several 'communicators' say that about an hour
before visible death (that is, before the breathing and heart-beat cease
and decomposition begins) *the dying man has often already shed his
Physical Body and stands, perfectly conscious, nearby.* (Compare Statement
No. 18.) He may still, usually for a short time—often only a few hours
—be attached to his body by the 'silver cord' (usually uniting head to
head). In this case he will be more or less aware of his Physical Body
and its surroundings (*e.g.*, people in the room).

Statement No. 7.—All agree that the gradual and natural process of
death in old age involves neither physical pain nor fear: many say that,
on the contrary, they found that *the act of dying was 'easy', and 'natural',
even 'delightful'*.

Statement No. 8.—This is the converse of No. 7. Being brought back
from the verge of death to physical life by stimulants, etc., does involve
pain and fear. *Those who return to earth-life do so with reluctance.*

Statement No. 9.—The actual shedding of the Physical Body is
seldom felt. (Where death occurs during sleep it could not be felt.) In
those cases in which it was felt, *some experienced a sensation either of
'falling' or of 'rising' while others had 'a momentary coma' 'darkness' or
'blackout'. This momentary 'darkness' is often described in symbolic terms:
the commonest is that of passing through a dark tunnel.* A 'communicator' of
Miss Cummins thought he had travelled through a 'dark tunnel' while
leaving his Physical Body. Another said, 'I saw in front of me a dark

tunnel. I stepped out of the tunnel into unknown country, into a new world.'

Statement No. 10.—Very many do not, for a time, realize that they have shed their Physical Bodies. Men of *average* morality and spirituality who die *naturally* in old age may not, on awakening, at first realize their transition. This is partly because the 'next' world of which *they* become aware ('Paradise') is very similar to the earth (Statement No. 11).

Very few *average* men whose death is *enforced* in the prime of life at first realize the fact of their transition. This is due to three factors. First, *they* have still to shed the vehicle of vitality, 'body-veil' or 'Denser Between Body' and *their* 'next' world (the 'earth-veil', 'Denser Between Worlds' or 'Hades') is even more earth-like than 'Paradise': the common and stable environment consists of the 'counterparts' of physical objects. Secondly, these people do not at first realize that the substance composing the 'Between Worlds' is ideo-plastic (as is ecto-plasm), that since it responds to their thoughts, feelings, expectations, hopes, fears etc., their environment may, in part, be self-created: in addition to the objective replicas of earthly houses, seas, mountains, etc. (forming the common environment), they may see 'thought-forms' (created either individually or collectively). They may not, at first, be able to recognize the latter as 'creations' (*e.g.*, Raymond's 'cigars'). Thirdly, since the 'body-veil' has no 'organs' and is not a vehicle of consciousness, it enshrouds consciousness, reducing it to 'sub-normal', dream-levels. The newly-dead in the 'Hades' state are nearest to mortals so that they most easily, and most often, communicate with mortals. But they 'know not anything' (Eccles. ix, 5): a number who communicated from 'Hades' conditions later 'returned' from 'Paradise' conditions to say that their earlier messages had been more or less misleading—they had largely been 'dreams'.

Those who die naturally, on awakening, tend to feel 'well', 'light', 'free', 'serene', 'peaceful', 'secure', 'alert', etc., and to find their environment 'natural' and 'bright'. *Those whose death is enforced* tend at first to be 'confused': they are 'bewildered' by what they see, and find their environment 'indistinct', 'unreal', 'misty', 'foggy' (even 'watery') and 'somewhat dreamlike'. Teachable and adaptable men, however, soon leave this temporary abnormal state. While the time (in our sense of the word) may be short, the experience may seem long. In any case, it ends when the 'body-veil' is shed and consciousness, now released, seems to expand considerably as it operates through the Psychical Body.

Statement No. 11.—Many say that death was 'not what was expected'. The process seemed 'natural', there was no 'abrupt change' in the self and the new environment was 'familiar', 'earth-like', 'substantial' and 'real'.

Statement No. 12.—Several who died thought at first that they might be dreaming. Most, however, knew that they were not (once any preliminary awakening was over).

Statement No. 13.—The total non-physical body, or 'double' (= the 'body-veil' as well as the Psychical and Spiritual Bodies) *usually left the Physical Body by way of the head.* Other exits were used in exceptional cases, where there was some 'weak' spot in the Physical Body (*see* 1b).

Statement No. 14.—A nebulous mass is first seen above the dying man. It usually floats horizontally over the recumbent Physical Body and is variously described as 'luminous', 'grey', 'smoke-like', 'steam-like', 'vaporous', 'cloudy', 'shadowy', 'misty', and 'hazy'.

Statement No. 15.—This cloudy form gradually becomes definite, until it resembles the discarded physical form (though looking younger and brighter).

Statement No. 16.—The distance above the discarded Physical Body usually varies from directly above to four feet.

Statement No. 17.—*Many 'communicators' described how, immediately after, death they saw their own Physical Bodies, in addition to the self-luminous non-physical body in which they stood.* (Many also saw the mourners round the bed and heard what was said, etc. Some eventually attended their own funerals.) Other 'communicators' did not describe seeing their own Physical Bodies or those of others. According to 'communications' (Statement No. 21) *there is some cognizance of physical matter so long as the newly-dead person is still in the 'body-veil' and especially if the 'silver cord' (that joins it to the Physical Body) has remained unbroken.*

Statement No. 18.—*Many also saw and heard their 'departed' friends and relations* (especially those whom they had 'called'—see Statement No. 2). Those who describe having these experiences fall into three approximately equal groups: some had them just before the Physical Body was shed (compare Statement No. 6), some had them immediately after it was shed, and the time of some cannot be determined. Statements 17 and 18 mean that *a man who dies naturally in old age has glimpses of two worlds—the physical world and the 'next' (in this case 'Paradise'): he has a certain amount of 'dual', or 'alternate', consciousness. But once the 'silver cord' becomes very thin or is actually severed his consciousness is of the 'next' world only.*

Statement No. 19.—Many say that the newly-discarded Physical Body is attached to the 'body-veil' and the latter to the Psychical Body by *a non-physical 'cord'* (as well as by numerous 'threads', such as intertwine to form the 'cord').

Statement No. 20.—*Until the 'silver cord' snaps or, in Biblical phraseology (Eccles. xii, 6), is 'loosed', decomposition does not commence in the Physical Body.* Until then (providing it is in fact re-habitable) a man can return to and re-animate his Physical Body. Once the cord is broken, however, return is impossible. (Note that in the case of Lazarus decomposition had not begun four days after death—John xi, 39.) It is said that the delay in decomposition until after the 'cord' is severed is due to the fact that 'vital currents' are collected by the Psychical Body and transmitted by way of the vehicle of vitality, to the Physical Body. Several 'communicators' warn against cremation or burial before the 'cord' is actually broken—*i.e.*, before decomposition sets in—since, in very rare instances (as, apparently, in the case of Lazarus), it may be a case of suspended animation.

Statement No. 21.—In the natural death of *average* men, the 'cord' may break immediately after, or within a few hours of, visible death. A definitely below-average person may have a thick and strong 'cord' and the period may extend to three or four days. In cases of enforced death in the prime of life (and especially where it is self-inflicted) the 'body-veil' may not be shed (in which case the cord is not 'loosed') for a period exceeding three or four days.

Statement No. 22.—After the 'cord' that unites the Physical Body to the 'body-veil' is 'loosed', the *average* man who dies naturally in old age enjoys *a period of recuperative sleep (sometimes with dreams) which lasts for an average period of three or four days of earth-time*. That period is mentioned in many independent accounts. (A man who is killed in the prime of life, on the other hand, tends to be awake at once.)

Statement No. 23.—The *post-mortem* sleep of the aged is due to the 'body-veil' being depleted of vital force, and the mind being fatigued. The newly-dead man is described as being in 'a veil', his condition resembling the chrysalis stage of insects. Once the 'body-veil' has been shed (= the 'second death'), and its cord 'loosed', it gravitates to its physical counterpart—from which it has seldom, if ever, been far distant. The two decompose simultaneously.

Statement No. 24.—The after-death 'sleep'-period may be lengthened and the 'sleep' deepened by certain factors: (a) a prolonged and severe last illness (causing mental exhaustion); (b) an exceptionally difficult and strenuous earth-life (also causing mental exhaustion); (c) a continued desire for physical sensation; (d) intense grief of 'living' friends (acting as a strong attracting force to the newly-dead and affecting him mentally—see Statement No. 27); (e) fixed ideas, and especially that there is no after-life (= Statement No. 4), and (f) the unteachability of exceptionally dull and unimaginative people. The opposite conditions tend to shorten the sleep-period and render it lighter and lighter. Thus, an above-average man who dies without exhausting illness, and whose friends are wise enough to replace selfish grief by wise prayers, may have little, if any, sleep. ['We shall not all sleep,' said St Paul (I Cor. xv, 51), 'but we shall all be changed, in a moment, in the twinkling of an eye. ...'] On the other hand, a below-average man who dies under unfortunate conditions may sleep for weeks or months of earth-time.

Statement No. 25.—Those who had a *post-mortem* sleep may have a *brief, preliminary or 'partial awakening'*. The newly-awakened man, and especially one who is relatively unevolved, may consequently experience a brief period of confusion: he has become conscious of his existence and identity but not of his surroundings. As one 'communicator' says, 'The spiritual senses have not yet begun to function'. In this brief period there may either apparently be no environment at all or the environment may seem dream-like and therefore unreal. Some of the newly-dead, on first awakening, wonder if they are in a dream: several speak of a brief period of 'confusion' and 'incertitude', while one mentioned 'a mere sense of identity, a point of self-awareness growing out of nothingness'.

Statement No. 26.—Many are spared even a brief period of confusion, since their consciousness of environment emerges simultaneously with that of identity: they have no 'partial awakening'. In these cases the first feeling described is one of 'peace', 'security', 'well-being', 'intense reality', etc. Some speak of 'astonishment' because death was 'not what was expected' (Statement No. 11): on the contrary, it was 'natural' and the surroundings were 'real', 'familiar' and 'earth-like'.

Statement No. 27.—Many complain that *excessive grief on the part of their still-embodied friends and relatives hurts them*. It hinders their progress into happier conditions. Several explain this: they say that the newly-dead are particularly sensitive to the thoughts and feelings of the physically-embodied. This explanation seems to be correlated with the 'call' (Statement No. 2) and with the ideo-plastic nature of the material that composes the 'body-veil' or vehicle of vitality.

Statement No. 28.—*The first wish of many communicators was to 'return'* (though they insist that they have not, in any sense, 'gone away') to assure their embodied friends of their survival of death and of their well-being. Many are said to make this attempt within the few weeks that follow death: *most find themselves unseen and unheard*. A number insist that they are free from illness and weakness and 'never felt better'.

Statement No. 29.—Several 'communicators' emphasize the value to the newly-dead of the prayers of the 'living'. (Compare Statements No. 24 and 27.)

Statement No. 30.—Related to the claims cited as Statements No. 27 and 29 is the frequent intimation that *suitable mortals (especially potential psychics) can 'co-operate' with 'ministering angels'* to help (i) other mortals, (ii) the dying, (iii) the newly-dead and (iv) the 'earthbound' (= those delayed in 'Hades' conditions).

Statement No. 31.—It has already been said (No. 10) that very many newly-dead men of average type do not, for some time, realize the fact of their transition. Where a man dies naturally in old age *the following factors may assist him to realize his transition:* (a) *the sight of his discarded Physical Body* (in addition to that of the Psychical Body in which he stands), mentioned in Statement No. 17; (b) *the sight of those whom he knows to have been 'dead' for some time* (some of whom he may have 'called'), mentioned in Statements 2 and 18; and (c) his *inability to make himself seen or heard by his 'living' friends* (Statement No. 28) and (d) *his ability to pass through walls, to defy gravity, etc.* Another factor that may affect realization of his altered condition is his idea of death and the after-life: false teachings that have become fixed ideas will hinder the process (Statement No. 24e). Where teaching corresponds to facts it will assist.

Statement No. 32.—There is a remarkable consensus of opinion among these 'communicators' that the environment (in the 'spheres', 'planes', 'realms', 'worlds', 'conditions', etc.) to which the newly-dead man awakes are not, as is usually taught in Protestant Churches, of a 'spiritual' nature—that he is neither in 'heaven' nor 'hell'. On the contrary, *newly-dead men of average type awake to conditions that are intermediate between those of the physical world and those of 'super-physical' or 'Spiritual' realms (the 'Heavens').* Different terms, yet all embodying this idea, are used in the numerous independent accounts: they include, 'the threshold' of and 'the anti-chamber' to 'the Spiritual World', 'the transitional state', 'the semi-spiritual sphere', 'the semi-material sphere', 'the inner, or invisible, earth-plane', 'the semi-state', 'the borderland', 'the in-between land', 'the between land', 'the anteroom', 'the clearing-house', *'Paradise'* (= *a park*), 'the preliminary sphere', 'the rudimentary sphere', 'the sedimentary sphere', the 'halting', 'jumping off' or 'resting place', 'Between conditions', 'Purgatory', 'the Astral Plane', 'the nexus stage', and 'the state between the two worlds'.

Statement No. 33.—The above accords with the invariable descriptions by average newly-dead men of their conditions as 'earth-like', 'familiar', etc. (Statement No. 11.)

Statement No. 34.—In the early stages of death a man is said to have a mechanical, non-emotional review of his past life (Statement No. 5). Later, after the 'body-veil' has been shed and the newly-dead man has awakened in the Psychical Body to 'Paradise' conditions, he experiences *a second review, one which is emotional, selective and responsible. This is said to, and clearly does, correspond to the 'Judgment' of the various religions.* It does not, however, as is taught on the basis of certain Biblical texts, take place at the same time for all men and that at the 'end of the Age'. On the contrary it is said to be an individual experience and to occur usually (in earth-time) some days, weeks or months after the shedding of the Physical Body. The process is described as one that cleanses from feelings and desires that are essentially of a selfish, physical and material nature. It also eliminates fears, anxieties, irritations and angers and 'complexes', so that one can pass on to more harmonious conditions. Its positive aspect is concerned with the distillation of wisdom garnered from the earth-life that has just closed. In Statement No. 24 a reason was given for quiet confidence and earnest prayer (in place of undue grief) on the part of the 'living' towards the newly-dead. A second reason is adduced: in quietness the newly-dead man can give full attention to the essential matters then in progress: he is reviewing his past life with emotions that are appropriate to the thoughts, words and acts reviewed, and his emotions are much more intense than when he occupied his Physical Body. The retarding and dulling effect of the latter no longer operates. He becomes aware not only of his own feelings, but of those that he caused in others. He sees motives, causes and connexions that escaped his observation during earth-life. Under these circumstances, he is obliged to accept responsibility for his life and to acknowledge himself as he is. This 'Judgment', which is inescapable self-knowledge, does not occupy a day (of earth-time): it is spread over a period that varies with the needs and capacities of the individual. It is not made by God from outside man but by the Real, Inner Eternal or Greater Self, the 'Over-soul' which necessarily expresses the will of God.

Statement No. 35.—On the basis of the 'Judgment', after a variable period of further adjustment in 'Paradise' conditions, each average man 'goes to his own place' in the super-physical or 'Spiritual' Spheres, the 'Heavens'. Although conditions are describable in poetic and symbolic language only, they are 'real', more so, indeed, than the physical earth. They are beyond time, space and form.

(2) ENFORCED DEATH IN PRIME OF LIFE

Statement No. 36.—In unexpected death there is no time to 'call' friends who have 'gone before'. Hence, discarnate friends may not know, for some time, of the 'passing'—they may not be able to come to the aid of a man who dies unexpectedly. (They do come later, being brought by others—see below.) This constitutes a temporary disadvantage.

Statement No. 37.—In sudden death the 'silver cord' may be severed at once.

Statement No. 38.—It is significant that, whereas in our accounts of gradual and natural death there are numerous references to the seeing, just before (or just after) visible death, of friends who were known to be 'dead' (see No. 18), in the accounts of sudden death few references are made to this phenomenon (just after death).

Statement No. 39.—With sudden death, the man tends to be (though he is not always) 'awake' at once (apart, that is, from the momentary coma that accompanies the actual shedding of the Physical Body, which, indeed, may not be noticed). This is because he is mentally alert at the time of death (whereas the man who dies in extreme old age is mentally fatigued). Such a man misses the (average) period of three or four days' 'sleep' of those who die naturally in old age. Both natural and enforced death must cause some shock, due to the change in 'vibration-rate'. In gradual death the 3–4 days' sleep permits a gradual adjustment; with sudden death this amelioration is not available. *The man who dies suddenly in his prime (and who does not have a period of sleep) awakens before his 'Denser Between Body' or 'body-veil' has been shed and consequently awakens to 'Denser Between Worlds', 'earth-veil' or 'Hades' conditions.* The disadvantage is, largely if not wholly, neutralized if he understands these matters and is aware of the possibility of death.

Statement No. 40.—*A man who is awake and who is yet enshrouded by the 'body-veil', or vehicle of vitality, may have difficulty in seeing in the 'earth-veil' or 'Hades' condition.* Again he may not at first see helpers who are at hand. *His views of the 'next' world tend, at least at first, to be vague, unsatisfactory and dream-like.*

Statement No. 41.—Where the 'silver cord' was 'loosed' at the same time as the Physical Body was shed, a man is similarly deprived of clear and continuous glimpses of the physical world. He will tend to regard the semi-physical 'doubles' or counterparts of physical objects as the physical objects themselves, seeing the latter only through a *'fog'* or *'mist'*; for him physical objects are 'out-of-focus'. Hence, descriptions of 'misty' and 'foggy' conditions are very common in the accounts of people who were forced to die in the prime of life, and absent from those of people who died naturally in old age. Again, the man who dies suddenly in his prime may, or may not, have the advantage of seeing his own Physical Body. Further, his bewilderment tends to prevent him realizing that he has 'died'. Still again, he may, or may not, have the opportunity of discovering that he is invisible and inaudible to mortals. All these possibilities in enforced death are disadvantages as compared with natural death. Well does the Prayer Book say, 'From sudden death, good Lord, deliver us'.

Statement No. 42.—The man who dies suddenly, unexpectedly and ignorant of after-death conditions is thus under several disadvantages. Death is more of a shock. Since it is particularly difficult for him to realize that he is 'dead', he is particularly liable to be bewildered. In extreme cases it may be weeks (of earth-time) before realization comes. *He knows that he is 'alive' (conscious), but does not know he is 'dead' (= out of normal contact with the physical world). Nor does he know that he has not yet made satisfactory contact with the normal 'next' world (= 'Paradise').* His religious 'teaching' on these matters may increase, rather than diminish, his confusion (Luke vi, 39): realizing that he is neither in the orthodox 'Hell', or the orthodox 'Heaven', and having been assured that, since the Scriptures mention these two states only, no other state exists, he is completely baffled and bewildered. That which might have been envisaged calmly and collectedly during earth-life has to be learned in a disordered state of mind after death.

The disadvantages possible to one who dies (1) suddenly in his prime, (2) unexpectedly and (3) without some knowledge of after-death states probably sound more disturbing than the events warrant. In point of fact, any bewilderment experienced by the *average* (or above-average) man is of brief duration, but considerable confusion may be suffered by one who is definitely evil or grossly sensual, one who seeks revenge or who has certain fixed erroneous ideas and is un-teachable (Mark x, 15): these may be 'earthbound', corresponding to the 'spirits in prison' (of sensuality, deliberate evil, false conceptions, etc.) to whom Jesus took the opportunity to 'preach' during His three-day period in the 'Hades' state (I Peter iii, 19). His 'preaching' doubtless took the form of explaining the processes by which they had forged their own prison-bars and indicating how they could be broken.

Although the man who dies suddenly in his prime may not have time to 'call' friends who have 'gone before', he is not without aid; there are, we are assured, those who undertake such special duties [see (a) State-ment No. 3 and (b) communications regarding 'co-operation']. These soon take him in charge, though it may be some little time before he is aware of their presence. They soon make him realize that his abnormal transition has resulted in a temporary abnormal state. They often bring the discarnate friends whom he had no time to 'call': the 'dead' man knows that these friends had 'passed on' some time before; this suggests that his own transition has occurred. This terminates his temporary bewilderment. A period of rest, under special conditions, is then enjoyed. It prepares the Psychical Body to work without being 'geared' down to the physical rate and eliminates the effects of the shock received. The newly-dead man awakes in 'Paradise', passes through his 'Judgment' and eventually 'goes to his own place' in the super-physical 'Heavens'.

(3) CORRELATION BETWEEN BODILY CONDITIONS, CONSCIOUSNESS AND ENVIRONMENTS

'Communications' indicate various levels of awareness. They are correlated with bodily conditions and the latter with environmental conditions. This correlation is so important a feature that we here give a résumé of the statements.

Those manifestations of consciousness that have filtered through the entire series of bodies (Spiritual, Psychical and Physical), that is 'every-day' consciousness, naturally seem to us mortals to be the normal, and indeed the maximum possible. Actually, they are very partial and very limited manifestations (compare the *kenosis*). Discarnates say the same as St Paul, that compared with what is possible, our consciousness during earth-life is a mere dream.

Immediately a man sheds his Physical Body, the 'outermost' layer of his total non-physical body is that which is named the 'Denser Between Body', vehicle of vitality and memory, or 'body-veil'. Since this has no 'sense organs' and does not transmit consciousness after the manner of the Physical, Psychical and Spiritual Bodies, so long as it remains the 'outermost' portion of the 'double' it causes a more pronounced *kenosis*, a greater limitation of consciousness, than the Physical Body. A man who dies in extreme old age takes an average of from three to four days to shed this 'after-birth', as it were. It is depleted of vitality. During that time, since he was greatly fatigued before shedding the Physical Body, he sleeps and dreams. Few 'com-munications' come through from old people until this period is over—and those that do 'come through' are often dream-like. On the other hand, a man whose death is enforced in the prime of life was awake and alert at the time of transition and he tends to be awake at once (except in cases of death by explosion): but his consciousness is not 'normal', much less 'super-normal'—it is 'sub-normal' and dream-like. Until it is shed, the 'body-veil' has a limiting and enshrouding effect on con-sciousness. [This condition may also occur during the earth-life, and especially in the case of potential 'physical' mediums. In the latter, since the 'body-veil' is relatively loosely associated with the Physical Body there is some tendency to awaken from sleep exceptionally slowly: during the transition period between actual sleep and the 'normal' state, consciousness gets through to, but stops short at, the 'body-veil'. This is the 'hypnagogic state' of psychologists.] The environment that corresponds to the dream-consciousness permitted by the 'body-veil' includes two different groups of phenomena, namely, the 'etheric' duplicates of physical objects (including the human body) and 'thought-forms', products of man's own mental activities. The first is the common and objective portion of the envir-onment (which is, therefore, earth-like), while the second is more or less private. Just as the substance of the 'body-veil' (related to ecto-plasm of 'materializations') is ideo-plastic, modelled automatically by the thoughts, feelings and images in men's minds, so the substance of the immediate 'next' world, the 'astral plane' or 'earth-veil' (from which the 'body-veil' is drawn and to which it eventually returns) is ideo-plastic. Hence, a person who is 'awake' in this brief transition period after death requires to be able to distinguish between the objective portions of his environment and the 'subjective' creations— pseudo-objects—some of which he himself may have created, others being products of collective thought. A man who has thought clearly and honestly during his physical embodiment soon learns, in the after-death state, to distinguish reality from illusion. The man whose death is enforced in the prime of life may take longer than the average three-to-four days to shed his 'body-veil' (since it is more or less highly vitalized at the time of death; it may, indeed, be 'super-charged' with vital energy).

The environment of which men who die suddenly in the prime of life are conscious (but which average men who die naturally are unaware, since they sleep through this brief stage in the successive death-experiences) clearly corresponds to the 'Amenta' of the Egyptians, the 'Hades' of the Greeks (and Romans), 'Sheol' of the Jews, 'Kama Loka' of the Hindus (and, following them, of the Theosophists), 'Bardo' of the Tibetans, 'Limbo' of the Scholastic theologians, the 'Lower Borderlands', 'Lower Astral', 'Plane of Illusion', 'Greyworlds', etc., of 'communicators'. What is described by these different names is essentially the same. Such a correspondence of human *experience* cannot be lightly disregarded.

The Psychical Body has 'sense organs', though differing from the physical sense organs. These permit 'super-normal' consciousness, with the exercise of such faculties as telepathy, clairvoyance, pre- and post-cognition. The corresponding environment is variously described as the 'Psychic World', 'Paradise' (not the true 'Heavens'), 'Summerland', the 'Third Sphere', the 'Third Heaven' (St Paul, II Cor. xii, 2), 'Svarga' (of Hindus), and Elysium. In these conditions earthly space and time are transcended (so that predictions may be correct but dates and times are often wrong): there is something analogous, however— rhythm and intensity of thought and feeling corresponds to our time, while affinity of thought and feeling corresponds to our space.

Our analyses do not go beyond the 'Paradise' stage (whether the transition occurred naturally or was enforced), but there are indications in many 'communications' of 'mystical', 'cosmic' or 'spiritual' consciousness in the Spiritual Body. The corresponding conditions, represented by the 'true' Heavens, are formless, timeless and spaceless. On this account the characteristic experience is one of unity and identity with one's fellow creatures and with God in whom all live and move and have their being. Such experiences can be described only by means of symbols. (*See* Dr. R. C. Johnson's *Watcher on the Hills*, Hodder & Stoughton, 1959.)

Appendix VI

STATEMENTS OF THE 'DEAD'
REGARDING OUR SLEEP-STATE

THE statements of the 'dead' regarding our being outside the Physical Body during sleep, etc. agree with those made by people who claim temporarily to have left the body and remembered their experiences. A large proportion of the latter specifically stated that they had no knowledge of psychic matters prior to undergoing the experience. The agreement between the statements assumes some importance when (as in several cases cited below), the 'dead' also, and the 'medium' through whom they communicated, insist that they had no previous knowledge of these phenomena. Note also that certain 'dreams' include features that characterize 'projections'—see Appendix IV.

Mrs Heslop who said 'had never read any book describing the experiences of spirit people' received 'communications' from her (deceased) husband who, she said, 'had no toleration for mysticism and occult matters'. They nevertheless contain the usual essential details, including references to the 'silver cord'. The communications were published in *Speaking Across the Border-Line* and *Further Messages across the Border-Line* (Charles Taylor). Heslop told her that 'practically everyone' has power to leave the Physical Body during sleep, since, *'the psychic body is nearly always externalized in sleep'*. He gave the reason for this exteriorization of the psychic body—that 'the physical frame needs absolute quiet' and should not be disturbed by the activities of the psychic body. He said, 'In most cases of "taking of rest in sleep", the ejected psychic body remains beside the sleeping form, ready at the least alarm to take possession again, or rouse the sleeper when it is necessary for him to awake. ... While you lie inanimate, it solves difficult problems for you, frequently in consultation with your spirit-guides. ... *When you possess occult power, your guides can bear your released psychic body into higher realms for spiritual refreshment* [cf. Statement No. 3 regarding 'deliverers']. It is ever hampering to this psychic body to be held in the flesh and it gladly floats away with the ministering spirits. ... *Through the communicating cord which connects the two bodies it returns to the physical portion* [cf. Statement No. 19]. The body is always guarded by watchful spirits ...'

Heslop also said, 'As psychic development proceeds you become conscious of these journeys into space, and the memory of what you have seen and heard is a priceless possession, a foretaste of the glory of the life to come (cf. Statement No. 1b]. But it is not always wise for these spirit journeys to be too well remembered, the contrast would make life unendurable, when times of stress come. ... We call upon you to help us in our work for those newly passed to this side [cf. Statement No. 30 regarding 'co-operation']. And you come in the night and aid us greatly while your physical frames are asleep. ... Now death is merely the severing of the psychic cord [cf. Statement No. 20]. The more you have functioned in these heavenly spheres while still on earth, the more familiar they will seem when you float away from your worn-out body' [cf. Statement No. 26].

Geraldine Cummins knew nothing of psychic matters. She received messages purporting to come from the deceased F. W. H. Myers (*Beyond Human Personality*, Ivor Nicholson & Watson, 1935) containing similar statements. She said, for example, that a (deceased) daughter 'met' her (living) parent during their sleep. Thus, '*when you sleep, your soul enters your double, or unifying body, and you then pass within your subliminal-self.* This self can and does communicate with the beloved— he or she making contact with you through his own subliminal-self. Such experience may not be brought within the bounds of your physical memory as a rule. But after death you will find this life that was known to you only in the depths of sleep registered in the memory of your double (the body your soul retains after your final farewell to earth). So, though a generation of years may have parted you from your loved one, you will come together again, not as strangers but as those who have enjoyed companionship with each other through the years.'

Again, 'In the period of deep slumber the human being goes out in his double and at times enters the subjective minds of those two or three discarnate beings who are bound to him by ties of warm affection.'

In her *Travellers in Eternity* (Psychic Press Ltd., 1948) Miss Cummins records a 'communicator' as saying, concerning a deceased woman, 'Because of her great love for them, she will be able to meet them (incarnate friends) when they sleep. *When living people fall asleep their soul leaves their body and the soul can then talk with and meet a spirit who is in another life.* In the Prayer Book this is called the Communion of Saints. ... Her boys will meet her and she will still talk to them and advise them. Only they will not be able to bring the recollection back— except, perhaps, only vaguely as a dream—but they will remember her words and advice and believe it to be their own thoughts.'

Elsa Barker 'had no preconceived ideas', since she had 'read practically nothing' on psychic matters. 'She was not and never had been, a spiritualist'. Her 'communicator' ('Judge D. P. Hatch') opposed indiscriminate mediumship. Nevertheless, the 'communications' contain essentially the same statements as those by clairvoyants, the supposed dead and those who claim to exteriorize from their Physical Bodies.

'*Reine*', *an 'ignorant' artists' model eighteen years of age, in hypnotic trance, relayed similar statements* from the supposed discarnate Vettellini to P. E. Cornillier (*The Survival of the Soul*, Kegan Paul, 1914). Although Cornillier had previous knowledge of psychic matters, the details given him by Vettellini quite often contradict his own views (see, for example, pp. 122, 142, 161, 181, 189, 357, 369, 370, 374, 412, 422, 431 and 457 of that book. It is noteworthy that Flammarion wrote to Cornillier—and it is cited in the latter's *The Prediction of the Future*— 'I have learned much from your pages, though my contact with Allan Kardec dates to 1861. From this you may infer that I have seen and heard a great deal. Of all I have seen and heard, Vettellini is undoubtedly the most remarkable personality.' Vettellini, the 'communicator', said, '*What causes sleep is a disunion between the astral (fluidic) body and the Physical Body.* The purpose of this disunion is to liberate sufficiently the Astral Body, so that it may go to gather, from the ambience, the vital force contained in the magnetic and cosmic currents, whose emission, or passage, is intensified and facilitated by the night. ... This sortie of the Astral Body for the purpose of gathering the nourishment necessary to organic life, is not to be confounded with the disengagement of highly evolved beings in quest of information, or influences that may develop their consciousness. The first is common to all animals, to everything that lives; the second [= 'astral projection'] is the privilege of a Spirit that has already attained a high degree of evolution. ... In a good sleep one should not dream.' Reine told Cornillier that, 'The superior Spirits' trained her psychic faculties during her periods of sleep. Much information was given by 'Vettellini' regarding the 'silver cord'.

'A.B.', communicating in *One Step Higher* (The C. W. Daniel Co. Ltd., 1937) said, 'The period of sleep is the most active in the twenty-four hours. *On earth the soul can escape from the body in sleep* and can stretch the cord by which it is attached to the body to such a length as to permit it to enter the state above that in which it is living, and to have intercourse with those who have passed beyond it. ... *The soul has departed temporarily for the purpose of becoming familiar with the spheres into which it will pass when the cord is broken by death.*

'In all states through which the soul passes there are times in which it sleeps and the soul projects itself into the sphere beyond. So we are taught—and, speaking from personal experience, nothing was strange or unfamiliar when I came here. I knew all about the place I came to: there seemed to have been no change. ...

'Sleep, however, has many degrees, and only when perfect sleep comes can that journey be made. An unconscious journey is accomplished in a moment when deep sleep is attained.'

In *Fragments from my Messages*, by A.L.E.H., we are similarly told 'Your consciousness lives a far more intense life during your sleeping than during your waking hours. ... *When you remember nothing of your dreams you have usually been in the spaces far beyond the earth*, in such a fine, rare atmosphere that your soul, which bears the conscious memory, cannot accompany your spirit there.'

Those who 'communicated' through Constance Wiley (*A Star of Hope*, The C. W. Daniel Co. Ltd., 1938) gave identical details. They said, '*You have a "body", just like a flesh-body, encased in the flesh-body and only leaving it when the body sleeps*. ... You receive rest to the Physical Body in sleep, while the spirit goes free and is carried to our world, there to meet loved ones who have gone before. ... During your hours of sleep you were working in our world. ... You have a very convincing way which helps especially because you are still in the flesh. ... If a mother and father, left on earth, and fit to be with their child who has passed on, each night the child is taken to meet those parents in their sleep-state, when their spirits have left their bodies. So the child is in constant touch with the parents, and ever will be, until they too pass into spirit. The child, therefore, does not grieve, not realizing that it has "died".' These messengers make other references to 'co-operation' of incarnates, during their sleep, with discarnates [cf. Statement No. 30]; they say that in earthquakes and other disasters (as with the newly-dead generally), 'You can help in this work—by prayer and in your sleep-life'.

The anonymous 'communicator' of *Life Beyond the Grave* (E. W. Allen) said, 'Whilst the body sleeps the spirit either remains near the body (and talks to spirit friends who may be near) or takes a journey to a distance. The spirit is often more lively when the body is asleep. ... Whilst the body is awake the spirit is asleep, or nearly so. ... When a man is asleep on the earth side of his life he is awake on the spirit side; the only difference between the two is that the spirit-body does not sleep while the natural body is awake—it walks about interspersed with the natural body, and looks to us like a man in his sleep (being, from our point of view, deaf, dumb and blind, or only half-awake ...').

The 'communicator' of F. W. Fitzsimons, *Opening the Psychic Door* (Hutchinson & Co. Ltd., 1933), said that, whereas 'advanced souls, who have been in the habit of leaving the body during sleep', require no help when they come to leave the body permanently at death, unevolved men may find some difficulty on dying and require some help' [cf. Statement No. 3].

Fitzsimons told his 'communicator' that, when he awoke in a morning he had memories of their being together; the reply was as follows.

'You quite frequently join me, in your astral form, while your body is sleeping and we accomplish a considerable amount of work together. Earth-bound, and other spirits needing help, listen and pay attention to what you say, because, by your appearance, they realize that you still have a Physical Body' [cf. Statement No. 30 regarding 'co-operation']. When Fitzsimons asked to be taken to a particular 'astral' locality he was told that a visit would not be possible during light sleep, that it could be made only during 'profound slumber'.

Fitzsimons had a friend who, like himself, was active and conscious in the Astral Body during sleep. He says, 'We determined to meet each other in my study (in our astral forms) and to see if we could remember when we awakened what had transpired. We agreed to record our remembrances independently, and afterwards to compare notes'. This they did and 'as time went on became quite proficient' in these exercises.

The 'communicator' of *Open the Door*, by Wilfred Brandon (Alfred A. Knoff, 1935) said, 'During natural sleep is the time when the soul is most active. It is then functioning on its own and without using the mechanism of the brain. This is when it has the opportunity to speak to those here. Usually it is concerned with the welfare of an absent friend. ... Many words of affection are exchanged in this way. We hope to see a more constructive use made of sleep. ... Make peace with every human being, including oneself, then know that in sleep we shall receive inspiration and encouragement for the coming day. ... By giving the soul its orders, we use sleep constructively.'

The 'communicator' of Kate Wingfield's *More Guidance from Beyond* (Philip Allan & Co., Ltd., 1925) said, 'The higher self is linked to the body as long as that exists. When the body is resting, the spirit is active above, gaining knowledge and working in many ways. ... The soul never sleeps. When outside the body, it is always learning or working, or in some way rising to a higher level, if the human being to whom it belongs is doing his best also during his waking hours. But if he is a bad person, the soul often goes to lower planes (in sleep) and does not learn at all. The soul is very active. It is none the less real because you cannot remember'.

'Claude', communicating to his mother (Mrs L. Kelway Bamber— *Claude's Book*, Psychic Book Club), told her, 'When your body sleeps, your soul comes over here and we spend hours together. You sometimes dimly remember things that happened, as in a dream. Thousands of people come over in this way every night, and are more awake and alive while here than on earth in their mortal bodies. To do this, people must be spiritually evolved to a certain degree. Sometimes we work among those who have just wakened in the spirit world and are bewildered and puzzled. ... You do this even better than I, as you are

still in a mortal body ... and feel more familiar to one who has just
come over. ... You are still controlled and limited by your earth-body
while connected with it' [cf. Statement No. 30. regarding 'co-operation'].

One 'communicator' told Lord Dowding (*Lychgate*, Rider & Co.)
'Living people, in sleep, not only work alongside those who inhabit the
astral and higher spheres, but they sometimes carry out the work of
meeting those who are killed in action, and helping them across the
Valley of the Shadow of Death' [= 'co-operation']. Another said,
'Quite a lot of people don't leave their earthly body [in the sleep state].
They sleep exactly above it. People who actively work over here have
been trained ...' Dowding commented, 'The work done seems to be at
least as important as anything that we do in our waking hours'.

A 'word of warning' is given to those who would force the exteriorization of the psychic body, by supposed 'communicators', just as it is
given by many of those who naturally have temporary out-of-the-
body experiences—Yram, etc. Thus, the communicator of Marjorie
Livingston's *The Element of Heaven* (Wright & Brown) said, 'Let no
man dare to come to us unbidden, for coming so shall that work be
unfinished which was given him to do. And he himself shall be found
unready, and shall have no joy in Paradise for many a long day to
come. You come to us in spirit, while you sleep, if so be your mind: let
that suffice, and to those impatient ones say, "What shall become of the
butterfly that is torn from its chrysalis before its time is ripe?" ' Again
he says, 'In your sleep hours you will come here and find all that you
need for the asking'.

J. S. M. Ward's 'communicator' (*Gone West*, Rider) told him that
many persons enter the astral plane [here = 'Hades'] in what they
think are dreams, and a few, but very few, enter the spirit plane [here
= 'Paradise']. 'Even those who do, seldom bring away a clear recollection. Far more people get on to the astral plane during sleep. They
come wandering along the fringe of it, as it were, often apparently
half-dazed, as if their connexion with their bodies rendered them only
partly conscious of the astral world in which they moved. The astral
body, of course, is often unable to leave the Physical Body owing to
the gross and material life such people live, and even when it can get
out of the physical, it cannot, or dare not, go any distance from it'

Ward's communicator also mentions the ideo-plasticity of the next-
world environment, a feature often described by those who temporarily leave their bodies [Statement No. 10], as well as by the supposed
dead. In certain conditions [= 'Hades'] *Ward could not see the landscape
very clearly, for it seemed all grey and shrouded in mist.* He was told that he
was more attuned to the brighter conditions and his 'communicator'
added, '*But to many spirits who know no brighter place, this seems full of*

colours, but not even to all of them. This is a land of change, a half-way house, as it were, between the physical and the spiritual plane [here = 'Paradise'], therefore it seems somewhat unreal and changing to denizens of either plane. So, too, the elements which form it are ever changing, and, being very malleable, often assume forms in consonance with the wills of those who pass through them, even when they are sleepers dreaming. Form which is eternal, goes to the spirit-plane: form in the half-way house is not stable (except where it is the living astral form)—the elemental forms have no stable form of their own'.

Appendix VII

ARNOLD BENNETT'S
RÉSUMÉ OF THEOSOPHICAL TEACHINGS

IN *The Glimpse* (Chapman and Hall, 2nd ed., 1909) Bennett gave an excellent account of an out-of-the-body experience in the first person and it is often cited as his own. However, according to *Arnold Bennett, a Biography* by Reginald Pound (Wm. Heinemann Ltd., 1952) a letter from Bennett to his sister shows that it was 'taken bodily' from Mrs Besant's books on Theosophy. It is extremely well written and we here quote extracts. The writer was supposed to be ill.

He said, 'I was looking at my bed. My brain worked with difficulty, but the argument was convincing: "I am looking *at* the bed, therefore I am not *in* the bed". I saw the bed framed in an oblong which was the doorway between the bedroom and my study. A body lay on the bed and I began to realize that it was mine. "I'm dead!" *I still had some sort of physical organism, patterned on the old* [cf. Statement No. 17]. *I was still* "I". *It was the relic on the bed that was not* "I".

'*Inez stood by the bed. I endeavoured to attract her attention, but could not* [cf. Statement No. 28]. *She passed out of the oblong. I then noticed a form floating over the bed. It resembled my body in shape, but was of a pale, greyish heliotrope colour.* [Bennett later described this form as 'the violet gaseous counterpart' of his Physical Body. It is often seen, by more or less clairvoyant observers of the process of dying, to leave, and float above, the body of dying persons. The phenomenon has been photographed on several occasions. Various names have been applied to it at various times and in various countries: among these are 'the Denser Psychic or Between Body'. We have called it the 'body-veil' from its effect on consciousness. It is said to be of an almost physical nature (not super-physical, or 'spiritual', in any sense) never to separate completely from the Physical Body during life, and to disintegrate with the physical body after death. Bennett gives this view when he groups it with the Physical Body (and not with certain subtler 'bodies' that he mentions) as the 'double envelope'].* It appeared to float. "My God" I thought, "How often am I to be multiplied? Dead? Yes. What they call dead!" But I knew then that there is no such catastrophe.

'I heard the voice of Inez: "Marion!" It told Marion [the maid-servant] the great fact regarding her master. They gazed at that body on the bed as if it were myself. I wanted to rouse them to their error, but was helpless. *They could not even discern the third "me" in my "Desire" or "Radiant", body* [= the Psychical Body] *floating above their heads.* [Compare, for plurality of bodies, the descriptions of Mrs Jeffrey, Miss Zoila Stables, Mrs Joy, Yram, Messrs Sculthorp, Turvey, Lind, etc.]

'The greyish heliotrope apparition rose higher from the bed and vanished out of my field of vision. I wished intensely to communicate with somebody how the interment of my body should be conducted.... Then Marion entered the room. Fatigue had mastered her and she had crept into my study to sleep. Soon after this, I was aware of partial, fleeting gaps in the physical continuity of the room—gaps that yawed and closed again. It was as though a whole series of phenomena were intermittently breaking through the physical phenomena. [Bennett was here beginning to experience higher psychic ('mental') phenomena, super-consciousness in the Psychical Body, corresponding to that of the 'Paradise', 'Summerland' or Third after-death state of supposed discarnate communicators. He called it the 'Radiant Plane'.]

'*I saw beautiful flashes of colour. Then I perceived that Marion was enveloped in colour. She was surrounded by a chromatic form, somewhat larger than herself. I could see her Physical Body within it, as a sort of nucleus of it. The colours, which were continually modified, were colours that I had never seen before. I knew that the envelope (or emanation) which I saw surrounding Marion always surrounded her; that it had only been invisible to eyes that could not see it.*' [Compare the account of Lord Geddes's doctor-friend. This 'envelope' Bennett later called the 'Radiant Body' and the 'Desire' (or Emotional) Body. His description agrees in every respect with those of the 'aura', 'psychic body', 'astral body', 'etheric body', etc. given by such clairvoyants as Leadbeater, Colville, Fletcher, Phoebe Payne, Eileen J. Garrett and Geoffrey Hodson, as well as with those of supposed discarnates.]

'*Then I observed that small shapes were escaping, one by one, from that part of the chromatic envelope which surrounded Marion's head. They floated away. Shapes more complex than spheres, shapes showing design, and the persistence of one design with minor variations! I traced them to a corner of the ceiling. Presently I could distinguish the gradual building-up of each of them in the recesses of that chromatic envelope. I thought, "They are her thoughts".* [These 'small shapes' that were projected from Marion's 'Radiant', or 'Desire' Body (= the Psychical Body) were clearly 'thought forms' in the theosophic sense. They are often described as seen by (1) the supposed dead, (2) 'living' clairvoyants and (3) those who, like Bennett, were temporarily out of their Physical Bodies. The accounts from all these sources agree with each other in every way. The fact that relatively few who had out-of-the-body experiences reported seeing thought-forms of this nature is explained on the basis of 'communications' from the supposed dead. They are seen by means of a particular 'organ' in the non-physical body, an 'organ' which operates only in men and women who are 'rather advanced'.]

'I watched these thoughts pass through the ceiling to the higher floor. They hovered caressingly around another chromatic human form ('aura') that lay on a trestle-bed. Within the coloured envelope was the Physical Body of a youth. I had seen him menially engaged about the exterior of Palace Court Mansions.

'Then the flight of Marion's thoughts ceased. I fixed my gaze on her body. She was asleep. The physical outlines of the room seemed to dissolve, to·return, trembling, distorted, then to dissolve again. *And then, slowly, I saw the chromatic envelope move entirely away from Marion's Physical Body. It floated an instant and finally swept upwards, following the direction of the stream of thoughts. And Marion calmly slept, dreaming.* [Marion, like the narrator himself, was temporarily exteriorized, in the chromatic envelope, the 'Radiant' or 'Desire' Body, corresponding to the Psychical Body. Although her Physical Body was 'incapacitated', unable to carry out her wish to visit the young man, her 'Radiant Body' was not; it followed her thoughts and went straight to the young man of whom she dreamed.]

'The physical world had almost dissolved away. I was now in the midst of a moving, shimmering "sea" of vapours. Everywhere was motion, vibration, change, close-woven radiance, and enchanting beauty. *There were exceedingly soft hues, unknown to my physical experience. I was under a spell of wonder. I gazed exactly as an infant gazes at a bright object. I was, in fact an infant. I knew that only long habit would enable me to see truly that which was before me. And I thought, how wondrous and lovely beyond visions was this spiritual world! But, although less substantial than air, it had substance, and I could throw it into agitation and deflect its ways. It was, and eternally would be, impossible even to conceive any phenomenon that was not fundamentally physical. Nothing could be supernatural. This gave me a feeling of comfortable security.*

'Through the transparent, prismatic, quivering "sea" floated shapes recalling those which had issued from the body of Marion more brightly, or more deeply, coloured than the "sea", each a dazzling object of beauty. Some wandered about without apparent purpose, and these were of vague outline; others, quite definite in form, though yieldingly plastic, passed onwards in straight paths, urgent, as if on a unique errand. In my earthly life I had stood in ecstasy before sunsets the beauty of which my imagination could not exceed; now I smiled at those moments. I steeped myself in the rapture of this new visual life.

'There was a jarring sound. It was caused by the abrupt blowing-to of a window. And instantly Marion's Radiant Body swept through the translucent, prismatic "sea" and came to rest within her Physical Body. And I thought, "The banging of the window has awakened Marion". It thrilled me to think that within that radiant body was concealed Marion's Physical Body, with its gross flesh, its clothes, the spectacles in the pocket of the apron. And I could not see it: it was hidden from me behind the dazzling veil of her chromatic envelope. I thought, "Was that her soul that fled and returned?" *I realized that her earthly body, instead of containing an ethereal counterpart, was contained in an ethereal counterpart.* I knew, rather than saw, that I too was a form resembling the ethereal radiant form of Marion. Was this the soul? ...

'The brilliant Radiant Body of Marion fascinated me. It was full of vibrations, currents, and shimmerings; more complex and puzzling than those of the fluid in which it floated at rest. I say 'at rest', but even its outline was never still, waving elastically from head to foot in scarce-perceptible undulations. Every part of it modified itself continuously. The whole was a miracle of adaptability. Indescribable!

'Then recommenced the emanation of clearly-defined floating shapes from the head of Marion's Radiant Body. They detached themselves, one after another, in the manner of bubbles, and floated away in a procession. *The inception of these shapes was to be seen in a whorl or volution of the omnipresent fluid, drawn into Marion's Radiant Body, matured there and then expelled. But as each shape floated away, I perceived that it had also had its effect on the Radiant Body itself, the general result being a structural cellular change.*

'*And this was my first view of the physical aspect of thought.*

'Now I noticed that two distinct species of thought-shapes were being thrown off from Marion's Radiant Body. One was violet-coloured, the other a delicate rose. Then a third appeared, a stream of vermilion shapes that darted off in a direction different from that of the other two. The vermilion shapes alarmed me and even the violet shapes inspired me with a certain antipathy. And I saw that the effects of these three kinds of thought-shapes on Marion's own Radiant Body were markedly dissimilar. I followed the vermilion shapes in their angry flight through the living luminance, and found that their objective was the form of another woman. *This form [= Radiant Body] was in an upright attitude, nearly still: its earthly counterpart was not, therefore, asleep.* Then I saw a number of less dazzling forms, horizontally disposed, in rows; and I reflected upon hospitals, barracks, hotels. But the horizontal forms were all forms of women. What could be the earthly solution?

'The vermilion shapes had resolutely voyaged, under the impulse of Marion's anger, to the vigil-keeping woman and assaulted her Radiant Body with extraordinary obstinacy. It was as though they were endowed with an energy, a hatred of their own; it was as if they lived with a vitality of their own. Sometimes they completely enveloped the attacked radiant form as in a vast menace.

'And then I traced an emanation of thought-shapes from the form which was being attacked. They were of extremely delicate and pure rosy tints. I followed them, in their turn, leaving the radiant form enmeshed in inimical vermilions. Their goal was the male form which I had previously learnt to be the goal of Marion's thoughts before she slept, and which I surely guessed her Radiant Body had visited during her dream. I recognized the stream of violet and rosy thought-shapes which Marion was still directing upon him.

'It was a stupendous spectacle, this soft besieging of the unconscious male form by the thought-shapes impelled by the two women distant from him and from each other. His transparent, glittering Radiant Body was surrounded by small appealing lucent shapes, each influential with its special energy. I grasped the significance of the different colourations. *The violet were the vehicles of desire and the rose were the messengers of affection. The vermilions were shapes of jealous hatred.* I then remembered having heard that the young man who was employed about the exterior of Palace Court Mansions had previously served in some outdoor capacity at a prison for women-convicts. I was observing the struggle between a parlour-maid and a female warder for the heart of an odd-job man! Only I was a witness of that aspect of it which was too radiant for the earthly eye to see. And I thought, 'If the hidden activity of such souls is so entrancingly resplendent, what must be the hidden activity of more advanced beings? [Compare John iv, 14; vii. 38; Syriac V, 'He that believeth in Me, out of his innermost being shall flow torrents of Living Waters'. Cf. also Matt. xiii, 43, etc.]

'*The solemn thing was that "they" themselves lived in ignorance of their own splendour, and of the fineness of their organism, and of the reach of their faculties. Their magnificence was veiled from them. They did not suspect the hundredth part of the powers which they possessed and constantly exercised. They were but awaking from unconsciousness to consciousness. They were building the future with terrific tools, and guessed it not.*

'As I watched the prismatic, Radiant Body of Marion creating and despatching thought-shapes amid the "sea" of fluid light, I could not help marvelling at the chasm between the self of which she was conscious [= the lesser self, or personality] and the self of which she was unconscious [= the Greater Self, Real, Inner, Eternal Self, or Individuality]. Since I could not see the earthly form of Marion, my fancy pictured it. She reclined in an easy chair, her tousled head against one of the ear-flaps. Commanded to relate what experiences she had passed through, she would have replied that she had gone into the study of her late master to rest, had thought considerably about a man whom she

loved, had fallen asleep and dreamed of him, had been awakened by a
noise, and had continued to think about her lover, with a certain preoccupation concerning another woman whom she knew to be interested in him. *She could not have even the dimmest surmise that she possessed
a body compact of light, that she had fabricated thought-shapes, and sent them,
charged with her vital energy, infallibly to fixed destinations, that she had
physically and eternally influenced other human beings at a distance, that her
Radiant Body had visited her lover where he lay, and finally, that she was
ceaselessly modifying her own Radiant Body and so deciding the tendencies of
her future. I wanted to warn her of the grave and lasting import of her
apparently trifling activities. And instantly I saw, wending from my Radiant
Body to hers, a series of pale rose-shapes.* Previously, I had emanated none
but grey or bluish shapes, vague in outline and without defined
direction. These new shapes followed one another purposefully in a
waving stream and surrounded Marion's Radiant Body, touching it in
soft contacts.

'Then I grew conscious of external vibrations which were setting up
vibrations within myself. I struggled against this but without success.
My Radiant Body was surrounded by prismatic thought-shapes. I saw
now that multitudes of these surged everywhere, but that most of them
were so tenuous and slight as to be scarcely visible. To distinguish them
from the medium in which they moved needed practice. Of the shapes
specially surrounding myself none save two species produced any
effect on me whatever. But those two species did assuredly affect me,
causing modifications of the substance of my Radiant Body. And then
I understood that *their power over myself depended on the correspondence
of their vibrations with certain of my own.* [Compare several sayings of
Jesus: 'To him that hath shall be given'—Luke xii, 48; 'The prince of
this world cometh and hath nothing in ME'—John xiv, 30; 'It hath
been said, "Love thy neighbour and hate thine enemy". But I say,
"Pray for them which despitefully use you" '—Matt. v, 43.]

'These two streams of thought were the messengers of Inez and
Marion. The women grieved at my departure. Little they guessed that,
weeping there, they were enveloped in light and that their thoughts,
urged by the intensity of their desires, were shooting forth in coruscat-
ing torrents to lure me back to earth-life. The shapes were continuously
arriving and with hysteric violence. I sought to shake them off. I saw,
with painful alarm, an impending tragedy, myself the victim and these
two women its ignorant cause. They could only attract me near themselves, to leave me beating once again, but vainly, against the shut
gates of humanity. They could never see me. I could not join them.
*Their grief meant nothing but disaster for me, torture, futility, a desolate
break in my evolution. To wish me back was to wish me evil, pain, danger
and retrogression.* [Compare what is said in innumerable independent

accounts by the supposed dead—that they are injured, depressed, smothered and held back by undue grief on the part of their still-embodied friends and relatives—Statement No. 27.]

'And then I was once more on the Radiant Plane in an atmosphere of moving colour. My mood lightened and I was alone. Not a single thought-shape now dogged me. Conceive the luminous air still flashing and sparkling in delicate hues: I have called it a "sea", but dismiss any idea of humidity. *That I should live in diffused light, in a visible atmosphere, in an environment of transparencies, seemed absolutely natural to me.*

'Save myself and this encircling air, the sole phenomena were the vague thought-shapes which constantly emanated from me, floating idly near for a time and then vanishing. I was alone. Before my death, my greatest pleasure had been in reflection. ... I said to myself, "Should this be likened to heaven or to hell?" It was neither distinctly a reward not distinctly a punishment. [In asking himself this question, Bennett repeats the question that, according to numerous 'communications' from the supposed dead, is often asked by newly-dead men and women who had 'fixed ideas' of the after-life, said to be erroneous ones, derived from the orthodox Protestant 'teachers' namely, that there are only two after-death states, 'heaven' and 'hell' and that there is 'no Scriptural authority' for anything intermediate between, or preliminary to, these. (This belief was, of course, an over-reaction against the purchase, in Pre-Reformation days, of Indulgences in the hope of escaping part of 'Purgatory'. The Roman Catholic Purgatory roughly corresponds to the 'Intermediate State', 'Borderlands', 'Between Worlds', 'Astral Plane', etc. of 'communications' from the supposed dead, and to the condition here described by Bennett.) The contention that nothing exists unless it has 'Scriptural authority' carries no weight. There is no Scriptural authority for Australia, New Zealand or America and their inhabitants, but they existed in Bible times. Bennett, then, was not in 'heaven' (a place of 'bliss') nor in 'hell' (a place of torment) but in a preliminary state, as he himself discovered. He was in that normal happy condition of the preliminary state that is known as 'Paradise', 'Summerland', or the 'Third Sphere', with an environment that is said to be partly of fixed, objective and common things and partly of forms that are created by the thoughts, feelings and expectations of the observer (and which therefore is more or less transitory and 'illusory'). Bennett now proceeds to describe his experience of the 'Paradise' state. His every wish was realized.]

'I had no sense of time nor of change. There was no morning, no night [cf. Rev. xxi, 25; xxii, 5]. I was set and fixed in a calm, omni-present beauty, inviolate. A desire awakened in me for companionship. There, near me, without surprise, but with rapture, I saw a woman. She was more radiant than any radiant creature I had yet seen. ... I shared eternity with this woman. ... An impossible ideal was realized. ...

'I descried a palace. It rose aloft in the luminiferous ether, glittering prismatically, somewhat brighter than the pulsating air, rather less bright than ourselves. It was like an edifice of pearl in a sun-steeped mist. ... I entered. Of course, it was a library. I was a bookman. It went beyond my dreams. I was free to read where I pleased.

'Then I found a doorway and saw, in the universal radiance, distant landscapes and seas. They were the majestic, absolute perfecting of earthly scenes. It was all mine. And, with the woman, I could wander in it, enfranchised from every care and preoccupation. ...

'Then I came to the first of the pavilions of music. I heard compositions that left me the ecstatic and silent victim of their power. It was in connection with this music that I first had intercourse with Beings other than the woman on the Radiant Plane. They were listening to the music and ready to converse. ...

'Enveloped in eternity, I lived amid universal nature, amid music, and amid the influences of the other arts, smoothly consorting with equal individualities and at moments withdrawing into absolute solitude that I might know what I was. *The existence was like a dream; but it was not a dream. It was a physical reality, visible, audible, tangible. A tie with the earlier plane seemed to be snapped: I had no sorrow.* ...

'*And then disturbing intuitions revisited me. ... After a long period of solitary reflection, a paramount idea took possession of me: I had not been in 'heaven'—every fine and beautiful desire that had actuated me in my earth-life had been REALIZED in my life on the Radiant Plane, and that to a degree transcendental and previously unimaginable. My plan for the extension and completion of my egoism had been executed. And another idea came. I myself had CREATED the woman, the palace, the literatures, the works of art, the garden, the music, the musicians and the landscapes—I had CREATED them all. Incomparably marvellous as they were, they were yet the toys which the spiritual child in me had CREATED for his education out of the all-permeating ethereal essence in which I existed. I had dreamed, but here one could not dream without CREATING realities. ... The elastic responsiveness [= the 'ideo-plasticity'] of the substance of the Radiant Plane was such that vision and physical fact were one* [cf. Statement No. 10].

'A force that sprang from the Soul of my soul compelled me to revisit my vast exploit. It was fading. ... It was melting like the dream it was. ... At last I was alone in the infinite vibrating atmosphere from which the miracle of my creative dream had been drawn, and into which it had been dissolved.

'*And then I felt that dissolution awaited me also. That trifling sloughing off of the earthly flesh was not death. Real death meant the end of desire* [and involved the shedding of the 'Desire', Emotional or 'Radiant'

Body]. *I spent tremendous force in urging myself into that real death. It was as if I cast off garment after garment of radiance; and I could see these abandoned shells floating weakly around me in the light. And then there visited me a beatific ministration—thought-shapes that were the thoughts of Inez. She was praying for the welfare of my soul.* [The 'communications' of supposed discarnates say that, whereas any undue grief on the part of still-embodied friends casts gloom on the newly-dead, prayer for their welfare is helpful and encourages—cf. Statement No. 29.]

'*Death is an awakening. I awoke. I emerged from stupor, dream, nightmare and illusion into REALITY. I had never hitherto once guessed that I was not awake.* [Compare (1) the *kenosis* and (2) 'Awake, thou that sleepest (in a body of flesh) Christ shall give thee Light'—Ephes. v, 14.] The limits of honest description are now reached [cf. II Cor. xii, 4]. I knew the Real. But I cannot convey any impression of it. ... *I reviewed my life from beginning to end. But I could note scarcely an odd hour that had not been devoted to the thickening of my prison bars* ... [== the 'Judgment' in the accounts of the supposed dead—cf. Statement No. 34].

At this point, Bennett, in his 'Mental Body', entered into conditions that were no longer psychical but mystical; they do not here concern us.

Appendix VIII

'THOUGHT-FORMS'

THE term 'thought-form' is used by those who discuss psychic phenomena in two distinct senses. In books on psychical research, and on spiritualism, a 'thought-form' generally refers to a mental reproduction of some physical object, *e.g.*, a chair, a table or a person's body: it thus often applies to an apparition of a person and when such an apparition corresponds to an actual person it is called a veridical hallucination. It is not usually supposed that the man represented by a veridical hallucination is there present, whether as a bodiless mind, or personality, or as a mind embodied in some sort of non-physical body: on the contrary, it is usually considered that such an apparition is merely a mental image which is received telepathically. According to psychic 'communications', however, while some veridical hallucinations are telepathic mental images ('thought-forms'), others are actually bodily (though non-physical) presences. Moreover (according to psychic 'communications'), images, thoughts, wishes, hopes, fears, indeed, all 'mental' phenomena and activities are not (as orthodox psychologists assume) purely mental, but have material accompaniments of a non-physical nature. They claim that there are material substances of a nature subtler than the physical.

The term 'thought-form' as used in theosophical literature generally (and in many spiritualistic books) often has a different meaning. According to these, the Physical Body of man is enveloped in an ovoid 'aura', which is related to the non-physical body. When a man has definite thoughts, wishes, desires, etc., this 'aura' throws off 'shapes' or 'forms' composed of non-physical substances; these they call 'thought-forms'; their outline and colour correspond to the nature of the thought, wish, desire, etc. An analogous physical phenomena is seen in 'the figures of Chladni'—if sand is strewn over a metal plate and a note is produced by drawing a violin-bow across the plate, the sand is so agitated as to form definite figures, patterns or forms. An account of this phenomenon was given by Margaret Watts Hughes (*The Eidophone Voice Figures*, Christian Herald Co. Ltd., 1904). Each note on the scale forms a recognizable pattern, so that a person who is conversant with the phenomenon, seeing the pattern only, can confidently say what note produced it.

In a similar way, thoughts and feelings are said to produce definite coloured forms and such forms are described (1) by the 'dead', (2) by 'living' clairvoyants and occasionally by those who claim temporarily to leave their bodies. The fact that all such accounts, given independently, agree (so that, as with sound-forms, the nature of the thought or feeling can be deduced from any given 'thought-form') indicates that 'thought-forms' are in some sense objective: that 'thoughts are things', or rather entities. We now give examples of 'thought-forms' from the three sources indicated.

(1) THE 'DEAD'

The 'communicators' of 'A.L.E.H.' (*Fragments from my Messages*, Women's Printing Society, Ltd.) said, 'There is a language of colour over here. We have far more shades than you. They serve us as the expression of our thought. *We are continually shaping them into varied patterns. ...*'

The 'communicator' of Hoey (*Truths from the Spirit World*, 1907) said that only those who are 'more spiritually advanced' are able to discern '*the actual forms that thought assumes*'. He added, 'for it materializes and is visible to those who have the inner vision'. Later he said that only that prayer which represents 'the strong will-effort of the heart and mind, expressing definitely what it requires' is able to produce thought-forms. He continued, 'The Higher Ego of every man is conscious of the thought-forms by which it is surrounded, and thus it is that some people and places have a depressing effect on you, whilst others seem to put fresh life into you. Be sure that those who depress and irritate you are constantly sending out gloomy thoughts or angry thoughts—whilst people who rest you, and make you feel happy, are sending out calm, loving thoughts. ... Cultivate a definiteness of thought and your thoughts shall indeed express themselves in forms, and help you to sway the minds of those who have not yet learned mind-control.'

The 'communicator' of Mabel Beaty (*Man Made Perfect*, Rider & Co. Ltd., 1929) was told, 'Whether for good or ill, a man's mental attitude towards life brings into existence certain vibratory forms which your minds call thoughts, but which have an existence independent of the one who thinks. Influences for health or disease are thus cast forth into the world to carry on an existence which will draw many within their own extending circles. Thoughts not only vibrate in the atmosphere, they take unto themselves *very definite forms, beautiful and geometrically perfect, or jagged edges and hideous, and poor in design and colour*.'

The same author (*The Temple of the Body*, Rider & Co. Ltd.) was also told, 'If a man thinks quietly, consecutively and reposefully on a certain subject he is really building *small but perfectly clear patterns* in the world of mental concepts. When well-planned thoughts on spiritual matters issue from a man's brain, they build up certain shapes; if of the more emotional kind, then the shape is not well-defined, but the cloud of colour may be very beautiful. *Hence certain shapes or designs may be seen by a highly-developed clairvoyant in a man's aura*' [cf. Mrs Gilbert and Mr Thomas, below].

Another communicator (*Spiritual Reconstruction*, Watkins, 1918) described a thought-form seen over a hospital as 'a beautiful form, like two large wings outspread, exquisite and harmonious in colouring'. He also said, '*Your thoughts often reach us in truly beautiful forms. I have seen exquisite flower-forms surrounding the loved ones here.*'

Anthony Borgia (*A.B.C. of Life*, Feature Books Ltd.) was told, 'Every thought that passes with force and purpose through the mind of an earth-dweller is projected from his mind as a thought-form. ...'

Alice Gilbert's deceased son (*Philip in Two Worlds*, Andrew Dakers) told her 'Round your Physical Body is this luminous outer "body" in which float your thought-images; in your case, usually in words. Some people's are all pictures, or geometrical figures or sounds.'

The Rev. C. Drayton Thomas (*The Life Beyond Death, with Evidence*, W. Collins & Co. Ltd., 1928) was informed that the 'dead' can not only 'read' the thoughts of the 'living' but have knowledge of the thoughts of others about us. He said, with regard to his son, that, when near him, he had found such thoughts 'sticking in his aura' [cf. Dr Walther, below].

(2) CLAIRVOYANTS

Dr Gerda Walther (*Journ. American S.P.R.*, 1932), though brought up in a materialistic philosophy, 'had experienced the human aura' years before she had heard that such things were claimed to exist. Like Mrs Garrett, Phoebe Payne, etc., she 'thought everybody had such experiences'. Eventually she saw a description by Steiner which agreed with her own observations and still later she found that Eastern writers gave identical descriptions. She consequently felt that 'there must be something in their statements'. In particular, she said, 'The descriptions of the auras, and of the significance of the colours of the auras in Leadbeater's *Man Visible and Invisible* and *Thought Forms* corresponds very closely to my own experience of these things ... before even I saw his books.' Dr Walther also pointed out that Nona, the control of Mrs Luisa Ignath, described the aura and its colours, together with their significance, in the same way as they appeared to her. Moreover, she had personal friends who also 'saw' auras, etc. and whose accounts agreed with her own. Like the supposed discarnate Mr Thomas, cited above, she said that 'sometimes there are embedded in the clouds or rays [= auras] thoughts or thought-fragments the persons from whom "they come" are just thinking of (though perhaps not in their conscious minds, and certainly without any need of uttering them aloud ...)'. Dr Walther had experiences that suggested that there is also something in the ideas of Chakras of Yoga philosophy.

Mrs Gwen Cripps sent drawings and descriptions to the present writer that clearly represented 'thought-forms' in the theosophic sense. She had not then seen the books by Leadbeater, etc., mentioned by Dr Walther. She also sent drawings of the Chakras.

Mrs Eileen J. Garrett (*Awareness*, Creative Age Press, 1943) found that 'thoughts are things possessing their own vitality, their own destiny, for ill or good'. In another book (*Adventures in the Supernormal*, Garrett Publications Inc., 1949) she tells how she 'began to feel and sense the thoughts of people as *forms of light* that moved to their destinies, impacting and dissipating according to their natures and the force with which they had been projected. I came to know that *thoughts are dimensional things* which become clothed with form and life as they are born.' In still another account (*My Life as a Search for the Meaning of Mediumship*, Rider & Co. Ltd.) Mrs Garrett called the human aura 'the surround'. She said, 'The impacts which I saw taking place in the 'surrounds' of people as they met, and reacted to each other's thoughts and emotions, constantly disturbed me. I saw how people's conflicts rocked them without their understanding why, and I became aware that people were thus the unconscious victims of each other's moods.' 'Thought,' she claimed, 'is an active force going forth from man's mind like a flash of lightning, which strikes and affects other minds as it moves and travels through space. It is so potent that it can make or mar us.' She suggested that, 'We should think constructively before allowing ourselves to be drawn into much of our useless living. ... Thought is the monarch of the world. ... Thought is the fundamental process of creation and nothing that has once manifested in the world is ever lost. ...'

Walter Carey (*Master Keys of Life and Death*, Rider & Co. Ltd.) said, 'Thoughts are things. Given a good brain in combination with a developed mental body, the act of *thinking creates thought-forms, which take shape and colour according to the type of thought*. These, like the aura, are visible to a comparatively small number of people, but they are just as real, or perhaps more so, than physical objects.

'If the thought is vague, the thought-form would be merely an undefined sort of cloud or coloured mist. Definite thought, however, produces very clear forms, in general shape something like flowers, sea-shells, or geometrical figures, which would be recognized and understood by one skilled in such matters. The length of time that these persist varies with the strength of the thought and the frequency of repetition'.

The Betty Book, by Stewart Edward White (Psychic Book Club,

1943) said, 'We are broadcasting even with our most secret thoughts and desires. We are accountable for what we send out.'

Phoebe Payne (*Man's Latent Power*, Faber & Faber Ltd., 1938) said that thoughts and emotions, 'and all influences termed spiritual' are 'definite forces, weaving forms which are recognizable at their own levels as objective manifestations.'

In collaboration with her husband, Dr L. J. Bendit, Phoebe Payne later wrote *The Psychic Sense* (Faber & Faber Ltd.). Like the supposed discarnate 'Philip', cited above, this clairvoyant used the term 'thought-form' to include both mental images (*i.e.*, 'pictures', copies of objects) and the geometrical forms of the Theosophists. She said, 'The best type of thought results in clear-cut, sharp-edged, well-focused forms, whereas emotion is essentially open and not outlined. ... Thought about concrete things produces images more or less like that thing. The more abstract the ideas, the more the images are likely to be geometrical or symbolic in design.'

Geoffrey Hodson (*The Science of Seership*, Rider & Co. Ltd.) described 'thought-forms' (resembling orthodox angels) which, as the result of the earnest prayers of certain parents, surrounded their 'dead' boy. The latter was a 'true lover of Nature' and Hodson said, 'Occasionally the higher Nature Spirits will enter one of these thought-forms and, by vivifying it, add to the prayer-force by which it was originally created and inspired'.

Many other examples exist of descriptions, by clairvoyants, of 'thought-forms', both those which are mental images that correspond to physical objects and those which are geometrical designs representing abstract thoughts, such as love and peace. There is, however, a whole book devoted to this subject by Annie Besant and C. W. Leadbeater (*Thought Forms*, Theosophical Publishing House, 1941): it gives both verbal descriptions and coloured illustrations of many 'thought-forms' in the theosophic sense.

(3) THOSE WHO ARE TEMPORARILY OUT-OF-THE-BODY

V. Turvey (*The Beginnings of Seership*, Stead's Publishing House, 1909), when out of his Physical Body saw thought-forms of the image-type which had been created by various men.

Arnold Bennett mentioned the geometrical type of thought-form.

Mr 'L.G.T.', writing to Muldoon (*The Case for Astral Projection*, Aries Press Ltd.) said that while out of his Physical Body, he saw what 'seemed to be a materialization of the thoughts of the person present'.

Bulford (*Man's Unknown Journey*, Rider & Co. Ltd., 1941), referred to *The Eidophone Voice Figures*, by Margaret Watts Hughes, describing and illustrating the 'sound-forms' ('Chladni's figures') produced when a violin-bow is drawn across a metal plate bearing a layer of sand, and said that 'thought-forms' (in the theosophic sense) were analogous, on their own 'plane'. Like Muldoon and others, he warned those who intended to attempt temporarily to leave their Physical Bodies to think none but harmonious thoughts. He said, 'Picture to yourself the invisible weaving of designs around you; these you carry wherever you go, and they make the atmosphere of your presence. ...'

Mr G. Rogers, an American whose exteriorization from the body is described by Muldoon and Carrington (*The Phenomenon of Astral Projection*, 1951), evidently saw the forms of abstract thoughts, since he said, 'All around me, suspended and floating in nothing, were the most beautiful symbols imaginable, some diamond-shaped, the outer part of one colour and the centre of another colour; others were round, several differently coloured in the centre. ...' In the same book (p. 145) illustrations are given of geometrical 'thought-forms' based on the work of French psychologists. Similar drawings, based on the teachings of the Kahunas ('Keepers of the Secret') of Polynesia, were published by Max Freedom Long (*The Secret Science Behind Miracles*, Kosmon Press Ltd., 1948).

Fate Magazine for June, 1955 carried an enquiry from Wm. Breakell. After discussing the after-life, etc. all evening, he went to bed where he saw 'bright discs about the size of a sixpence, of a yellow-gold colour, gently floating over the bed'. When the eyes were closed he could not see them. They were doubtless 'thought-forms' impregnated with ectoplasm, *i.e.*, partially 'materialized'.

(4) THE CORRELATION OF INDEPENDENT DESCRIPTIONS

In order to illustrate the fact that specific 'thought-forms' independently described by the 'dead' and the 'living' agree both in form and colour, the 'thought-form' of anger may be taken.

According to the deceased communicator of *The Coming Light*, writing in 1918, 'The mental cloud over India is dark ... *emitting flame* at times'. He added, 'This is how we perceive mental states' and warned against the thoughts of revenge that were brooding in that land. Similarly, the deceased 'Private Dowding', communicating, spoke of 'turbulent sensual and fearful thoughts, which resembled *'crimson darts'*. It is interesting to note that the clairvoyants Besant and Leadbeater, in their book on *Thought Forms*, illustrated (their fig. 23) 'steady anger' as a *crimson dart*. St Paul's phrase (Ephes. vi, 16) is also significant; he said that only 'faith would quench the *fiery darts* of the wicked'.

When it is remembered that droplets of *water-vapour* (clouds), under the influence of cold, etc. automatically take definite geometrical patterns (snow-flakes) and those *vibrations of the air* which produce the sensations of sound also automatically take different forms according to their rate, etc., the statements quoted above regarding forms being automatically assumed by definite thoughts and feelings become highly credible. The agreement which exists between independent accounts suggests something objective.

So much for the probable objectivity of 'thought-forms' in the theosophic sense. As to the objectivity of 'thought-forms' in the sense of mental images (*e.g.*, images of cups, chairs, men's Physical Bodies, etc.) there can be no doubt that some such images are objective, since they have not only often been described by clairvoyants (and by the 'dead'), but have often been photographed. (Indeed, those psychical researchers who deny that any 'materializations' are direct products of the 'dead' rely for their argument on the objectivity of mental images of the dead.)

Appendix IX

EVIDENCE, DIRECT AND INDIRECT

WHEN psychic or mystical experiences are under consideration, there is often a tendency to demand evidence that, in the nature of things, cannot, and never will be, forthcoming. The various kinds of evidence and their applicability were reviewed in a popular manner by B. Abdy Collins (*Death is not the End*, Psychic Book Club, 1941).

It will suffice here to point out that, in the present writer's opinion, the theory of survival, the case for a non-physical body and the reality of out-of-the-body experiences can all be accorded a very high degree of probability. They seem, to him, to be as well established as the theory of evolution.

In a recent book, *Is Evolution Proved?* by Dewar and H. S. Shelton (Hollis and Carter, 1947), the former advanced reasons for regarding the theory of evolution as non-proven. Although Shelton considered that this is 'proved', he stated his opinion only with a necessary qualification. He asked, 'What kind of proof is possible?' and replied, 'I think the proof in a general way is perfectly sound so far as is possible in a case of this kind'. Pointing out that any evidence in support of the theory must necessarily be of an *indirect* nature, he continued, '*This indirect evidence is of the kind and quality which would naturally be expected*'. [Italics by present writer.]

When similar qualifications are made in respect to the evidence for the theory of survival, the latter is, we claim, as well founded as that of evolution. It is, indeed, remarkable how near to Shelton's criteria of evidence for evolution are Dr Hereward Carrington's criteria of evidence for survival. Writing in his *Primer of Psychical Research* (Ives Washburn, N.Y.), published fifteen years before Shelton gave his views, after expressing his considered opinion that 'there is a great deal of evidence' in favour of survival, and that in a matter less momentous to mankind 'one would be tempted to say that sufficient evidence *had* been obtained to *prove* the claim made'. Carrington asked, 'How is such evidence to be obtained?' He continued, 'If a distant relative were to return after an absence of some twenty years and call you up by telephone, how would you assure yourself of his identity if you were in some manner prevented from seeing him? ... He would have to narrate a number of detailed, personal, perhaps trivial, incidents which only he would be supposed to know; and *if you obtained enough of these* you would be inclined to say to yourself, "Sure enough, that is so-and-so speaking to me at the other end of the line. Only he would know those facts". *That is precisely the kind of evidence that we want in obtaining proof of personal identity*'. [Italics by the present writer.]

Echoing Shelton's words, we maintain that, in relation to the theories of the 'astral body', astral projection and the survival of bodily death, the evidence which we adduce 'is of a kind and quality which would naturally be expected'. Although this evidence, like that for the theory of evolution, is necessarily of an indirect nature, it is otherwise inexplicable.

DURATION OF VACATION →		(1) PERMANENT	(2) TEMPORARY
(B) NATURAL	BODY (DEDUCED)	SOUL BODY, (a) COMPLETE AND (b) UNENSHROUDED BY VEHICLE OF VITALITY	SOUL BODY, (a) INCOMPLETE (BECAUSE OF CORD) AND (b) SLIGHTLY ENSHROUDED BY VEHICLE OF VITALITY
	ENVIRONMENT	HIGHEST: GLORIFIED EARTH ('PARADISE')	INTERMEDIATE: EARTH, OR GLIMPSES OF 'PARADISE' OR BOTH
	CONSCIOUSNESS	(3) VERY MANY SEE REVIEW, 'SILVER CORD' AND HELPERS (2) UNDERGO A 3-DAY SLEEP (1) HIGHEST – SUPER-NORMAL (WITH TELEPATHY, ETC.)	(3) SOME SEE REVIEW,'SILVER CORD' & HELPERS (2) NO 3-DAY SLEEP (1) HIGH – INCLUDES GLIMPSES OF TELEPATHY, ETC.
(A) ENFORCED	BODY (DEDUCED)	SOUL BODY, BUT ENSHROUDED BY VEHICLE OF VITALITY (WHICH IS FULL OF VITAL ENERGY)	
	ENVIRONMENT	LOWEST: EARTH AND/OR DREAM-WORLD ('HADES')	
	CONSCIOUSNESS	(3) VERY FEW SEE THE REVIEW OF PAST LIFE, THE 'SILVER CORD' OR DISCARNATE HELPERS (2) NO DEFINITE SLEEP: ARE AWAKE AT ONCE (1) LOWEST – SUB-NORMAL (DREAM) TO ALMOST NORMAL	

(Left margin label: TYPE OF VACATION)

CORRELATION OF PERMANENT, TEMPORARY, NATURAL & ENFORCED VACATIONS OF THE BODY (READ UPWARDS)

ACKNOWLEDGEMENTS

For permission to make extracts from copyright material, the author is grateful to the following publishers. (The Case-numbers are given in parentheses after the title of the work concerned.) Apologies are rendered for any inadvertent omission from this list.

Messrs George Allen & Unwin, Ltd.: *Unbidden Guests*, by Wm. Oliver Stevens, 1949 (147); *The Mystery of Dreams*, by Wm. Oliver Stevens, 1950 (15, 112).
American Magazine, 1929 (92).
The Aquarian Age (2).
Aquarian Press: *Philip in the Spheres*, by Alice Gilbert, 1952 (77).
Aries Press Ltd., Chicago: *The Case for Astral Projection*, by Sylvan J. Muldoon (5, 85, 86, 98, 135, 136).
Arthurs Press Ltd.: *Encyclopedia of Psychic Science*, by Dr Nandor Fodor, 1933.
Author-Partner Press Ltd.: *The Prediction of the Future*, by P. E. Cornillier, 1947 (80).
G. Bell & Sons, Ltd.: *The Meaning of Dreams*, by Dorothy Grenside, 1923 (45).
Basil Blackwell & Co. Ltd.: *Beyond the Five Senses*, by Miss L. M. Bazett, 1946 (78).
J. Burns & Co. Ltd.: *Report on Spiritualism by the Committee of the London Dialectical Society*, 1873 (54, 121).
Cassell & Co. Ltd.: *Resurrection*, by Wm. Gerhardi, 1934 (32); *Man is a Spirit*, by J. Arthur Hill, 1918 (29, 39, 133, 151); *Brief Darkness*, by Gladys Osborn Leonard, 1942 (44).
Chapman & Hall Ltd.: *The Glimpse*, by Arnold Bennett, 2nd ed., 1909 (30).
Collins & Co. Ltd.: *Thirty Years of Psychical Research*, by Charles Richet (transl. by Stanley de Brath), 1923 (28, 114).
Creative Age Press Inc., N.Y.: *Telepathy*, by Mrs Eileen J. Garrett, 1941 (33); *Awareness*, by Mrs Eileen J. Garrett, 1943 (75).
Fate, 1953 (42), 1954 (121).
Funk, Wagnalls' Co. Ltd.: *The Psychic Riddle*, by I. K. Funk (93).
Harrap & Co. Ltd.: *In Search of the Hereafter*, by Reginald M. Lester, 1952 (62).
Heath Cranton Ltd.: *A Book of True Dreams*, by Mary Monteith, 1929 (58, 79).

Hodder & Stoughton, Ltd.: *The Spirit of the Hills*, by E. S. Smythe, 1937 (148).

James Clarke & Co. Ltd., *The Supreme Adventure*, by Robert Crookall, 1960.

John Lane the Bodley Head Ltd.: *Glimpses into Infinity*, by Frank Hives, 1931 (59).

Light, 1912 (106); 1954 (105, 156).

Longmans, Green & Co. Ltd.: *The Varieties of Religious Experience*, by Wm. James, 28th imp., 1917 (107, 128, 129); *Out of the Body*, by John Oxenham, 1941 (11).

J. C. Moore, Ltd.: *The Seeress of Prevorst*, by Dr F. Kerner (transl. C. Crowe), 1845 (38).

Occult Review, 1908 (142).

Penguin Books Ltd.: *With Mystics and Magicians in Tibet*, by Mme Alexandra David-Neel, 1936 (92).

Pitman & Co. Ltd.: *Incidents of My Life*, by D. D. Home, 1864 (34).

Prediction, 1936 (27, 74, 95, 96, 153); 1937 (101, 102), 1938 (103), 1950 (55); 1951 (52); 1952 (9); 1953 (1, 158–160).

Psychic Book Club: *The Last Crossing*, by Gladys Osborn Leonard, 1937 (44).

Psychic News: 1952 (73); 1954 (17, 116).

George Redway: *Shadow Land*, by Mme d'Espérance, 1897 (43).

Rider & Co. Ltd.: *Focus on the Unknown*, by Alfred Gordon Bennett, 1953 (104); *A Search in Secret Egypt*, by Paul Brunton (51); *Life's Hidden Secrets*, by F. Collinge, 1952; *Man's Unknown Journey*, by Staveley Bulford, 1941 (88); *Astral Projection*, by Oliver Fox (31), *Why We Survive Death*, by H. E. Hunt (46); *I Was In The Spirit*, by Sigrid Kaeyer (57); *My Occult Case Book*, by Frank Lind (63, 65); *The Projection of the Astral Body*, by Sylvan J. Muldoon and Hereward Carrington (20, 124); *The Phenomena of Astral Projection*, by Sylvan J. Muldoon and Hereward Carrington (22, 138, 139, 140, 147); *Man Outside Himself*, by H. F. Prevost Battersby (122, 134); *The Possibility of Miracles*, by Anna Maria Roos; *Ghosts with a Purpose*, by Elliott O'Donnell, 1951 (16); *The Mystery of the Human Double*, by Ralph Shirley (87); *Life Now and Forever*, by A. J. Wills (7), *After Life*, by Wm. Wilson (130); *Practical Astral Projection*, by 'Yram' (84).

George Ronald: *Acquainted with the Night: a Book of Dreams*, by Nancy Price (81).

Routledge, Trench, Trübner & Co. Ltd.: *Footfalls on the Boundary of Another World*, by Robert Owen, 1860 (14); *A Theory of the, Mechanism of Survival*, by W. Whatley Smith, 1920 (119); *The Secret of the Golden Flower: A Chinese Book of Life*, by Richard Wilhelm (83).

Society for Psychical Research: Proc. vii (55); viii (3, 4); Journ. (6, 36, 108, 151, 154); Americal Society, 1923 (111), 1939 (110).

Spectator: 1930 (42).

Spiritualist Press Ltd.: *What Mediumship is,* by Dr. Horace Leaf, Ph. D. (60); *Through the Psychic Door,* by F. Wood (132).

Stead's Publishing House: *The Beginnings of Seership,* by Vincent Turvey (21).

Student Christian Movement Press Ltd.: *The Truth about Spiritualism,* by Canon Anson (12).

The Tuttle Co. Rutland, U.S.A.: *My Travels in the Spirit World,* by Caroline Larsen, 1927 (56).

Two Worlds: 1952 (48, 137); 1954 (24).

Watkins and Co. Ltd.: *The Prodigal,* 1921 (118); *Experiences,* Anon., 1926 (143).

Youth Book Club Ltd.: *Escape to the Sea,* by Fred Rebell, 1951 (61).

Especial thanks are due to the following, who sent first-hand accounts of their experiences, together with permission for their inclusion in this book: Mr C. L. Banks, Mrs D. E. Boorman, Mr Percy Cole, Mrs Gwen Cripps, Mr J. H. Dennis, Mrs Gussie Dowell, Mr Wm. E. Edwards, Mrs E. Hatfield, Mrs Howard W. Jeffrey, Sr., Miss Marjorie Johnson, Mrs I. M. Joy, Mrs 'M. A. E.', Mrs R. Ivy 'Prothero', Mr J. Redgewell, Mrs Peggy Roberts, Mr F. C. Sculthorp, Mrs E. F. Sheridan, Miss Zoila C. M. Stables, the Revd. Dr J. R. Staver, Mrs Mary Tarsikes, Mrs H. E. Wheeler and Mrs H. D. Williams.

All who are interested in this subject owe a deep debt of gratitude to Sylvan J. Muldoon of Darlington, Wis., U.S.A. The present writer expresses his personal thanks to his friend Mr Muldoon.

INDEX TO CASES GIVEN IN THE TEXT

	Case No.
'A', Mrs	156
Addison, Miss Cromwell	95
Anon.	37, 119
Anon., (a lady)	143
'A.P.H.' (Harrow)	101
Baeschley, M.	28
Banks, Mr C. L.	99
Bazett, Miss L. M.	78
Bennett, Mr Alfred Gordon	104
Bennett, Arnold	30
Bensusan, Mr S. L.	160
Bertrand, Revd. L. J.	4
'Bill'	152
Blakeley, Miss Elizabeth	1
Boorman, Mrs D. E.	68
Bounds, Mrs Elizabeth	116
Brooks, Miss Helen	55
Brown, Mr Jeffrey H.	73
Brunton, Dr Paul	51
Bulford, Mr Staveley	88
Burgess, Mr Claude	109
Burton, Capt.	29
Callan, Lt. C. F.	149
Carrington, Dr (friend of)	117
Cole, Mr Percy	126
Collins, Mrs F.	96
Colonel, A	6
Costa, Mr G.	145
Cripps, Mrs Gwen	90
Crump, Mr Basil	115
David-Neel, Mme Alexandra	82
Dennis, Mr J. H.	49
Dowell, Mrs Gussie	25
Dreisch, Mrs	110
Eden, Bishop (case of)	12
Edgerton, Mr J. C.	135
Edwards, Mrs Wm. E.	70
Eeden, Dr Frederick van	79
Einarsson, Mr G. J.	22
Ellison, Mr N. F.	36
Espérance, Mme d'	43
Fancher, Miss Molly	23
'F.B.', Mrs	106
Fisher, Mrs Phyllis	113
Fox, Mr Oliver	31
Funk, Dr I. K. (doctor-friend)	93
Garrett, Mrs Eileen J.	75

Garrett, Mrs Eileen J. (nurse of)	33
Geddes, Lord (doctor-friend)	19
Georginus	38
Gerhardi, William	32
Gibier, Dr P. (engraver friend of)	41
Gilbert, Mrs Alice	77
Grenside, Miss Dorothy	45
Griggs, Miss Catherine	111
'H', Mr	86
'H', Mrs	108
Hamilton, Miss Gail	5
Hartmann, Dr Franz	142
Hatfield, Mrs E.	123
Hepworth, Revd. Dr George	40
'H.F.P.', Mrs	105
Hinton, Miss Beryl	133
Hives, Mr Frank	59
Home, Mr D. D.	34
Hotel Guest, The	147
Hout, Dr R. B.	74, 153
Huntley, Mr F.	39
Hymans, Mr M. D.	125
'Janie'	16
Jeffrey, Mrs Howard W.	69
Johnson, Miss Marjorie T.	53
Joy, Mrs I. M.	97
Kaeyer, Miss Sigrid	57
Kelley, Dr George	2
Lady, A (from Dallas, Texas)	136
Lady, A	42
Land, Mrs A.	27
Landa, Mr B.	138
Larsen, Mrs Caroline D.	56
Leaf, Dr Horace, F.R.G.S.	60
Leonard, Mrs Gladys Osborn	44
Leslie, Mrs Francis	9
Lester, Lt.-Col. Reginald M.	62
Lind, Mr Frank	65
Ludlow, Mr F.	141
'M.A.B.', Miss	122
'M.A.E.', Mrs	47
Mare, Walter de la	127
'M.D.',	157
Monteith, Miss (doctor-friend)	58
Morrell, Mr Edward	35
Muldoon, Mr Sylvan J.	20
'N.D.' (Pontypool)	103
Newby, Miss Margaret	52

	Case No.		
Officer, An	150	Staver, Revd. Dr J. R.	71
Ogston, Sir A.	18	Steele, Miss Emma	109
Okeden, Miss Hermione	87	Stevens, Mr	112
Ostby, Dr O. A.	85	Stuart-Young, Mr J. M.	137
Oxenham, Mr J.	11	Symonds, Mr J. A.	107, 128
Palmer, Mrs G. S.	158	Tankerville, Countess Leonora	8
Parker, Mrs D.	140	Tarsikes, Mrs Mary	13
Patient, A dysentery	10	'T.D.', Mrs	115
Pelley, Mr Wm. Dudley	92	'T.S.' (Dorset)	102
Peters, Miss Dorothy	48	Tuberculosis Patient, A	159
'P.L.', Miss	46	Turvey, Mr Vincent	21
Porter, Mrs J.	139	Varley, Mr Cromwell F.	54, 121
Price, Miss Nancy	81	Vlasek, Mrs Mary	89
'Prothero', Mrs R.	146	Wheatley, Mr Horace E.	24
'Prodigal', The	118	Wheeler, Mr J. C.	144
Rebell, Mr Fred	61	Wheeler, Mrs H. E.	94
Redgewell, Mr J.	26	Wilhelm, Mr Richard	83
'René, C.'	80	Williams, Mrs H. D.	91
Roberts, Mrs Peggy	67	Wills, Mr A. J.	98
Rose, Dr O.	7	Wilmot, Mr S. R.	50
'S', Mr	14	Wilson, Dr Wm.	130
Sculthorp, Mr F. C.	64	Wiltse, Dr A. S.	3
Seton, Mr Ernest Thomson	131	Wirt, Mr B. B.	76
Sheridan, Mrs E. F.	66	'Woman, A Gifted'	129
Simons, Dr C. E.	154	Wood, Dr Frederick H.	132
Smith, Mrs C. H.	100	'W.S.', Miss	63
Smith, Dr Enid	17, 124	Wyld , Dr George	120
Smythe, Mr F. S.	148	'X', Mr	114
Soldier, A	151	'X', Mrs	134
Stables, Miss Zoila C. M.	72	Yeoman, Miss I. V.	15
		'Yram'	84